T0233963

This book discusses the connection between two areas of semantics, namely the semantics of databases and the semantics of natural language, and links them via a common view of the semantics of time. It is argued that a coherent theory of the semantics of time is an essential ingredient for the success of efforts to incorporate more 'real world' semantics into database models. This idea is a relatively recent concern of database research but it is receiving growing interest.

The book begins with a discussion of database querying which motivates use of the paradigm of Montague Semantics and discusses details of the intensional logic ILs. This is followed by a description of the author's own model, the Historical Relational Data Model (HRDM) which extends the RDM to include a temporal dimension. Finally the database querying language QEIII is defined and examples illustrate its use. A formal model for the interpretation of questions is presented in this work which will form the basis for much further research.

**FORMAL SEMANTICS AND PRAGMATICS
FOR NATURAL LANGUAGE QUERYING**

**Cambridge Tracts in Theoretical
Computer Science**

*Managing Editor* Professor C.J. van Rijsbergen, Department of Computing Science,
University of Glasgow

**Titles in the series**

# FORMAL SEMANTICS AND PRAGMATICS FOR NATURAL LANGUAGE QUERYING

JAMES CLIFFORD
*New York University*

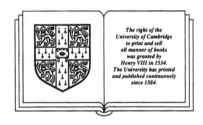

## CAMBRIDGE UNIVERSITY PRESS

*Cambridge*

*New York   Port Chester   Melbourne   Sydney*

PUBLISHED BY THE PRESS SYNDICATE OF THE UNIVERSITY OF CAMBRIDGE
The Pitt Building, Trumpington Street, Cambridge, United Kingdom

CAMBRIDGE UNIVERSITY PRESS
The Edinburgh Building, Cambridge CB2 2RU, UK
40 West 20th Street, New York NY 10011–4211, USA
477 Williamstown Road, Port Melbourne, VIC 3207, Australia
Ruiz de Alarcón 13, 28014 Madrid, Spain
Dock House, The Waterfront, Cape Town 8001, South Africa

http://www.cambridge.org

© Cambridge University Press 1990

First published 1990
First paperback edition 2004

A catalogue record for this book is available from the British Library

ISBN 0 521 35433 1 hardback
ISBN 0 521 60274 2 paperback

*Dedicated to the memory of Peter Connelly*

# Contents

# List of Figures

# CHAPTER ONE

# INTRODUCTION

It is difficult to imagine a successful semantic theory that does not include time as an integral component. Yet all of today's major data models – models which purport to provide a general theory on how to represent information for convenient and rapid storage and retrieval on digital computers – completely ignore this essential aspect of semantics. In this work we examine the connection between two areas of semantics, namely the semantics of databases and the semantics of natural language, and link them together via a common view of the semantics of time. In the first part we argue that an essential ingredient for the success of efforts to incorporate more *real world* semantics into database models is a coherent theory of the semantics of time. We describe such a database theory, and then proceed to present a formally defined English database query language whose semantic theory makes explicit reference to the notion of denotation with respect to a moment of time.

The idea that time might be an important consideration in providing an enriched database semantics is not new to this work, but it is nonetheless a relatively recent concern of database research. [Bub77], [Ser80], [Klo81], [And81], [AM82], [CW83], [Sno84], [GV85], [CC87], [GY88], and [CC88a] are among the many works that have lately investigated ways in which time might be added to a database model. Two recent surveys of the literature on time and databases, [BADW82] and [Sno86], and a recent international conference, [TAI87], provide excellent references to the growing interest and literature in this field. Our own approach (first presented in [Cli82a] and [CW83] and further investigated in [CC87]) owes a debt to the philosophical tradition represented in such works as [Car47], [Pri67], and [RU71], and particularly in the works of the logician Richard Montague [Mon74]. This tradition makes a case for a far more pervasive theory of the importance of time in a theory of meaning than one which asserts that time is just one among many equally important aspects.

In Chapter 2 we present a brief introduction to the Montague Semantics (MS) framework, including a definition of the intensional logic $IL_s$. Then in Chapter 3 we present a formal definition of the Historical Relational Database Model (HRDM), our formal incorporation of a semantics for time within the context of the relational

1

database model ([Cod70]). Unlike much of the recent database work involving time, we do not attempt to incorporate any notions of how time is encoded (e.g., in the Julian calendric system.) Such theories are important, but it seems that before exploring some of the minutiae of time a theory that captures more of its essence is needed. Theories concerned with months of the year or days of the week are best discussed at the level of interfaces or data representation schemes, and not at the level of a basic semantic theory. We therefore present a very general theory, one which ascribes only the simplest and most intuitive properties to time (order and density) and defines a very simple relationship between time and the other elements of the relational database model.

Our emphasis, as discussed in Chapters 3 and 4, is on the centrality of time with respect to database modelling, and we argue that time is central to our understanding of database semantics. We present the point of view that it is not simply expressions such as "previous employee" or "salary increase" that require reference to the notion of time for their understanding, but rather that every aspect of database theory is understood better when its relationship to the phenomenon of time is considered. In particular, a new insight into the nature of the database distinction between *key* and *non-key* attributes is provided by an understanding of their relationship to time.

In order to make a concrete presentation of these ideas, we present them within the context of two well-known database models, the relational model [Cod70] and the entity-relationship model [Che76]. We adopt the relational model both because it is a well-studied and formalized database model, and because it is increasingly being used as a model for implemented systems. The entity-relationship model is used not simply because of its growing popularity as a tool for modelling database semantics, but also because its ontological theory – that the world consists of entities and relationships among them – is in close accord with the ontology of the philosophical logic tradition.

In the latter part of this work we argue that a fully formalized account can successfully be given for both the syntax and the interpretation of an English database query language. Moreover this account is independent of any performance model of how a processor (for example, a computer) might go about understanding such a language. The language theory that we present, with syntax paired with semantics, is once again a direct outgrowth of the work of Richard Montague, who argued quite seriously in a number of papers for the contention that there is "no important theoretical difference ... between formal and natural languages" ([Mon70a, p.188 in [Mon74]].) Working within the framework of Montague's syntactic and semantic theory we present a formalized fragment of English questions designed for the purposes of database querying.

Numerous systems for providing natural language access to databases have been described in the literature, including [WKN81], [Wal78], [Har78], and [HSSS78]. While these systems are dissimilar in a number of different respects, they all share what to us is the same defect, namely the lack of any fundamental formal theory of the semantics of the database or the semantics of the English query language.

We view the development of these and other such systems as belonging to the first phase in the development of a formal theory of the semantics of database and of database querying, much as the early years in the design of computer languages such as FORTRAN were part of the first phase in the development of a theory of programming-language semantics. It awaited the impact of formal language theory, coupled with a theory of syntax-directed translation, for the area of programming language theory to be born. To complete an analogous development in the area of natural language querying would require the impact of formal language theory and a theory that coupled the syntax and the semantics of English. Many linguists today believe that Montague's theory of universal grammar [Mon70c] is the first successful attempt at formalizing such a uniform syntactic and semantic theory of natural language. We believe that some such formal theory of a query language is an important first step towards the development of provably correct and reliable natural language processing systems. For inherent in the notion of program *correctness* is the concept of a standard against which a program is to be judged.

In Chapter 5 we present an informal overview of a fragment of English for database querying which we call QE-III. We discuss the kinds of properties and abilities that a database query language in English should possess. Principal among these are an account of question semantics that possesses close analogs in database theory, an account of the semantics of multiple-WH questions, an account of the semantics of time, and a grammar that is conducive to a computer implementation. After examining a number of partial solutions to these problems, we introduce the notion of pragmatics as an additional formal component of our language's theory. We argue that assigning to the pragmatic component the task of providing a representation for the answer(s) to a question is both appropriate and elegant. Finally we discuss several other recent attempts at developing a formal theory of questions.

After this informal presentation we provide in Chapter 6 a formal definition of the query fragment QE-III as a Montague Grammar. This fragment represents a simplification of the semantic theory of Montague's fragment, presented in [Mon73] and known in the literature as PTQ, that offers a natural correspondence to the semantics of queries in a database context. An excellent introduction to the formal semantic approach to linguistic analysis which has come to be known as Montague Semantics can be found in [DWP81]. The fragment is provided with a formal syntax, semantics, and pragmatics, each component designed with the database application in mind. These components of the QE-III language are based upon the language $IL_s$ introduced in Chapter 2. The inclusion of a formal pragmatic component is an interesting extension to the traditional conception of a Montague Grammar. Among the major extensions to the PTQ fragment embodied in QE-III are the inclusion of time-denoting expressions and temporal operators, an analysis of verb meanings into primitive meaning units derived from the database schema, and of course the inclusion of certain forms of direct questions. These extensions, and the semantics with which they are provided, are motivated by the ultimate goal of database access, but they are equally interesting in their own right. The syntactic theory presented is in some cases admittedly naive, for we have been primarily interested in getting the interpretation right.

A more complete discussion of the details of the features of the QE-III fragment is presented in Chapter 7, where numerous example derivations and translations of typical database queries are examined and discussed. We also discuss briefly how QE-III can be adapted to different database domains, and how the logical translations of the English queries expressed in QE-III can be translated into a data manipulation language like the historical relational algebra of [CC87]. The chapter concludes with a discussion of some of the limitations of the fragment and of some possibilities for further extensions. Finally, we conclude in Chapter 8 with a review of the major ideas of the book and with a discussion of future work that this research suggests.

# CHAPTER TWO

# MONTAGUE SEMANTICS

## 2.1  Overview of the Approach

In a series of papers culminating in [Mon73], henceforth PTQ, Richard Montague embarked upon a program of providing a formal syntax coupled with a model-theoretic semantics for increasingly sophisticated fragments of English. The semantics for the PTQ fragment is given indirectly, as follows. The set of sentences of the fragment is defined inductively from a set of Basic Expressions (words). Direct translations into an Intensional Logic (IL) are provided for each of the Basic Terms. Each of the formation rules in the inductive definition is coupled with a translation rule which specifies the translation into IL of the output of the rule as a function of the translations of the input(s) to the rule. Thus the interpretation of any English sentence in the fragment is given by means of the model-theoretic interpretation given by the semantics of the logic to its corresponding representation in IL.

Subsequent to the presentation of the PTQ fragment, a number of researchers (e.g. [Tho72], [Ben74], [Par75], [Tho76], [Kar77], [Ben79], [Dow79], [Hir83], and [Hin88]) have explored various extensions to the PTQ fragment. These extensions have been motivated by the desire to provide a formal syntax and semantics to a larger set of English syntactic constructs; occasionally they have necessitated changes or extensions to the underlying logic IL. [DWP81] provides an excellent introduction to the area known as Montague Semantics, while [vB88] surveys the entire field of intensional logic.

In this chapter we describes the logic $IL_s$, an extension to IL which is motivated by the desire to provide a formal basis for the semantics of English querying of historical databases. In particular $IL_s$ allows variables and constants over indices. In explaining why IL lacks variables (and constants) over indices, [Gal75] states that "IL was intended as a formal logic with intensional features close to those of natural language, and in natural language we do not refer explicitly to contexts of use." Thus IL contains a number of modal and tense operators (e.g., $\Box$, $\Diamond$, $\mathcal{F}$, $\mathcal{P}$) that allow indirect reference to indices other than the (implicitly understood) *current index*, but does not allow names for specific indices. Natural language queries to an HDB, however, frequently require explicit reference to the time(s) at which the query is to be evaluated.

In the HRDM model which we shall shortly present, the set $T$ consists of the names of all of the possible times with respect to which data can be stored. An English query fragment for such a database must have Basic Expressions corresponding to such times, and a logic which is to provide the semantics for such a fragment must therefore allow constants over times in its syntax. The logic $IL_s$ is designed to serve this need. It is basically the logic $Ty_2$ presented in [Gal75], except that we have included more logical connectives and quantifiers as primitive symbols. Moreover we shall simplify the model theory, so that an index consists solely of a time rather than an ordered pair consisting of a time and a *possible world*. Extending the logic to include other components such as a possible-world component, or multiple time-dimension components, to the index is straightforward.

The chapter is organized as follows. Sections 2.2 and 2.3 give the formal definitions of the syntax and semantics of $IL_s$, and then the relationship between $IL_s$ and Montague's IL is discussed in Section 2.4. The last section contains an informal discussion of the logic and its model theory; readers unfamiliar with intensional logic and Montague Semantics may wish to refer ahead to this section as an aid to following the earlier, more dense definitional sections.

## 2.2  The Language $IL_s$

The set of Types for $IL_s$ is the smallest set $T$ such that:

1. $e, t$ and $s \in T$, and

2. if $a, b \in T$, then $<a, b> \in T$.

The primitive symbols of $IL_s$ are the following:

1. for each $a \in T$, a denumerable set of variables $v_{0,a}, v_{1,a}, v_{2,a} \cdots$

2. for each $a \in T$, a denumerable set of constants $c_{0,a}, c_{1,a}, c_{2,a}, \ldots$

3. the following improper symbols: $\lambda, (,), =, \neg, [,], \forall, \exists, \exists!, \rightarrow, \leftrightarrow, <, \ll, \wedge, \vee, \subseteq$

The Meaningful Expressions of type $a$, denoted $ME_a$, are defined as follows:

1. every variable of type $a$ belongs to $ME_a$

2. every constant of type $a$ belongs to $ME_a$

3. if $A \in ME_{<a,b>}$ and $B \in ME_a$, then $A(B) \in ME_b$

4. if $A \in ME_b$ and $x$ is a variable of type $a$, then $\lambda x A \in ME_{<a,b>}$

5. if $A, B \in ME_a$, then $[A = B] \in ME_t$

6. if $\phi, \psi \in ME_t$, and $x$ is a variable, then $[\neg\phi], [\phi \wedge \psi], [\phi \vee \psi], [\phi \to \psi], [\phi \leftrightarrow \psi], \forall x \phi, \exists x \phi,$ and $\exists! x \phi \in ME_t$

7. if $A, B \in ME_s$, then $[A < B] \in ME_t$

8. if $A \in ME_s$ and $B \in ME_{<s,t>}$, then $[A \ll B]$ and $[B \ll A] \in ME_t$

9. if $A, B \in ME_{<a,t>}$, then $[A \subseteq B] \in ME_t$

## 2.3 Semantics of $IL_s$

A model $M$ for the language $IL_s$ is an ordered 4-tuple $M = < E, S, <, F >$ defined as follows:

1. $E$ is a non-empty set (the set of basic entities)

2. $S$ is a non-empty set (the set of times)

3. $<$ is a linear ordering on S

4. $F$ is a function which assigns to each constant $c_{n,a}$ an element in $D_a$, which is defined recursively over the set of Types $T$ as follows:

   - $D_e = E$
   - $D_t = \{0, 1\}$
   - $D_s = S$
   - $D_{<a,b>} = D_b^{D_a}$, *i.e., the set of all functions from $D_a$ to $D_b$*

Let **As(M)** be the set of all value assignments over M, i.e. all functions $g$ on the set of variables of $IL_s$ such that $g(x_{n,a})$ is in $D_a$ for every variable $x_{n,a}$ of type $a$. If $g \in \mathrm{As(M)}$, $y$ is a variable of type $a$, and $Y \in D_a$, then $\mathbf{g(y|Y)}$ denotes the value assignment $g'$ whose value is given as follows:

$$g'(z) = \left\{ \begin{array}{ll} Y & \text{if } z = y \\ g(z) & \text{otherwise} \end{array} \right\}$$

Finally, we define the Denotation of the expression $A_a$ (i.e., A is of type a) with respect to a model $M$ and a value assignment $g$, which we write as $Den_{M,g}(A_a)$ by the following recursion on the expression $A_a$ of $IL_s$:

1. $Den_{M,g}(x_a) = g(x_a)$

2. $Den_{M,g}(c_{n,a}) = F(c_{n,a})$

3. $Den_{M,g}(A_{<a,b>}(B_a)) = Den_{M,g}(A)(Den_{M,g}(B))$

4.

$$Den_{M,g}(\lambda x_a A_b) = \left| \begin{array}{l} \text{the function } f \text{ on } D_a \text{ whose value} \\ \text{at } X \in D_a = Den_{M,g'}(A_b), \\ \text{where } g' = g(x_a|X) \end{array} \right.$$

5.

$$Den_{M,g}([A \ = \ B]) = \left| \begin{array}{ll} 1 & \text{if } Den_{M,g}(A) = Den_{M,g}(B) \\ 0 & \text{otherwise} \end{array} \right.$$

6.

$$Den_{M,g}(\neg \phi_t) = \left| \begin{array}{ll} 1 & \text{if } Den_{M,g}(\phi) = 0 \\ 0 & \text{otherwise} \end{array} \right.$$

7.

$$Den_{M,g}(\forall x_a \phi_t) = \left| \begin{array}{l} 1 \quad \text{if for every } X \in D_a, Den_{M,g'}(\phi) = 1 \\ \quad \text{where } g' = g(x_a|X) \\ 0 \quad \text{otherwise} \end{array} \right.$$

8.

$$Den_{M,g}(\exists x_a \phi_t) = \left| \begin{array}{l} 1 \quad \text{if there exists an } X \in D_a \text{ such that} \\ \quad Den_{M,g'}(\phi) = 1, \text{ where } g' = g(x_a|X) \\ 0 \quad \text{otherwise} \end{array} \right.$$

9.

$$Den_{M,g}(\exists! x_a \phi_t) = \left| \begin{array}{l} 1 \quad \text{if there exists a } unique \ X \in D_a \text{ with} \\ \quad Den_{M,g'}(\phi) = 1, \text{ where } g' = g(x_a|X) \\ 0 \quad \text{otherwise} \end{array} \right.$$

and similarly for $[\phi_t \wedge \psi_t]$, $[\phi_t \wedge \psi_t]$, $[\phi_t \rightarrow \psi_t]$, and $[\phi_t \leftrightarrow \psi_t]$.

10.

$$Den_{M,g}([A_s < B_s]) = \left| \begin{array}{ll} 1 & \text{if } Den_{M,g}(A) < Den_{M,g}(B) \\ 0 & \text{otherwise} \end{array} \right.$$

11.

$$Den_{M,g}([A_s \ll B_{<s,t>}]) = \left| \begin{array}{l} 1 \quad \text{if, for every } t \in D_s \text{ such that} \\ \quad Den_{M,g}(B)(t) = 1, \text{ it is also} \\ \quad \text{the case that } Den_{M,g}(A) < t \\ 0 \quad \text{otherwise} \end{array} \right.$$

12.

$$Den_{M,g}([B_{<s,t>} \ll A_s]) = \begin{vmatrix} 1 & \text{if, for every } t \in D_s \text{ such that} \\ & Den_{M,g}(B)(t) = 1, \text{ it is also} \\ & \text{the case that } t < Den_{M,g}(A) \\ 0 & \text{otherwise} \end{vmatrix}$$

13.

$$Den_{M,g}([A_{<s,t>} \subseteq B_{<s,t>}]) = \begin{vmatrix} 1 & \text{if, for every } X \in D_a, \text{ whenever} \\ & Den_{M,g}(A)(X) = 1, \text{ it is also} \\ & \text{the case that } Den_{M,g}(B)(X) = 1 \\ 0 & \text{otherwise} \end{vmatrix}$$

## 2.4   $IL_s$ and Montague's IL

The logic $IL_s$ differs from IL primarily in treating $s$ as a basic type along with $e$ and $t$; the formula-constructing operations of the two logics are the same. It is easy to see that this makes the set of Types $T_{IL_s}$ strictly larger than the set of types $T_{IL}$, and that therefore the language IL is a proper subset of the language $IL_s$. We can therefore proceed as in [Gal75] to define, for each expression $A_a$ of IL, the translate of $A_a$ in $IL_s$, denoted by $|A_a|*$. In what follows, $i$ is to be considered a particular, distinguished variable of type $s$, say $x_{0,s}$.

1.  $|x_{n,a}|* = x_{n,a}$

2.  $|c_{n,a}|* = c_{n,<s,a>}(i)$

3.  $|A_{<a,b>}(B_a)|* = |A_{<a,b>}| * (|B_a|*)$

4.  $|\lambda x_a A_b|* = \lambda x_a |A_b|*$

5.  $|[A_a = B_a]|* = [|A_a|* = |B_a|*]$

6.  $|\neg\phi|* = \neg|\phi|*$, and similarly for $|[\phi \wedge \psi]|*$, $|[\phi \vee \psi]|*$, $|[\phi \rightarrow \psi]|*$, $|[\phi \leftrightarrow \psi]|*$, $|\exists x\phi|*$, and $|\forall x\phi|*$.

7.  $|{}^\wedge A_a|* = \lambda i |A_a|*$

8.  $|{}^\vee A_{<s,a>}|* = |A_{<s,a>}| * (i)$

9.  $|\phi|* = \forall y_s |\phi|*$

10. $|\mathcal{F}\phi|* = \exists y_s[[i < y_s] \wedge \lambda i |\phi| * (y_s)]$

11. $|\mathcal{P}\phi|* = \exists y_s[[y_s < i] \wedge \lambda i |\phi| * (y_s)]$

We note also that for the convenience of some of our translations from English we have defined four additional primitive symbols, $\exists!$, $<$, $\ll$, and $\subseteq$ in $IL_s$, and therefore the following formula schemata are without a simple equivalent in IL (though they could be defined in IL):

1. $\exists! x_a \phi$

2. $[A_s < B_s]$

3. $[A_s \ll B_{<s,t>}]$ and $[B_{<s,t>} \ll A_s]$

4. $[A_{<a,t>} \subseteq B_{<a,t>}]$.

There is an obvious meaning-preserving relationship between these two logics in the following sense. Recall that in IL the set of Types $T$ is defined as follows:

1. $e, t \in T$

2. if $a, b \in T$, then $< a, b > \in T$

3. if $a \in T$, then $< s, a > \in T$

A model $M$ for IL, $M = < E, S, <, F >$ is defined as for $IL_s$, except for a difference in the interpretation function $F$. In IL the function $F$ assigns to each constant $c_{n,a}$ an element in $D_{<s,a>}$ defined as follows:

- $D_e = E$

- $D_t = \{0, 1\}$

- $D_{<a,b>} = D_b^{D_a}$

- $D_{<s,a>} = D_a^S$

Given a language IL and its model $M$, we define a corresponding language $IL_s$ and model $M_s$ that will satisfy the property that, for every expression $A_a$ in the language IL, its translate $|A_a|*$ will have the *same meaning* in the model $M_s$ as $A_a$ has in the model $M$. We have effectively done this already in defining the translate $|A_a|*$. For every constant $c_{n,a}$ of IL we associate a corresponding constant $c'_{n,<s,a>}$ in $IL_s$ such that $F_{IL}(c_{n,a}) = F_{IL_s}(c'_{n,<s,a>})$. In the case of variables, for a given variable assignment $g$ for IL, we simply choose any variable assignment $g_s$ which is an extension of $g$, i.e., such that for all variables $x_{n,a} \in IL, g_s(x_{n,a}) = g(x_{n,a})$. As a result of our definition of $|A_a|*$, it follows immediately that, when evaluated in their respective models with respect to a time $t$, the two expressions $A_a$ and $|A_a|*$ have the same denotation. More formally, $Den_{M,g,t}(A_a) = Den_{M_s,g_s}(i|t)(|A_a|*)$.

The following points bear emphasizing with regard to the translations from English into the logic $IL_s$ as compared to IL:

1. For each constant $c_a$ of IL, we will use a corresponding constant $c_{<s,a>}$ in $lL_s$, such that $F_{IL_s}(c_{<s,a>}) = F_{IL}(c_a)$. For example, for $J_e$ of IL, we use $J_{<s,e>}$ in $IL_s$, and for $walk'_{<<s,e>,t>}$ of IL, we use $walk'_{<s,<<s,e>,t>}$ in $IL_s$

2. From the definition of $|c_a|*$ above, we see that any constant we use must be applied as a function to the distinguished time variable $i$, e.g. $|J_e|* = J_{<s,e>}(i)$, and $|walk'_{<<s,e>,t>}|* = walk'_{<s,<<s,e>,t>>}(i)$.

Two points should be made regarding this change to $IL_s$. First the somewhat confusing process in IL by which a constant of type $a$ is mapped by the interpretation function $F$ to its sense (function from indices to $D_a$) disappears in $IL_s$, where the more *normal* interpretation function $F$ maps a constant of type a to an element in $D_a$. (Note that it was confusion about this aspect of IL that led Montague to make a small error in defining the semantics of IL; Thomason, the editor of [Mon74], amended the definition in footnote 10, p.259.) The second and related point stems from the aforementioned difference in the treatment of constants. In IL, a constant is interpreted as denoting its sense or intension, but at *evaluation time* it is interpreted as denoting its extension with respect to the *current index*. This *hidden* function application (of an intensional expression to an index) is made explicit in $IL_s$ as follows: to evaluate an expression $A$ with respect to a time $s$ in $S$, we form the expression $(\lambda i\, A)(s)$ and then evaluate this expression in the model. (Alternatively, we could make the stipulation that the only variable assignments $g$ that are of interest to us are those that satisfy the property that $g(i) = s$.) For example, we evaluate a formula $\phi$ by forming the expression $[\lambda i\, \phi](s)$, so that the formula $walk'_*(i)(J(i))$, intended to denote the proposition that John walks, would be evaluated with respect to a time $s$ by forming the formula:

$$[\lambda i(walk'_*(i)\ (J(i)))](s)$$

which reduces by $\lambda$-conversion to

$$walk'_*(s)(J(s)).$$

This formula explicitly indicates that the constants $walk'_*$ and $J$ are to be evaluated at the index $s$.

## 2.5 Informal Discussion of $IL_s$

Probably the best way to get a feeling for what these definitions say is to set up a small language and model and provide some examples. Before doing that, we wish to point out a standard way of referring to expressions of type $< a, t >$ for any type a. Such an expression denotes a function from $D_a$ into $\{0,1\}$ and can therefore be thought of as the characteristic function of a set of objects in $D_a$. Accordingly we will often speak of, e.g., sets of individuals, when we should more formally speak of functions from individuals to $\{0,1\}$. For example, over a universe consisting of the set $\{a,b,c,d,e\}$, the set $\{a,c,e\}$ is equivalently represented by the following characteristic function:

$$\begin{bmatrix} a & \to & 1 \\ b & \to & 0 \\ c & \to & 1 \\ d & \to & 0 \\ e & \to & 1 \end{bmatrix}$$

In order to illustrate some examples we assume a language that contains the following constants of the indicated types:

- Peter, Liz, Elsie, and THE_BOSS of type $<s,e>$

- 85, 86, 87, 88, and 89 of type $s$, and

- EMP of type $<s,<e,t>>$

and that our model $M = <E, S, <, F>$ is defined as follows:

- $E = \{\mathbf{Peter, Liz, Elsie}\}$

- $S = \{1985, 1986, 1987, 1988, 1989\}$

- with $<$ the obvious ordering on $S$.

Assume that the interpretation function $F$ makes the obvious assignments to the time constants. The other constants are interpreted as follows:

$$F(Peter) = \begin{bmatrix} 1985 & \to & \mathbf{Peter} \\ 1986 & \to & \mathbf{Peter} \\ 1987 & \to & \mathbf{Peter} \\ 1988 & \to & \mathbf{Peter} \\ 1989 & \to & \mathbf{Peter} \end{bmatrix}$$

$$F(Liz) = \begin{bmatrix} 1985 & \to & \mathbf{Liz} \\ 1986 & \to & \mathbf{Liz} \\ 1987 & \to & \mathbf{Liz} \\ 1988 & \to & \mathbf{Liz} \\ 1989 & \to & \mathbf{Liz} \end{bmatrix}$$

$$F(Elsie) = \begin{bmatrix} 1985 & \to & \mathbf{Elsie} \\ 1986 & \to & \mathbf{Elsie} \\ 1987 & \to & \mathbf{Elsie} \\ 1988 & \to & \mathbf{Elsie} \\ 1989 & \to & \mathbf{Elsie} \end{bmatrix}$$

These functions, from times to individuals, are what we have defined above as *individual concepts (ICs)*: they are intended to represent the **sense** of a name, since they pick out the individual referred to by the name at every index. The ICs above all share the additional property of being **constant ICs** (or **rigid designators**): in each time $S_i$ they pick out the same individual. Compare how $F$ interprets the constant THE_BOSS:

$$F(THE\_BOSS) = \begin{bmatrix} 1985 & \to & \textbf{Liz} \\ 1986 & \to & \textbf{Peter} \\ 1987 & \to & \textbf{Peter} \\ 1988 & \to & \textbf{Peter} \\ 1989 & \to & \textbf{Elsie} \end{bmatrix}$$

This function is also an IC, but it is not a constant IC. Later we shall see how this distinction between constant and unconstrained ICs will be related to the database concepts of key and descriptive attributes, respectively. We can think of this function as representing the **role** of the boss, in that it tells who fills that role in every time. The interpretation of EMP will be a function which, for any time, picks out a set of individuals (the intended interpretation being that set of individuals who are EMPloyees at that time):

$$F(EMP) = \begin{bmatrix} 1985 & \to & \{\textbf{Liz}\} \\ 1986 & \to & \{\textbf{Peter}, \textbf{Liz}\} \\ 1987 & \to & \{\textbf{Peter}, \textbf{Liz}\} \\ 1988 & \to & \{\textbf{Peter}\} \\ 1989 & \to & \{\textbf{Elsie}\} \end{bmatrix}$$

Such a function is often called a **property** of individuals. Notice that we have used set notation instead of the following more cumbersome, though equivalent, representation by characteristic functions:

$$F(EMP) = \begin{bmatrix} 1985 & \to & \begin{bmatrix} \textbf{Peter} & \to & 0 \\ \textbf{Liz} & \to & 1 \\ \textbf{Elsie} & \to & 0 \end{bmatrix} \\ 1986 & \to & \begin{bmatrix} \textbf{Peter} & \to & 1 \\ \textbf{Liz} & \to & 1 \\ \textbf{Elsie} & \to & 0 \end{bmatrix} \\ 1987 & \to & \begin{bmatrix} \textbf{Peter} & \to & 1 \\ \textbf{Liz} & \to & 1 \\ \textbf{Elsie} & \to & 0 \end{bmatrix} \\ 1988 & \to & \begin{bmatrix} \textbf{Peter} & \to & 1 \\ \textbf{Liz} & \to & 0 \\ \textbf{Elsie} & \to & 0 \end{bmatrix} \\ 1989 & \to & \begin{bmatrix} \textbf{Peter} & \to & 0 \\ \textbf{Liz} & \to & 0 \\ \textbf{Elsie} & \to & 1 \end{bmatrix} \end{bmatrix}$$

Consider now the expression EMP(86). Since EMP is of type $< s, < e, t >>$ and 86 is of type $s$, this expression is well-formed and is of type $< e, t >$. Its interpretation is given by applying the function which is the interpretation of EMP to the interpretation of 86, viz. 1986, yielding the set {**Peter, Liz**}.[1].

Thus we see that the interpretation rules give the expected meaning to EMP(86) in the given model, viz. the set of individuals who are EMPloyees in 1986. Consider now the expression EMP(86)(Elsie)(86), of type $t$. The denotation of this expression is *computed* by *applying* the set {**Peter,Liz**}. (considered as a function) to the argument **Elsie** to obtain the value 0 (False); i.e., Elsie is not an EMPloyee in 1986.

Now, suppose we wanted to form an expression whose denotation was a function from times to those individuals who were **not** the boss at those times. Such an expression will be of the same type as the constant EMP, viz. $< s, < e, t >>$, and can be constructed from the constants we have so far defined using $\lambda$-abstraction over the set of times and the set of individuals. In order to do this we need to use two variables in the logic: a variable $i$ of type $s$, i.e. a variable over times, and a variable $u$ of type $e$, a variable over individuals. We already know that the interpretation function $F$ gives the interpretation of each non-logical constant. The variable assignment $g$, as in first-order languages, provides the denotation of variables. Explicitly, for every variable $y$ of type $a$, $g(y) \in D_a$. With these two variables we can form an expression which denotes the function we want, viz.:

$$\lambda i \lambda u [\neg THE\_BOSS(i)(u)].$$

The denotation of this function, let us call it N_T_B, is specified by our model $M$ as follows:

$$N\_T\_B = \begin{bmatrix} 1985 & \rightarrow & \{\textbf{Peter}, \textbf{Elsie}\} \\ 1986 & \rightarrow & \{\textbf{Liz}, \textbf{Elsie}\} \\ 1987 & \rightarrow & \{\textbf{Liz}, \textbf{Elsie}\} \\ 1988 & \rightarrow & \{\textbf{Liz}, \textbf{Elsie}\} \\ 1989 & \rightarrow & \{\textbf{Liz}, \textbf{Peter}\} \end{bmatrix}$$

The denotation indicates that in each year one and only one person is not not the boss (viz., the one who IS the boss.) (Of course an alternative definition might want to limit the universe to only those individuals who are actually employees and not the boss at a given time.)

Finally, we consider an example that makes explicit reference to time, the formula which translates the sentence "Elsie was the boss":

$$\exists i [[i < now] \wedge THE\_BOSS(i)(Elsie)(i)]$$

If we assume that **now** (of type $s$) is interpreted as 1989, this formula will be True just in case there is some time $i$ prior to 1989 at which Elsie was "the boss." It is

---

[1]Again, more precisely, its characteristic function. Henceforth we will blur the distinction and use the two representations interchangeably as convenient.

easy to see that with respect to the model $M$ this formula is False, and the inductive definition of the interpretation of the language $IL_s$ appropriately has this formula denote 0.

This completes our informal discussion of the language $IL_s$ and its semantics. In the following chapter we present a detailed discussion of the model-theoretic implications of a historical relational database.

# CHAPTER THREE

# THE HRDM MODEL

## 3.1 Motivation for Historical Databases

The relational database model proposed by Codd [Cod70] views a database as a collection of "time-varying relations of assorted degrees" [Cha78]. However the model itself incorporates neither the concept of time nor any theory of temporal semantics. Our research suggests that the concept of time can be of interest in real-world databases, and presents a technique for incorporating a semantics of time into a database model. The relational model is used as the formal database framework within which the work is cast, but it is not an essential ingredient in the work discussed. Indeed in [CC88a] we address the issue of modelling the temporal dimension of data within the context of an *object-oriented database model*.

A great deal of attention has been given lately to the role that formal logic can play in providing a formal mathematical theory to unify the theory and semantics of database concepts and operations ([GM78] is an excellent reference for these issues.) We believe that this is a healthy trend that can only serve to clarify and make precise otherwise vague ideas and theories. Moreover, a great deal of the meta-theory of formal logic can be applied directly toward the understanding and the proof of many notions in database theory. In this work we propose the concept of a **historical database** as a tool for modelling the changing states of information about some part of the real world. Most conventional databases are *static*, representing a snapshot view of the world at a given moment in time; changes in the real world generally are reflected in the database by changes to its data, thereby *forgetting*, as it were, the old data. By contrast, a historical database is a model of the dynamically changing real world. Changes in the real world are reflected in such a database by establishing a new state description; no data is ever *forgotten*. As such the historical database can be viewed intuitively as a collection of static databases organized in a coherent fashion. We will provide here a detailed description of such an organization and a discussion of the usefulness of the historical database concept for modelling the real world (or some *possible world*) more closely than is possible with a static database.

[Bub77] provides a good overview of the issues involved in incorporating a temporal dimension in databases.

We believe that providing a formal semantics for a database model is of paramount importance to its usefulness. The concept of time is crucial to all databases, but is only treated implicitly in the existing database models. Databases exist in time and model changes that occur temporally in the world via database state changes. In order to have a proper understanding of how an explicit representation of time interacts with all of the data in the database it is not enough simply to allow users to utilize *time attributes* where they seem appropriate. By incorporating a general temporal semantics directly within the database model we not only spare the user the task of defining such a semantics, but we also can ensure that time is treated in a uniform and consistent manner. Moreover, if the temporal semantics is built into the model implementations of a historical database can take advantage of this standard semantics to increase the efficiency of database operations. The basis which we suggest for the semantics of a historical database model is the formulation of an intensional logic $IL_s$, a modification of the language IL of Richard Montague [Mon73], whose work has profoundly influenced current research in linguistics and the philosophy of language.

The major reason for preferring a Montague-type logic over other formulations of temporal or intensional logics (as in [RU71]) is the framework he provides [Mon73] for defining a formal syntax and semantics of English using IL. The development of the historical database model is part of our research into the larger area of Natural Language Database Querying (NLQ). Our approach is motivated by the desire to develop a framework for NLQ that is founded squarely on a fully formalized syntax and semantics in the sense of Montague [Mon73], and suggestive of a formalized pragmatics as well. In the latter chapters of this book we discuss the translation of English database queries into the logic $IL_s$, and provide a general schema for defining an English query language specific to a given database domain. The model theory of the logic $IL_s$ has directly influenced our view of the objects in the historical database. In particular, database attributes are viewed in our historical database model as **functions** from moments in time to values (in the appropriate domain), and $IL_s$ gives us the power to speak directly about these *higher-order* objects and to incorporate them into a general temporal semantics for the database. We can therefore express both static and dynamic constraints (as discussed in [NY78]) in the same language, by quantifying over variables of the appropriate types.

It should perhaps be noted that a historical database, as we define it, is a theoretical object, and a rather large one at that; no remarks in this work should be construed as referring to any techniques for implementing this object. Obviously a direct implementation would be extremely cost-prohibitive for any real database. Reasonable implementations that eliminate much of the inherent data redundancy of the formal model are not difficult to imagine. We are currently in the process of exploring a number of different implementations and algorithms for an HDB; an early implementation as a Pascal front-end to the relational DBMS Ingres ([Sto86]) was reported in [Shi86].

In Section 3.2 we begin our discussion by providing the motivation behind the historical database concept; this leads to a central idea in our approach, namely the concept of an object's *lifespan*, which we discuss in Section 3.3. Before the formal presentation of the HRDM model in Section 3.5, we present in Section 3.4 a *stepwise development* of a historical relational database for a very simple database example consisting of a single relation. We present this discussion in terms of the entity-relationship view of data semantics ([Che76]) modified slightly to incorporate the a semantics for time. In Chapter 4 we will expand our example to encompass a larger database of historical relations, using a version of the entity-relationship department-store database described in [Cha78].

In a database modelling information over time, the status of an *object* – is it interesting to the enterprise or is it not? – will change over time. For example, in a personnel database, throughout the period during which a particular person is employed by a company, information about that person can be assumed to be of interest and so will be recorded in the database. But in general it can be assumed that the database itself will have existed before and will continue to exist after the employment period of any particular employee.

The *birth* of an object $O$, with respect to a database, refers to the point in time when the database first records any information about $O$. Similarly, its *death* occurs when the object ceases to be modelled. Historical databases, however, need also to support the notion of *reincarnation*, since a death is not necessarily terminal. For example, employees can be hired, fired, and subsequently rehired; students may drop in and out of school. For this reason the historical database must be able to support object reincarnation, to allow for tracking such reincarnation events as well as the individuals so reincarnated. But database *objects* model not simply individuals (parts, suppliers, students, courses, etc.) but also relationships among individuals (shipments, enrollments). Unlike the standard Entity-Relationship model ([Che76]), which allows for only one instance of a given relationship (one part-supplier pair, e.g.), the historical model must model relationships over time, allow for *reincarnated* relationships, and enforce referential integrity constraints with respect to the temporal dimension. For example, a student can only take a course at time t if both the student and the course exist in the database at time t.

Early work on historical databases, (e.g. [Klo81,KL83,CW83] ) recognized this problem and proposed the incorporation of a time-stamp, e.g. a STATE attribute, and a Boolean-valued EXISTS? attribute to each tuple as a solution. The database was seen as a three-dimensional cube, wherein at any time $t$ a tuple with EXISTS? = True was considered to be meaningful, otherwise it was to be ignored. As discussed in a classification scheme proposed in [SA85], other subsequent and contemporaneous efforts at defining *historical* database models (e.g. [Ben82,Lum84,Sno84,ABM84]) continued to examine more succinct or perspicuous representations along this tuple-based line. [Cli82b] was the first to suggest incorporating the temporal dimension at the attribute level. This idea was further refined in [Cli85] and was also the basis for

| emprel | | | |
|---|---|---|---|
| **EMP** | MGR | DEPT | SAL |
| John | John | Linen | 25K |
| Mike | John | Linen | 17K |
| Elsie | Elsie | Toy | 26K |
| Liz | Liz | Hardware | 30K |
| Rachel | Liz | Hardware | 29K |
| Peter | Liz | Hardware | 29K |

**Figure 3.1: Relation emprel on Scheme EMPREL**

the model proposed in [GV85].

These developments can be seen as efforts in the direction of associating the temporal dimension with a smaller component of the model – at first with the relation itself (the *cube* metaphor), later with each tuple (e.g., the notion of *tuple homogeneity* in [GV85]), and finally with each attribute value. We believe that the orthogonal notions of tuple and attribute lifespans provide for the suitable level of uniformity and flexibility in the temporal dimension.

## 3.2   Informal Presentation of HRDM

Consider a static database with a relation scheme EMPREL(<u>EMP</u> MGR SAL DEPT) and a relation emprel on EMPREL. A typical query to such a relation, of the sort that has been treated in the literature, might be: "What is employee John's salary?" In the relational algebra this would be expressed as $\pi_{SAL}(\sigma_{EMP=John}(emprel))$. A first-order language would express this same query as something like

$$\{z|\exists x \exists y[emprel(John, x, y, z)]\}$$

where $x$,$y$, and $z$ are individual variables and *John* is an individual constant. In order to answer such a query, a Data Manipulation Language (DML) simply accesses the relation instance emprel on EMPREL, such as the one in Figure 3.1. In recent database literature (e.g. [Min78], [Rei78a], [Cha78]) such a relation instance has been termed the *extension* of the relation scheme EMPREL, a term borrowed from logic.

One could imagine other sorts of queries that casual users might want to ask about the employees in this company, e.g.:

- "Has John's salary risen?"

- "When was Peter rehired?"

- "Did Rachel work for the toy department last year?"

- "Has John ever earned the same as Peter?"

- "Will the average salary in the linen department surpass 30K within the next 5 years?"

Time-dependent questions of this sort are not handled by existing static database models or systems, and have not received adequate attention within the database literature (although such papers as [Bub77], [NY78], [CB79], [LMP79], [Ser80], and [Klo81] discuss from various points of view the need for a temporal semantics for databases). Real database administrators faced with the need to process particular instances of queries of this sort have undoubtedly used some version of the technique that we present here of incorporating a time attribute into the database, and providing this attribute with a special significance. We are interested in developing a unified and formal theory of database semantics that includes time. In other words, given the need for maintaining a historical record of changing data, and a language (English) that makes (explicit or implicit) reference to the concept of time, we would like a theory that provides a database semantics capable of interpreting sentences in the language correctly, i.e., in a way that corresponds with our intuitive understanding of the relation of time to the semantics of the real-world.

Let us consider more closely the query "Has John's salary risen?" Even with time represented explicitly in the database, there is no apparent simple relational algebraic formulation for this query. With the first-order representation for John's salary given above, as a first guess we might imagine that $RISE(\{z|\exists x\exists y[emprel(John, x, y, z)]\}$ would represent this new query, where RISE is a predicate symbol. However even with a *functional dependency* (FD) [Mai83] that ensured that John had only one salary, say 25K, it clearly makes no sense to ask whether 25K "rises." In order to answer this question, more data is needed than the current extension of John's salary: the values of John's salary for some other point(s) of time (in this specific instance, in the past) are needed. In the model that we present we will identify such things as SALaries, not with individual dollar amounts, but with dollar amounts in the **role** of an EMPloyee's salary.

It is not difficult to see that if we need to keep track of *when* the facts we record in our database are to be considered *true*, then we need to *time stamp* these facts in some way. Exactly how we propose to do this, and how this proposal will extend the concept of and intuition about relations is the subject of the remainder of this chapter. For the moment we take a simplified look at this suggestion and discuss some of the issues involved. A first point to notice is that the expression

$$\{z|\exists x\exists y[emprel(John, x, y, z)]\}$$

has, in these two queries, two very different meanings. The simple query

$$\{z|\exists x\exists y[emprel(John, x, y, z)\}]$$

denotes the extensional value 25K, the salary that John is making **now**. However the second query

$$RISE(\{z|\exists x\exists y[emprel(John,x,y,z)]\})$$

is not to be interpreted as asking $RISE(25K)$. Some other meaning, involving more than the current extension of John's salary, must be given to John's salary in order to determine whether the predicate $RISE$ is true of it. This other meaning for John's salary, we shall see, is what is called (in intensional logic) its **intension**. (The terms extension and intension are given formal definitions in intensional logic, and will be defined formally here. They should not be confused with their usage in some database papers where the term "intension," e.g. in [Rei78a], is used to refer to axioms which constrain the set of possible models for the database.) It may be helpful to think of them in terms of roles, which at any moment of time might be filled by any appropriate individual.

The concept of intension dates back to Frege [Fre92] and his distinction between the sense and denotation of an expression in a language. A full discussion of the history of these concepts in logic is beyond the scope of this work; [Car47], [DWP81], and [vB88], among others, provide a useful introduction to these issues. Roughly speaking, the extension of a linguistic expression is some *object* or element of the appropriate kind in the model for that language. The extension of a name is some individual in the model; the extension of a formula is one of the objects *True* or *False*; the extension of a set is some collection of individuals, etc. The concept of intension, on the other hand, is meant to capture the notion of the *sense* or *idea* or *meaning* of an expression. This somewhat vague idea is formalized in Montague's IL by defining the intension of any expression as a function from a set of points of reference (variously called *possible worlds* or indices) to extensions. Thus the intension of a name (called an **individual concept (IC)**) is a function which, given any index, picks out some individual as the referent of that name *at that index*. Similarly the intension of a set (called a **property**) picks out some collection of individuals which is the referent of the set-name at each index, and the intension of a formula (called a **proposition**) is that function which, for any index, tells whether the formula is True or False at that index.

For example, suppose that we are interested in maintaining a yearly record of the emprel relation, say for the period of the last five years. If we define a set of times, say $S = \{1977, 1978, 1979, 1980, 1981\}$, as the *complete* set of indices or points of reference of interest to us, then the intension of a name in our language will be a function from this set $S$ to individuals in the model. Thus, considering the employee John we might have the intensions depicted in Figure 3.2 for the names "John," "Department-of-John" and "Salary-of-John" (assuming for the moment some linguistic mechanism for constructing these names). The function that is the intension of "Department-of-John," for instance, represents the **role** of John's department and tells what department *fills* that role in each state.

We can now imagine a DML that could examine such a database and provide an affirmative answer to our query "Has John's salary risen?" In subsequent chapters

$$
\begin{bmatrix}
1977 & \rightarrow & John \\
1978 & \rightarrow & John \\
1979 & \rightarrow & John \\
1980 & \rightarrow & John \\
1981 & \rightarrow & John \\
& (a) &
\end{bmatrix}
\quad
\begin{bmatrix}
1977 & \rightarrow & linen \\
1978 & \rightarrow & linen \\
1979 & \rightarrow & linen \\
1980 & \rightarrow & shoe \\
1981 & \rightarrow & shoe \\
& (b) &
\end{bmatrix}
\quad
\begin{bmatrix}
1977 & \rightarrow & 25K \\
1978 & \rightarrow & 25K \\
1979 & \rightarrow & 27K \\
1980 & \rightarrow & 27K \\
1981 & \rightarrow & 30K \\
& (c) &
\end{bmatrix}
$$

(a) Intension of "John" (b) Intension of "Department-of-John" (c) Intension of "Salary-of-John"

**Figure 3.2: Three Intensions**

we will present a formalization of these ideas in terms of the relational database model using the intensional logic $IL_s$. We also discuss the application of this logic to database querying in natural language, and to the unified expression of various kinds of data constraints.

## 3.3 Lifespans

In order to address these temporal issues (and also, as we shall see, the related issue of evolving database schemas) we introduce the lifespan notion. For instance, the lifespan of an employee, with respect to the personnel database, would *explicitly* represent the temporal dimension of the information about that employee. Queries or other data operations that refer to that employee outside of that lifespan will be treated specially, because the database is not modelling that employee during those time periods.

The question arises, what is an appropriate *object* with which to associate such a lifespan? In particular, data models distinguish between the schema and the instance, and provide constructs of both types. Most attention in historical database research has focussed on the database instance, since in general it is the *data objects* whose lifespans will be of interest. In the relational model the database instance can be looked at as a hierarchy as in Figure 3.3, the database being composed of a set of relations, and each relation composed of a set of tuples.

The addition of a temporal component adds a third dimension to the relational model, as depicted in Figure 3.4. Restrictions on the way in which this new dimension interacts with the other two result in a variety of different *temporal extensions* to the relational model. If, for example, we associate a lifespan at the database level of the hierarchy in Figure 3.3, our database will look like Figure 3.5, i.e., a collection of relations which are homogeneous in the temporal dimension. (Although in this figure the lifespan is shown as a single, connected interval of time, this is not necessarily the case.) Associating the lifespan at this level commits us to a database in which

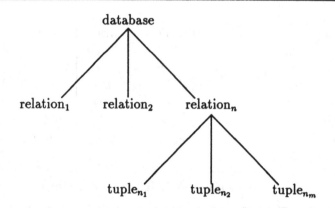

**Figure 3.3: A Relational Database Instance**

each relation and each tuple has the same lifespan. Because this is so stringent a constraint, it has not, to our knowledge, been the subject of any serious research.

If we instead associate a lifespan with each relation, then we can have a database which looks like Figure 3.6, where each relation can be defined over different periods of time, but each tuple in a given relation is homogeneous in the temporal dimension, as in [GV85].

Finally, if we associate the lifespan at the tuple level, we have a database that consists of tuples which, for any given relation, can look like those in Figure 3.7.

The choice of which level is appropriate involves a tradeoff between the cost of maintaining proliferating lifespans, on the one hand, and the flexibility that finer and finer lifespans provide, on the other. In terms of complexity, the overhead for the database or relation approach is quite small, and is proportional to the size of the schema. The cost of the tuple lifespan approach is proportional to the size of the database instance. [Cli85] argues that associating the temporal dimension with each attribute provides for more user control of the different temporal properties of individual attributes.

Orthogonal to the database instance and its components is the relational database schema and its components. Some work has been done in considering the schema to be a time-varying component of the database (e.g. [Nav80], [Shi86]), but this work has not been done within a single, unified model for historical databases. The database schema, as illustrated in Figure 3.8, consists of a set of relation schemas, each of which, ignoring constraints, can be considered to be the set of attributes for that relation.

A single lifespan assigned to the database schema (or relation schema) itself would presumably indicate the period of time during which the entire database (or relation) was defined or, in a sense, operational. This does not seem to buy us very much. However, assigning a lifespan to each attribute in a relation scheme, allows the user

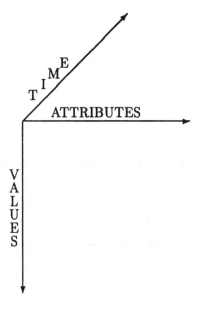

**Figure 3.4: The Three Dimensions of a Historical Database**

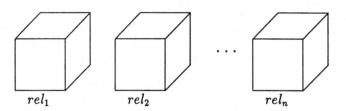

**Figure 3.5: One Lifespan Associated with Entire Database**

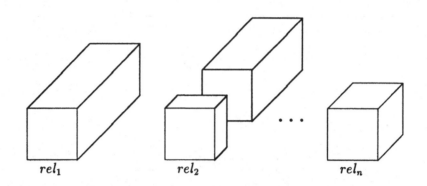

**Figure 3.6: Lifespans Associated with Each Relation**

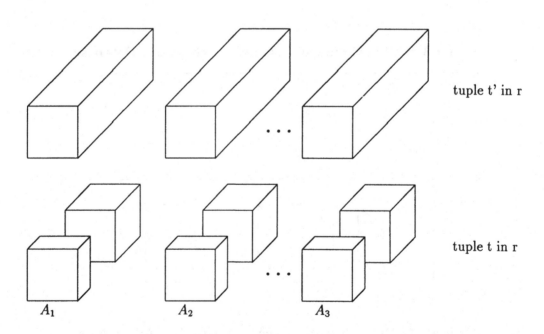

**Figure 3.7: Lifespans Associated with Each Relation Tuple**

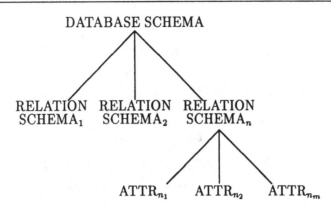

Figure 3.8: Relational Database Schema

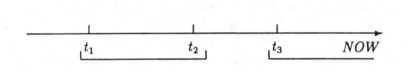

Figure 3.9: Lifespan of Attribute **DAILY-TRADING-VOLUME**

to explicitly indicate the period of time over which this attribute is defined in that relation, thereby allowing for the possibility of *evolving schemes*. (Then the lifespan of the relation schema would be the union of the lifespans of all of the attributes in the schema, and we need the constraint that the lifespan of the key attributes must be the same as the lifespan of the entire relation schema.)

As an example, consider a database that records stock market information, including an attribute Daily Trading Volume.

Its lifespan might, for example, be $\{[t_1, t_2], [t_3, NOW)\}$, as indicated in Figure 3.9, where for the period $[t_1, t_2]$ this information was recorded, after which it became too expensive to collect and so it was dropped from the schema. Subsequently, at time $t_3$ and continuing through the present, perhaps a cheap outside source of this information was discovered and so the schema was expanded to once again incorporate this attribute.

The lifespan of an attribute within a given relation is orthogonal to the notion of the lifespan of a tuple in a relation, as shown in Figure 3.10.

Consider the value of attribute $A_n$ for tuple$_m$, i.e., the **XXX**'d box in the lower

$$\text{ls} = L_1$$

|  | $A_1$ | $A_2$ | ... | $A_n$ |
|---|---|---|---|---|
| $tuple_1$ |  |  |  |  |
| $tuple_2$ |  |  |  |  |
| ... |  |  |  |  |
| $tuple_m$ |  |  |  | XXX |

$$\text{ls} = L_2$$

**Figure 3.10: Interaction of Tuple and Attribute Lifespans**

right hand corner of the matrix of Figure 3.10. Over what period of time is it defined in the database? The tuple provides information about an *object* which is assumed to be defined in the database over the lifespan $L_2$, but the attribute is only defined over the lifespan $L_1$. Clearly the *object* can only have a value for this attribute in the database over the intersection $L_1 \cap L_2$ of these two lifespans.

Figure 3.11 represents an example within the HRDM model to be presented in Section 3.4; lifespans are associated with tuples and also with attributes, and so tuples are heterogeneous in their temporal dimension. The lifespan of any particular value is limited both by the lifespan of the tuple and the lifespan of the attribute. (It is worth pointing out that in the most general or flexible historical model we would associate a lifespan with each *value* in a relation, and so allow for a completely heterogeneous temporal dimension, but at the cost of maintaining a distinct lifespan for each value.)

## 3.4   Intuitive Presentation of Historical Databases

We proceed under the assumption that an enterprise wishes to maintain a **historical database,** i.e. one that models the dynamic nature of that part of the real world that is its concern. To simplify the discussion we again consider only our entity relation scheme EMPREL as representing the entire database; later we will present a more formal view, and include both entity and relationship relations. We suppose that we are given three **static relation** instances emprel$_1$, emprel$_2$, and emprel$_3$ (Figure 3.12), i.e., instances each of which represents a single state of the world as modelled in the relational database.

We will proceed first to develop in stages a *feel* for the concept of a historical database, in order to provide some intuition for the more formal treatment given later. We will use the EMPREL entity relation scheme as our running example. The first step is to incorporate a method for time-stamping the tuples (*facts*) in our database. One obvious way to do this would be to add a new attribute, say STATE, to the relation scheme, creating the scheme EMPREL'(STATE EMP MGR DEPT

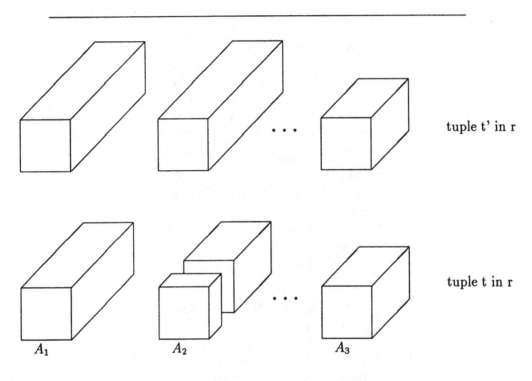

Figure 3.11: Tuple and Attribute Lifespans

| emprel₁ | | | |
|---|---|---|---|
| **EMP** | MGR | DEPT | SAL |
| John | John | Linen | 23K |
| Mike | John | Linen | 17K |
| Elsie | Elsie | Toy | 26K |
| Liz | Liz | Hardware | 30K |
| Rachel | Liz | Hardware | 29K |
| Peter | Liz | Hardware | 29K |

| emprel₂ | | | |
|---|---|---|---|
| **EMP** | MGR | DEPT | SAL |
| John | John | Linen | 25K |
| Mike | Elsie | Toy | 20K |
| Elsie | Elsie | Toy | 27K |
| Rachel | Rachel | Hardware | 28K |
| Sharon | Rachel | Hardware | 25K |

| emprel₃ | | | |
|---|---|---|---|
| **EMP** | MGR | DEPT | SAL |
| Beth | Beth | Linen | 23K |
| Elsie | Elsie | Toy | 27K |
| Rachel | Peter | Hardware | 28K |
| Sharon | Peter | Hardware | 25K |
| Peter | Peter | Hardware | 33K |

Figure 3.12: **Three Static Relation Instances**

| emprel'₁ | | | | |
|---|---|---|---|---|
| **STATE** | **EMP** | **MGR** | **DEPT** | **SAL** |
| S1 | John | John | Linen | 23K |
| S1 | Mike | John | Linen | 17K |
| S1 | Elsie | Elsie | Toy | 26K |
| S1 | Liz | Liz | Hardware | 30K |
| S1 | Rachel | Liz | Hardware | 29K |
| S1 | Peter | Liz | Hardware | 29K |

| emprel'₂ | | | | |
|---|---|---|---|---|
| **STATE** | **EMP** | **MGR** | **DEPT** | **SAL** |
| S2 | John | John | Linen | 25K |
| S2 | Mike | Elsie | Toy | 20K |
| S2 | Elsie | Elsie | Toy | 27K |
| S2 | Rachel | Rachel | Hardware | 28K |
| S2 | Sharon | Rachel | Hardware | 25K |

| emprel'₃ | | | | |
|---|---|---|---|---|
| **STATE** | **EMP** | **MGR** | **DEPT** | **SAL** |
| S3 | Beth | Beth | Linen | 23K |
| S3 | Elsie | Elsie | Toy | 27K |
| S3 | Rachel | Peter | Hardware | 28K |
| S3 | Sharon | Peter | Hardware | 25K |
| S3 | Peter | Peter | Hardware | 33K |

**Figure 3.13: Three Extended Static Relations**

SAL). Each tuple $t$ in an instance emprel$_i$ would then be extended accordingly, by adding the value $S_i$ for the attribute STATE. The extended relations emprel$'_i$ are shown in Figure 3.13. Formally,

$$emprel'_i = \{t | t(EMPREL) \in emprel_i \wedge t(STATE) = S_i\}$$

We thus adopt an obvious notational convenience that a relation instance $r_i$ is to be associated with state $S_i$.

We would like to view these new relation instances emprel$'_i$ as providing historical information about the changing values of the attributes of the **objects** denoted by values of the key, in this instance about EMPloyees. In order to visualize more clearly what is going on, it is helpful to picture a historical relation as a *three-dimensional relation* or *relation cube*, each plane of which is a *static* or planar relation instance on EMPREL for a given state of the world $S_i$. Time adds the third dimension to the normal flat-table view of relations. In a tabular relation we understand that a

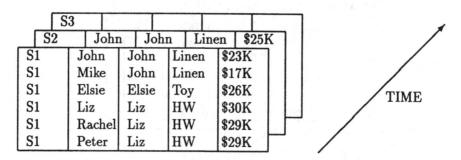

| STATE | EMP | MGR | DEPT | SAL |
|-------|-----|-----|------|-----|
| S3 | John | John | Linen | $25K |
| S2 | John | John | Linen | $25K |
| S1 | John | John | Linen | $23K |
| S1 | Mike | John | Linen | $17K |
| S1 | Elsie | Elsie | Toy | $26K |
| S1 | Liz | Liz | HW | $30K |
| S1 | Rachel | Liz | HW | $29K |
| S1 | Peter | Liz | HW | $29K |

**Figure 3.14: Historical Relations as Three-Dimensional**

row or tuple in a tabular relation corresponds to the information about a particular object, and a column corresponds to the Active Domain of a particular attribute. We now propose to view each non-key attribute, such as SAL, as a set of function values filling application-specific roles related to the objects given by the key values, e.g. John's SALary, Mike's SALary, etc. If we continue with the approach of extending each tuple with a STATE attribute, it will be necessary – in order to see more easily exactly what individuals fill these roles in each state – to *line up* the entities in the cube by sorting on the key attribute). Figure 3.14 illustrates such a cube for the emprel relation.

Figure 3.14 also illustrates a problem that must be solved if we are to model the temporal dimension correctly, viz. that some EMPloyees are not represented in every state. For example, John is not an EMPloyee in state S3, and therefore there is no tuple for John in the plane for S3 in this cube. Given the query "What is John's salary in S3?" we would want our model to give us the power to say, not that there is no such employee, but rather that John does not work for us in S3.

In order to provide a metaphor through which these issues can be examined we in-troduce the concept of a **completed relation**. Later this notion will be incorporated into a more formal definition of a number of assumptions on the interpretation of a historical database, assumptions with the same flavor as the Closed World Assump-tion of Reiter [Rei78b] but expanded to incorporate the temporal dimension. In order to indicate which entities are of interest in any state, we could use a special Boolean-valued attribute EXISTS?. In those states in which an entity does not exist as an EMPloyee, EXISTS? would be 0 for that EMP, and all of the other attributes would be given the value "⊥", a distinguished entity whose meaning is that no individual fills the role of that attribute, i.e., that the attribute does not apply. A *completed* *relation* will have a tuple in each state for every entity that is an EMPloyee in *any* state in the entire database. In this way we could follow objects and their attributes throughout all of the states of the database. To do this we must specify precisely all of the objects (key values) that are represented in any relation instance, and extend with a null tuple each instance that does not represent information about this object.

We formalize these ideas as follows: given a relation scheme $R'(\underline{STATE\ K}A_1 \ldots A_n)$ and an instance $r'_i$ on $R'$, we define the **Active Key Domain (AKD)** of $r'_i$ on $R'$ to be the set of all key values (entities) in the relation instance $r'_i$, i.e.:

$$AKD(r'_i) = \pi_K(r'_i)$$

We then extend this definition to a set of instances $I = \{r'_1, \ldots, r'_n\}$ on $R'$ by defining the **Complete Active Key Domain (CAKD)** of a set of instances as

$$CAKD(I) = \bigcup_{AKD(r'_i)} \text{ for all } r'_i \in I.$$

CAKD(I) is exactly the set we need – it represents all of the EMP entities about which any information is stored in the database.

We then extend each relation instance $r''_i$ so that it has a tuple for each entity in CAKD(I), the set of all *possible* EMPloyees that are *actual* in some state. Now by construction the projection of each expanded instance $r''$ onto the attribute K will correspond to *all* of the entities, i.e.:

$$\pi_K(r''_i) = CAKD(I).$$

If the entity k is an actual entity in state $S_i$, then in the expanded relation $r''_i$ the tuple $t''_k$ will have $t''_k(EXISTS?) = 1$ and will agree with the tuple $t'_k$ in $r'_i$ on every other attribute. On the other hand if k is not an actual entity in state $S_i$, then the tuple $t''_k$ will have $t''_k(EXISTS?) = 0$, but the distinguished value "$\perp$" for every other attribute other than STATE, indicating the *inapplicability* of this information for this entity, i.e., that no individual fills the roles of these attributes for that entity. Formally, we define the **completed relation** as follows:

$$\begin{aligned} r''_i = \ & \{t|t(R') \in r'_i \wedge t(EXISTS?) = 1\} \cup \\ & \{t|t(K) \in CAKD(I) - AKD(r'_i) \wedge \\ & t(STATE) = S_i \wedge t(EXISTS?) = 0 \wedge \\ & t(A) = \perp \ \forall A \in \{A_1, \ldots, A_n\}\}. \end{aligned}$$

The three completed EMPloyee relation instances are shown in Figure 3.15, arranged in a consistent (but arbitrarily chosen) order on key values.

The three-dimensional cube representation of the completed relation, such that the *i*th plane of the cube is $r''_i$, was already shown in Figure 3.14. In fact, HRDM

| emprel″₁ | | | | | |
|---|---|---|---|---|---|
| **STATE** | **EMP** | **EXISTS?** | **MGR** | **DEPT** | **SAL** |
| S1 | John | 1 | John | Linen | 23K |
| S1 | Mike | 1 | Mike | Linen | 17K |
| S1 | Elsie | 1 | Elsie | Toy | 26K |
| S1 | Liz | 1 | Liz | Hardware | 30K |
| S1 | Rachel | 1 | Rachel | Hardware | 29K |
| S1 | Peter | 1 | Peter | Hardware | 29K |
| S1 | Sharon | 0 | ⊥ | ⊥ | ⊥ |
| S1 | Beth | 0 | ⊥ | ⊥ | ⊥ |

| emprel″₂ | | | | | |
|---|---|---|---|---|---|
| **STATE** | **EMP** | **EXISTS?** | **MGR** | **DEPT** | **SAL** |
| S2 | John | 1 | John | Linen | 25K |
| S2 | Mike | 1 | Mike | Toy | 20K |
| S2 | Elsie | 1 | Elsie | Toy | 27K |
| S2 | Rachel | 1 | Rachel | Hardware | 28K |
| S2 | Sharon | 1 | Sharon | Hardware | 25K |
| S2 | Peter | 0 | ⊥ | ⊥ | ⊥ |
| S2 | Beth | 0 | ⊥ | ⊥ | ⊥ |
| S2 | Liz | 0 | ⊥ | ⊥ | ⊥ |

| emprel″₃ | | | | | |
|---|---|---|---|---|---|
| **STATE** | **EMP** | **EXISTS?** | **MGR** | **DEPT** | **SAL** |
| S3 | Beth | 1 | Beth | Linen | 23K |
| S3 | Elsie | 1 | Elsie | Toy | 27K |
| S3 | Rachel | 1 | Rachel | Hardware | 28K |
| S3 | Sharon | 1 | Sharon | Hardware | 25K |
| S3 | Peter | 1 | Peter | Hardware | 33K |
| S3 | John | 0 | ⊥ | ⊥ | ⊥ |
| S3 | Liz | 0 | ⊥ | ⊥ | ⊥ |
| S3 | Mike | 0 | ⊥ | ⊥ | ⊥ |

**Figure 3.15:** *Completed* **Relations**

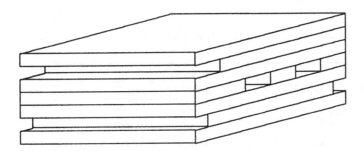

**Figure 3.16: A Historical Relation as a 3-D Structure**

is a more general model than this, allowing lifespans consisting of multiple, disjoint intervals of time. The picture in Figure 3.16 is a more accurate representation of the general *shape* of a historical relation.

The concept of a completed relation, combined with the EXISTS? attribute and the distinguished value $\perp$, is a convenient *metaphor* allowing us to refer in any state to any entity (EMP) that is actual at any time in the database, and we can visually follow the changes in the facts about each EMPloyee through a three-dimensional row of the cube. Gradually we will introduce enough of the theory of $IL_s$ to show how it can be applied to a historical database to provide a comprehensive database semantics capable of treating time-dependent queries and constraints.

In fact we could extend this metaphor, if we so desired, to allow us to consider all of these relation instances as comprising a single relation on the scheme EMPREL. We can easily combine them into one large relation by taking their union. In so doing we could view a historical relation $r_h$ on a relation scheme $R''(STATE\ K\ EXISTS?\ A_1 \ldots A_n)$ for a set of instances $I = \{r_1, r_2, \ldots, r_m\}$ as the union of the completed relations $r_i''$ that we have just constructed (Figure 3.17). There are no tuples lost in taking this union (i.e., there were no duplicates) because of the manner in which we have constructed each instance. Moreover we know that {STATE, K} would be a key of $r_h$. Finally, for each $S_i \in S$ the corresponding completed relation $r_i''$ is embedded in $r_h$, since

$$r_i'' = \sigma_{STATE=S_i}(r_h).$$

A **historical relational database**, then, is a collection of historical relations over the same set of states. In what follows we will continue to use the term **static database** as a general term to describe those familiar databases which attempt to model only *one* state of the world.

| emprel$_h$ | | | | | |
|---|---|---|---|---|---|
| **STATE** | **EMP** | EXISTS? | **MGR** | **DEPT** | **SAL** |
| S1 | John | 1 | John | Linen | 23K |
| S1 | Mike | 1 | John | Linen | 17K |
| S1 | Elsie | 1 | Elsie | Toy | 26K |
| S1 | Liz | 1 | Liz | Hardware | 30K |
| S1 | Rachel | 1 | Liz | Hardware | 29K |
| S1 | Peter | 1 | Liz | Hardware | 29K |
| S1 | Sharon | 0 | $\perp$ | $\perp$ | $\perp$ |
| S1 | Beth | 0 | $\perp$ | $\perp$ | $\perp$ |
| S2 | John | 1 | John | Linen | 25K |
| S2 | Mike | 1 | Elsie | Toy | 20K |
| S2 | Elsie | 1 | Elsie | Toy | 27K |
| S2 | Rachel | 1 | Rachel | Hardware | 28K |
| S2 | Sharon | 1 | Rachel | Hardware | 25K |
| S2 | Peter | 0 | $\perp$ | $\perp$ | $\perp$ |
| S2 | Beth | 0 | $\perp$ | $\perp$ | $\perp$ |
| S2 | Liz | 0 | $\perp$ | $\perp$ | $\perp$ |
| S3 | Beth | 1 | Beth | Linen | 23K |
| S3 | Elsie | 1 | Elsie | Toy | 27K |
| S3 | Rachel | 1 | Peter | Hardware | 28K |
| S3 | Sharon | 1 | Peter | Hardware | 25K |
| S3 | Peter | 1 | Peter | Hardware | 33K |
| S3 | John | 0 | $\perp$ | $\perp$ | $\perp$ |
| S3 | Liz | 0 | $\perp$ | $\perp$ | $\perp$ |
| S3 | Mike | 0 | $\perp$ | $\perp$ | $\perp$ |

Figure 3.17: Completed Relation

The development of the historical relation emprel$_h$ in this section has been very informal; we have utilized the metaphor of a completed relation because viewing a historical database as a three-dimensional object aids our intuition. The technique of time-stamping each tuple is a fairly simple idea, and many databases have kept information such as salary histories in a similar way. In this approach the STATE and EXISTS? attributes are considered *distinguished* attributes that are an intrinsic part of the historical database model, and not ordinary attributes under the user's direct control. By this means an explicit temporal semantics could be incorporated directly within the framework of the relational model, provided that the model were extended to include a special treatment for these attributes.

We have tried in this section to provide a reasonable intuition about the added dimension that time contributes to database semantics. The approach that we will take in the subsequent sections of this book will be slightly different, and closer to the approach of the intensional logic which was its inspiration. Rather than time-stamping each tuple – which is in effect what the STATE attribute approach accomplishes – we will incorporate the temporal component at the individual *attribute value* level by viewing the value of each attribute as a function from time to values, i.e., as an *intension*. In either case, however, it is important that the *model*, and not the user, provide a temporal semantics by the interpretation that it gives to the representation of the temporal dimension, and to its interaction with all of the other elements in the basic relational model. Through the technique of Meaning Postulates ([Car47], [Mon73]), which are axioms that constrain the set of allowable models, the user can be provided with the facility to make certain modifications to the general temporal semantics provided in the general historical relational model. In the next section we proceed to define more formally our concept of historical relations.

## 3.5   Historical Relations in HRDM

Let $T = \{\ldots, t_0, t_1, \ldots\}$ be a set of **times**, at most countably infinite, over which is defined the linear (total) order $<_T$, where $t_i <_T t_j$ means $t_i$ occurs before (is earlier than) $t_j$. (For the sake of clarity we will assume that $t_i <_T t_j$ if and only if $i < j$.) The set $T$ is used as the basis for incorporating the temporal dimension into the model.

For the purposes of this discussion the reader can assume that $T$ is isomorphic to the natural numbers, and therefore the issue of whether to represent time as intervals or as points is simply a matter of convenience. Using the natural numbers allows us to restrict our attention to closed intervals ( a closed interval of $T$, written $[t_1, t_2]$ is simply the set $\{t_i | t_1 \leq t_i \leq t_2\}$ ). In [CR87] we discuss more elaborate structures for the time domain of historical databases.

A **lifespan** $L$ is any subset of the set $T$.

In order to provide for derived lifespans, we allow (similar to [GV85]) for the usual set-theoretic operations over lifespans. That is, if $L_1$ and $L_2$ are lifespans, then so are

1. $L_1 \cup L_2$

2. $L_1 \cap L_2$

3. $L_1 - L_2$

Since lifespans are just sets, defined over a universe $T$, the semantics of these operators is apparent.

Let $D = \{D_1, D_2, \ldots, D_{n_d}\}$ be a set of **value domains** where for each $i$, $1 \le i \le n_d$, $D_i \neq \emptyset$. Each value domain $D_i$ is analogous to the traditional notion of a domain in that it is a set of atomic (non-decomposable) values.

Using the sets $T$ and $D$ we define two sets of temporal mappings, one called $TD$ from the set $T$ into the set $D$, and the other called $TT$ from $T$ into itself.

The set $TD = \{TD_1, TD_2, \ldots, TD_{n_d}\}$ where for each $i$, $1 \le i \le n_d$, and each $TD_i = \{f_i | f_i : T \to D_i\}$ is the set of all partial functions from $T$ into the value domain $D_i$.

The set $TT = \{g | g : T \to T\}$ is the set of all partial functions from $T$ into itself.

The set of temporal functions $TT$ serves a similar role in the model to each of the sets $TD_i$, but is defined separately to make explicit the distinction in the model between those values representing times, and those that do not.

Let $U = \{A_1, A_2, \ldots, A_{n_a}\}$ be a (universal) set of **attributes**.

All attributes in the historical relational data model are defined over sets of partial temporal functions. Specifically,

$$HD = (TD \cup \{TT\}) = \{TT, TD_1, TD_2, \ldots, TD_{n_d}\}$$

is the set of all **historical domains**.

Among the functions in each of the set of functions in $HD$ are some that are constant-valued, i.e., they associate the *same* value with every time in their domain. Let $CD$ be the set derived from $HD$ by restricting each of the sets of functions in $HD$ to only those functions having a constant image. That is, for each set of functions $TD_i$ (and in $TT$) in $HD$ restrict $TD_i$ (and $TT$) to only those functions that map their domain to a single value.

We will sometimes want to restrict a function $f$ with domain $D$ to a smaller domain $D' \subseteq D$; we will denote this restricted function by $f \mid_{D'}$.

A **historical relation scheme** $R = < A, K, ALS, DOM >$ is an ordered 4-tuple where:

1. $A = \{A_{R_1}, A_{R_2}, \ldots, A_{R_n}\} \subseteq U$ is the set of **attributes of R**. We will sometimes abuse notation and refer to $A$ as the **scheme of R**; no confusion should arise.

2. $K = \{A_{K_1}, A_{K_2}, \ldots, A_{K_m}\} \subseteq A$ is the set of **key attributes of R**

3. $ALS : A \to 2^T$ is a function assigning a **lifespan** to each attribute in $R$. We will refer to the lifespan of attribute $A$ in relation scheme $R$ as $ALS(A, R)$.

4. $DOM : A \to HD$ is a function assigning a **domain** to each attribute in $R$, with the restrictions that

   (a) for all key attributes $A_i$, $DOM(A_i) \in CD$, i.e., the key attributes must all be constant-valued, and

   (b) the domain of each of the partial functions in any $DOM(A)$ is contained within $ALS(A, R)$.

We refer to the underlying value set of attribute $A$ (i.e., the ranges of the functions in $DOM(A)$) as the **value-domain of A**, denoted $VD(A)$. The value-domain corresponds to the traditional notion of the domain of an attribute.

A **tuple $t$ on scheme $R$** is an ordered pair, $t = <v, l>$, where

1. $t.l$, the **lifespan of tuple $t$**, is a lifespan, and

2. $t.v$, the **value of the tuple $t$** is a mapping such that

$$\forall \text{ attributes } A \in R, t.v(A) \text{ is a mapping in } t.l \cap ALS(A, R) \to DOM(A).$$

Since we associate a lifespan with both a tuple in a relation and an attribute in a scheme, we can derive the lifespan of the value of an attribute $A$ in a tuple $t$ in relation $r$ on scheme $R$, which we will denote as $vls(t, A, R)$. This lifespan represents the set of times over which the value is defined, and is given by:

$$vls(t, A, R) = t.l \cap ALS(A, R).$$

We can extend this definition to a set of attributes $X = \{A_1, \ldots, A_n\}$ as follows:

$$vls(t, X, R) = t.l \cap ALS(A_1, R) \cap \ldots \cap ALS(A_n, R)$$

For simplicity we will refer to the value $t.v$ of tuple $t$ as follows. The value of tuple $t$ for attribute $A$ will be denoted by $t(A)$. $t(A)(s)$ is the value of tuple $t$ for attribute $A$ at time $s$. Similarly, $t(X)(s)$ represents the value of tuple $t$ for a set of attributes $X$ at time $s$. Since $t(A)$ is a function with domain $t.l \cap ALS(A, R)$, the value of $t(A)(s)$ is **undefined** for any $s$ not in this time period. In this context undefined means that the attribute is not relevant at such times, and thus does not exist. Figure 3.18 presents the *employee* database as it actually represented at the conceptual level in HRDM. Each $n$-tuple has a value component, consisting of $n$ function values for each attribute, and a lifespan which is some subset of the universe of times, $T$.

A **historical relation $r$ on $R$** is a finite set of tuples $t$ on scheme $R$ such that if $t_1$ and $t_2$ are in $r$,

$$\forall \ s \in t_1.l \text{ and } \forall s' \in t_2.l, t_1.v(K)(s) \neq t_2.v(K)(s).$$

| | employee | | | |
|---|---|---|---|---|
| **EMP** | **MGR** | **DEPT** | **SAL** | **lifespan** |
| $\begin{bmatrix} S1 & \rightarrow & John \\ S2 & \rightarrow & John \end{bmatrix}$ | $\begin{bmatrix} S1 & \rightarrow & John \\ S2 & \rightarrow & John \end{bmatrix}$ | $\begin{bmatrix} S1 & \rightarrow & Linen \\ S2 & \rightarrow & Linen \end{bmatrix}$ | $\begin{bmatrix} S1 & \rightarrow & 23K \\ S2 & \rightarrow & 25K \end{bmatrix}$ | $\{S1, S2\}$ |
| $\begin{bmatrix} S1 & \rightarrow & Mike \\ S2 & \rightarrow & Mike \end{bmatrix}$ | $\begin{bmatrix} S1 & \rightarrow & John \\ S2 & \rightarrow & Elsie \end{bmatrix}$ | $\begin{bmatrix} S1 & \rightarrow & Linen \\ S2 & \rightarrow & Toy \end{bmatrix}$ | $\begin{bmatrix} S1 & \rightarrow & 17K \\ S2 & \rightarrow & 20K \end{bmatrix}$ | $\{S1, S2\}$ |
| $\begin{bmatrix} S1 & \rightarrow & Elsie \\ S2 & \rightarrow & Elsie \\ S3 & \rightarrow & Elsie \end{bmatrix}$ | $\begin{bmatrix} S1 & \rightarrow & Elsie \\ S2 & \rightarrow & Elsie \\ S3 & \rightarrow & Elsie \end{bmatrix}$ | $\begin{bmatrix} S1 & \rightarrow & Toy \\ S2 & \rightarrow & Toy \\ S3 & \rightarrow & Toy \end{bmatrix}$ | $\begin{bmatrix} S1 & \rightarrow & 26K \\ S2 & \rightarrow & 27K \\ S3 & \rightarrow & 27K \end{bmatrix}$ | $\{S1, S2, S3\}$ |
| $\begin{bmatrix} S1 & \rightarrow & Liz \end{bmatrix}$ | $\begin{bmatrix} S1 & \rightarrow & Liz \end{bmatrix}$ | $\begin{bmatrix} S1 & \rightarrow & Hardware \end{bmatrix}$ | $\begin{bmatrix} S1 & \rightarrow & 30K \end{bmatrix}$ | $\{S1\}$ |
| $\begin{bmatrix} S1 & \rightarrow & Rachel \\ S2 & \rightarrow & Rachel \\ S3 & \rightarrow & Rachel \end{bmatrix}$ | $\begin{bmatrix} S1 & \rightarrow & Liz \\ S2 & \rightarrow & Rachel \\ S3 & \rightarrow & Peter \end{bmatrix}$ | $\begin{bmatrix} S1 & \rightarrow & Hardware \\ S2 & \rightarrow & Hardware \\ S3 & \rightarrow & Hardware \end{bmatrix}$ | $\begin{bmatrix} S1 & \rightarrow & 29K \\ S2 & \rightarrow & 28K \\ S3 & \rightarrow & 28K \end{bmatrix}$ | $\{S1, S2, S3\}$ |
| $\begin{bmatrix} S1 & \rightarrow & Peter \\ S3 & \rightarrow & Peter \end{bmatrix}$ | $\begin{bmatrix} S1 & \rightarrow & Liz \\ S3 & \rightarrow & Peter \end{bmatrix}$ | $\begin{bmatrix} S1 & \rightarrow & Hardware \\ S3 & \rightarrow & Hardware \end{bmatrix}$ | $\begin{bmatrix} S1 & \rightarrow & 29K \\ S3 & \rightarrow & 33K \end{bmatrix}$ | $\{S1, S3\}$ |
| $\begin{bmatrix} S2 & \rightarrow & Sharon \\ S3 & \rightarrow & Sharon \end{bmatrix}$ | $\begin{bmatrix} S2 & \rightarrow & Rachel \\ S3 & \rightarrow & Peter \end{bmatrix}$ | $\begin{bmatrix} S2 & \rightarrow & Hardware \\ S3 & \rightarrow & Hardware \end{bmatrix}$ | $\begin{bmatrix} S2 & \rightarrow & 25K \\ S3 & \rightarrow & 25K \end{bmatrix}$ | $\{S2, S3\}$ |
| $\begin{bmatrix} S3 & \rightarrow & Beth \end{bmatrix}$ | $\begin{bmatrix} S3 & \rightarrow & Beth \end{bmatrix}$ | $\begin{bmatrix} S3 & \rightarrow & Linen \end{bmatrix}$ | $\begin{bmatrix} S3 & \rightarrow & 23K \end{bmatrix}$ | $\{S3\}$ |

**Figure 3.18: Example Historical Relational Database in HRDM**

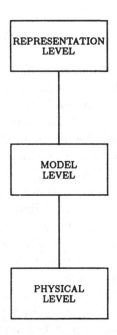

**Figure 3.19: Levels in Historical Relational Data Model**

If $r = \{t_1, t_2, \ldots, t_l\}$ is a relation on $R$, then $LS(r)$, the lifespan of relation $r$, is just:

$$LS(r) = t_1.l \cup t_2.l \ldots \cup t_l.l.$$

In the subsequent chapter we will describe the need for an interpolation function to deal with the issue of incompletely specified time functions as the values of $TV$ attributes. For our purposes we can assume that $t(A)(s)$ is the value of attribute $A$ at time $s$ for tuple $t$, regardless of *how* that value is obtained (for example, it might be stored directly in the relation, or computed by means of an interpolation function from stored values.)

Put slightly differently, we can assume that the model consists of three levels, the representation level, the model level, and the physical level, as in Figure 3.19. At the physical level are the file structures and access methods, at the model level each attribute in a tuple has as its value a *total* function from $vls(t, A, R)$ into some value domain, while at the representation level these functions may be represented more succinctly using intervals and allowing for value interpolation.

For example, assume that the lifespan of a particular value for some $t(A)$ is $S = vls(t, A, R)$. We can imagine a situation in which, for some $S' \subseteq S$, at the representation level $t(A)$ is a function from $S'$ to the value-domain of $A$. Then the mapping from the representation level to the model level must include, for any such attribute, an **interpolation function** $I$:

$$I : VD(A)^{2^S} \rightarrow VD(A)^S$$

which maps each such *partially-represented function* into a total function from $S$. As another example, we might imagine that values constrained to be constant-valued functions might, at the representation level, be represented as simple <lifespan, value> pairs (e.g., $< [t_i, t_j], Codd >$). (For example, in Figure 3.18, all of the constant-valued EMP functions could be represented in this more succinct fashion.)

These two types of lifespans, attribute and tuple, constrain the value of every attribute in every tuple as follows. The tuple lifespan indicates the periods of time during which the tuple bears information; a tuple has no value at points in time other than those in its lifespan. Moreover, each attribute in a relation has an associated lifespan, and so attributes in a tuple are further restricted to have no value outside of their own lifespan. Taken together, these two conditions imply that there is no value for an attribute in a tuple for any moment in time not in the intersection of the lifespans of the tuple and the attribute.

The temporal component of HRDM can thus be viewed as a third dimension to the relational model, as we have already seen in Figure 3.4. The algebra for the relational model provides a unary operator for each of its *two* dimensions (Select for the value dimension, Project for the Attribute dimension). The historical relational algebra extends the definition of these two operators to operate on historical relations, and adds a third operation (Time-Slice) for the added temporal dimension. The binary Join operation is also extended to join two historical relations. To access the third dimension, a When operator *extracts* purely temporal information.

We omit a complete discussion of the algebra of HRDM here and present only those aspects which are essential to follow the examples and discussion in subsequent chapters. For a complete presentation of the HRDM algebra and its expressive power, the reader is referred to [CC87] and [CC88b].

The essential operators of the HRDM algebra are the following:

1. **Project** ($\pi$): This operator is equivalent in definition to its standard relational counterpart, and has the effect of reducing the set of attributes over which each of the tuples $t$ in its operand, a relation $r$, is defined, to those attributes contained in a set of attributes $X$.

$$\pi_X(r) \;=\; \{t(X)|t \in r\}$$

2. **Select-If** ($\sigma{-}IF$): This variant of the select operator selects from a relation $r$ those tuples $t$ each of which for some period within its lifespan has a value for a specified attribute $A$ that satisfies a specified selection criterion. The period

of time within the lifespan is specified by a lifespan parameter $L$. The selection criterion is specified as $A\theta a$, where $\theta$ is a comparator and $a$ is a constant. (It is also possible to compare one attribute with another in the same tuple.) A parameter, $Q$, of the Select-If operator is used to denote a quantifier that specifies whether the selection criterion must be satisfied for all ($\forall$) times in the specified subset of the tuple's lifespan, or that there exists ($\exists$) at least one such time.

$$\sigma\text{--}IF_{(A\theta a, Q, L)}(r) \;=\; \{t \in r | Q(s \in (L \cap t.l))[t(A)s\theta a]\}$$

3. **Select-When** ($\sigma\text{-}WHEN$): This operator is similar to the $\exists$-quantified Select-If operator. However, the lifespan of each selected tuple is restricted to those times *when* the selection criterion is satisfied.

$$\sigma\text{--}WHEN_{A\theta a}(r) \;=\; \{t | \exists t' \in r[t.l = \{s | t'(A)(s)\theta a\} \land t.v = t'.v|_{t.l}]\}$$

4. **$\theta$-Join:** Like its counterpart in the standard relational data model this operator combines tuples from its two operand relations. With $\theta$-join two tuples are combined when two attributes, one from each tuple, have values at some time in the intersection of the tuples' lifespans that stand in a $\theta$ relationship with each other. The lifespan of the resulting tuple is exactly those times when this relationship is satisfied.

Let $r_1$ and $r_2$ be relations on schemes $R_1$ and $R_2$, respectively, where $A \in R_1$ and $B \in R_2$ are attributes.

$$\begin{aligned}
r_1[A\theta B]r_2 \;=\; & \{t | \exists t_{r_1} \in r_1 \exists t_{r_2} \in r_2[t.l = \{s | t_{r_1}(A)(s)\theta t_{r_2}(B)(s)\} \land \\
& t.v(R1) = t_{r_1}.v(R1)|_{t.l} \land \\
& t.v(R2) = t_{r_2}.v(R2)|_{t.l}]\}
\end{aligned}$$

5. **Static Time-Slice** ($\mathcal{T}_{@L}$): This operator reduces a historical relation in the temporal dimension by restricting the domains of the functions assigned to the attributes of each tuple $t$ of the operand relation $r$ to the intersection of the lifespan of tuple $t$ and the set of times $L$.

$$\mathcal{T}_{@L}(r) \;=\; \{t | \exists t' \in r[l = L \cap t'.l \land t.l = l \land t.v = t'.v|_l]\}$$

6. **Dynamic Time-Slice** ($\mathcal{T}_{\odot A}$): The dynamic time-slice also reduces a relation in the temporal dimension, and is applicable to relations that include in their scheme an attribute $A$ whose domain consists of partial functions from the set of times into itself. Under this operation the lifespan of each tuple $t$ in the operand relation is reduced to those times that also occur in the range of values of its attribute $A$.

$$\mathcal{T}_{\odot A}(r) \;=\; \{t | \exists t' \in r[\text{for L, the image of } t(A), t.l = L \wedge t = t'|_L]\}$$

**Other Operators** In addition to the above categories of operators, the **HRDM** algebra includes several of what we term *structural* operators because they are used to restructure a relation without changing the information content of that relation. Each of these operators, **union-merge** ($\cup_o$), **intersection-merge** ($\cap_o$), and **difference-merge** ($-_o$), first computes the set-theoretic operator indicated by their prefix, and then in the resulting relation combine into a single tuple several tuples that, based on their key values, denote the same entity. Various types of structural operators are often found in extensions to the relational data model, historical or otherwise.

The **HRDM** algebra also includes an operator **WHEN**, denoted $\omega$. Applied to a historical relation, this operator returns a value defined as the union of the domains of all of the functions assigned to attributes of tuples in that relation. This operator can be viewed as a temporal-based *aggregate* operator.

$$\omega(r) \;=\; LS(r)$$

Since the semantics of the HRDM model depends upon the formalization of $IL_s$, the next chapter provides an intuitive discussion of this logic and its model theory with particular emphasis on how the two paradigms, intensional logic and historical relations, are interrelated in this work. As already pointed out in Chapter 2, readers familiar with Montague's formulation of IL [Mon73] will see that in $IL_s$ we have reformulated IL to include $s$ as a basic type, along the lines suggested in [Gal75].

# CHAPTER FOUR

# INTENSIONAL LOGIC AND HRDM MODEL

## 4.1 Introduction

In this Chapter we describe the relationship between HRDM and the logic $IL_s$ and its model theory. This relationship is first presented formally, and is then followed by an informal discussion that emphasizes insights that it can provide into the way that a database models the *real world*, and into the nature of entities and relationships, of key and non-key attributes, of queries and data constraints, and of the interaction of *time* with all of these concepts. The formalism is presented in the interests of completeness and rigor, but it is easy to get lost in some of the notation; the informal discussion provides a better overview both of how the temporal dimension is incorporated into, and how it affects, the traditional relational model.

In Chapter 2 we described the syntax and semantics of the language $IL_s$. To be more precise we should rather say the family of $IL_s$ languages, any particular language in this family being determined by the set $C$ of non-logical constants. The historical relational database concept presented in Chapter 3 will now be related to the discussion of the intensional logic as follows. First we show that a particular $HRDB$ scheme defines a particular logic in the family of $IL_s$ languages that provides a formal expression of the historical database semantics and that serves as the target language for translations from our English Query Language which will be described in the latter half of this work. Second, we show how the interpretation of the set of non-logical constants of this applied $IL_s$ is given by an instance of an *hrdb* on this scheme at any moment in its history.

### 4.1.1 Introduction

In $IL_{s}$, as in Montague's formulation of IL, all functions are defined to be functions that take only one argument. It is well known, however (see discussion in [Chu41]) that any function of $n$ arguments can be represented by an equivalent function of one argument whose value is a function of $n - 1$ arguments. Thus, e.g., if $f$ is a function of two arguments, $(f(a))(b)$ represents the value of $f$ for the arguments $a, b$. $f(a)$ represents a function of one variable whose value for any argument $x$ is $(f(a))(x)$. We shall abbreviate this notation as $f(a)(x)$ or as $f(<a, x>)$, and assume that the generalization to functions of $n$ arguments is obvious. Thus if $g$ is a function of $n$ arguments, $g(x_1)(x_2)\ldots(x_n)$ or $g(<x_1, x_2, \ldots, x_n>)$ abbreviates $(((g(x_1))(x_2))\ldots)(x_n)$, which represents the value of the $n$-ary function $g$ for the arguments $x_1, x_2, \ldots, x_n$.

In our discussion of functions we will have occasion to speak of particular *function spaces*, i.e., the set of all functions with the same domain and the same range. For example the set of all functions with domain $S$ (times) and range $E$ (individuals) is written $E^S$. Recalling our notation for the denotation sets corresponding to a given type in $\text{IL}_s$, this function space can also be written $D_e^{D_s}$, and represents the set of all ICs. We will sometimes refer to a given function in this function space as being of **type** $<s, e>$, although strictly speaking we should rather say that if, e.g., $X$ is a term in the language $\text{IL}_s$ that names this function then $X$ is of type $<s, e>$. In general a function from $A$ to $B$ will be said to be of type $<A, B>$. Many of the non-logical constants that we will be discussing will be of types such as $<s, <e, <e, \ldots, <e, t> \ldots >>>$, where there are $n$ $e$'s before the $t$. Instead of this cumbersome notation, we will abbreviate such a type as $<s, <e^n, t>>$.

**Definition:** We say that $X$ is an $<A_1, A_2, \ldots, A_n>$-value for a relation scheme $R(\ldots A_1 A_2 \ldots A_n \ldots)$ if $X = <x_1, x_2, \ldots, x_n>$ where $x_i \in DOM(A_i)$, $1 \leq i \leq n$. If $n = 1$ we sometimes omit the braces and say simply that $X$ is an $A_1$-value.

We have chosen in this work to adopt the entity-relationship view of data semantics [Che76] as applied to the relational model for two main reasons. First, we view the constraints that the entity-relationship model makes upon the database view of an enterprise as rather *natural* constraints that accord with our intuition. Second, these same constraints appear to have direct logical analogues in the kinds of objects – entities and relationships and properties – contained in the model theory of our logic. Since Montague's Intensional Model Theory and Chen's Entity-Relationship (ER) Model are two *independent* efforts to characterize real-world semantics, we feel that the similarity in some of their concepts strengthens their intuitive appeal. The constraints of the entity-relationship model applied to the historical database concept, combined with some simple assumptions on how to interpret a historical database, allow us to define a reasonably straightforward mapping between any relational *hrdb* that conforms to these constraints and an $\text{IL}_s$ model.

We proceed to define the entity-relationship constraints that we place upon the more general HRDM model presented in Chapter 3, and then define first the $\text{IL}_s$ language that a given HRDM scheme defines, and second the model $M_{HRDB}$ for that language that is induced by an instance *hrdb* on this scheme. It is assumed that the reader has some familiarity with the basic ideas of the ER Model [Che76] and its mapping to the relational model. In particular, the notion of simple objects being represented as *entity relations* and associations between (among) simple objects as *relationship relations*.

<u>Definition</u>: A **historical entity relation** is a historical relation $r_h$ on a scheme of the form $(\underline{K}\ A_1 \ldots A_n)$ with the following constraints:

1. $K$, and $A_1 \ldots A_n$ are as in an entity relation.

2. An entity can belong to only one *entity-set*. That is, if $r_1$ is a historical entity relation on $R_1(\underline{K_1}\ A_1 \ldots A_m)$ and $r_2$ a historical entity relation on $R_2(\underline{K_2} A_1' \ldots A_n')$ then for any $t_1 \in r_1$ and $t_2 \in r_2$, $t_1(K_1) \neq t_2(K_2)$.

3. For any tuple $t$ in $r_h$, and any time $s \in t.l$, the value of $t(K)(s)$ must be defined; similarly for any time $s' \in t.l \cap ALS(A_i)$, $1 \leq i \leq n$, the values of $t(A_i)(s')$ must be defined.

4. For any tuple $t$ in $r_h$, and any state $s \in T - t.l$, the entity represented by $t(K)$ is said not to exist in the state $s$, and the values of $t(A_i(s))$, $1 \leq i \leq n$ are all *undefined*.

<u>Definition</u>: A **historical relationship relation** is a relation $r_h$ on a scheme of the form $(\underline{K_1 \ldots K_n A_1 \ldots A_m})$ with the following constraints:

1. $K_1 \ldots K_n$ and $A_1 \ldots A_m$ are as in relationship relations.

2. for any tuple $t$ in $r_h$, and any time $s \in t.l$, the values of $t(K_i)(s)$, $1 \leq i \leq n$ must all be defined; similarly for any time $s' \in t.l \cap ALS(A_i)$, $1 \leq i \leq m$, the values of $t(A_i)(s')$ must be defined.

3. for any tuple $t$ in $r_h$, and state $s \in T - t.l$, the relationship represented by $t(K_1 \ldots K_n)$ is said not to exist in state $s$ and the values of $t(A_i(s))$, $1 \leq i \leq m$ are all *undefined*.

Moreover, the following inter-relational constraints must be satisfied:

4. Only one relationship is allowed among (between) the same entity sets. That is, it is not permitted to have more than one historical relationship relation whose object key is $K_1 \ldots K_n$.

5. For each historical relationship relation $r_h$ with entity keys $\{K_1, K_2, \ldots, K_n\}$, there must exist, for each of the $K_i$, a corresponding historical entity relation $r_i$, such that for each tuple $t$ in $r_h$ and each time $s \in t.l$ there must exist in the relation $r_i$ corresponding to $K_i$ a tuple $t'$ such that $t'(K_i(s)) = t(K_i)(s)$.

6. A role attribute A can appear as a role attribute in at most one relation. If role attribute $A$ in $r_1$ is an entity attribute $K$ in $r_2$, then for each tuple $t$ in $r_1$ and each time $s \in t.l$, there must be a $t'$ in $r_2$ with $t(A)(s) = t(K)(s)$.

Both of these inter-relational constraints ensure that if an entity $k$ participates in a relationship or fills a role in a state $s$, then the existence of $k$ in state $s$ must be predicated in the entity relation for $k$. All of these constraints are essentially the same as in the general entity-relationship model, extended to include a temporal semantics.

<u>Definition:</u> We will sometimes wish to refer to database entities or relationships by the neutral word **object** or **object of arity** $n$. If $n = 1$ this term refers to an entity, whereas if $n > 1$ it refers to an $n$-ary relationship.

<u>Definition:</u> Henceforth, by a **historical database (hrdb)** we shall mean a collection of historical entity and historical relationship relations that satisfy the above constraints, which we shall refer to as the **historical entity-relationship constraints.**

## 4.1.2   The $IL_s$ Language Defined by an HRDB Scheme

The information in an *hrdb* is organized in the form of historical entity and historical relationship relations. We represent this information in the logical model by some set of functions which are defined implicitly by the database. In this section we give the *names* of the functions that are needed to represent the *hrdb* as a portion of an intensional model. These names are simply a set of non-logical constants that define a particular $IL_s$ language. In this section we will only briefly discuss the sorts of functions denoted by these constants; in the following section we will show how any instance of an *hrdb* induces the interpretation of these constants.

For each *HRDB* scheme we will define six sorts of constants, corresponding to *domain values, time values, entity attributes, role attributes, relationships,* and the *associations* between objects (entities or relationships) and their role-attributes. In the discussion to follow we will have occasion to make reference to a sample database to exhibit some of the ideas that we discuss. We will therefore define a simple historical database based on the department-store relational database example in [Cha78]:

<u>Historical Entity Relation Schemes</u>
EMPREL(<u>EMP</u> MGR DEPT SAL)

DEPTREL(<u>DEPT</u> FLOOR)

ITEMREL(<u>ITEM</u> TYPE)

<u>Historical Relationship Relation Schemes</u>
SALESREL(<u>DEPT ITEM</u> VOL)

We will also have occasion to use the instances over these schemes shown in Figures 4.1 - 4.4.

| emprel | | | | |
|---|---|---|---|---|
| **EMP** | **MGR** | **DEPT** | **SAL** | *lifespan* |
| Peter | $\begin{bmatrix} S2 & \to & Elsie \\ S3 & \to & Liz \end{bmatrix}$ | $\begin{bmatrix} S2 & \to & Hardware \\ S3 & \to & Linen \end{bmatrix}$ | $\begin{bmatrix} S2 & \to & 30K \\ S3 & \to & 35K \end{bmatrix}$ | $\{S2, S3\}$ |
| Liz | $\begin{bmatrix} S2 & \to & Elsie \\ S3 & \to & Liz \end{bmatrix}$ | $\begin{bmatrix} S2 & \to & Toy \\ S3 & \to & Hardware \end{bmatrix}$ | $\begin{bmatrix} S2 & \to & 35K \\ S3 & \to & 50K \end{bmatrix}$ | $\{S2, S3\}$ |
| Elsie | $\begin{bmatrix} S1 & \to & Elsie \\ S2 & \to & Elsie \end{bmatrix}$ | $\begin{bmatrix} S1 & \to & Toy \\ S2 & \to & Toy \end{bmatrix}$ | $\begin{bmatrix} S1 & \to & 50K \\ S2 & \to & 50K \end{bmatrix}$ | $\{S1, S2\}$ |

Figure 4.1: Relation emprel

| deptrel | | |
|---|---|---|
| **DEPT** | **FLOOR** | *lifespan* |
| Toy | $\begin{bmatrix} S1 & \to & F1 \\ S2 & \to & F2 \\ S3 & \to & F2 \end{bmatrix}$ | $\{S1, S2, S3\}$ |
| Hardware | $\begin{bmatrix} S1 & \to & F2 \\ S2 & \to & F2 \end{bmatrix}$ | $\{S1, S2\}$ |
| Linen | $\begin{bmatrix} S2 & \to & F3 \\ S3 & \to & F3 \end{bmatrix}$ | $\{S2, S3\}$ |

Figure 4.2: Relation deptrel

| itemrel | | |
|---|---|---|
| **ITEM** | **TYPE** | *lifespan* |
| Ball | $\begin{bmatrix} S1 & \to & 5 \\ S2 & \to & 0 \\ S3 & \to & 10 \end{bmatrix}$ | $\{S1, S2, S3\}$ |
| Game | $\begin{bmatrix} S1 & \to & 6 \\ S2 & \to & 6 \end{bmatrix}$ | $\{S1, S2\}$ |
| Glove | $\begin{bmatrix} S1 & \to & 7 \\ S2 & \to & 5 \end{bmatrix}$ | $\{S1, S2\}$ |

Figure 4.3: Relation itemrel

| salesrel | | | |
|---|---|---|---|
| **DEPT** | **ITEM** | **VOL** | *lifespan* |
| Toy | Ball | $\begin{bmatrix} S1 & \to & 3 \\ S2 & \to & 3 \\ S3 & \to & 4 \end{bmatrix}$ | $\{S1, S2, S3\}$ |
| Toy | Game | $\begin{bmatrix} S1 & \to & 6 \\ S2 & \to & 6 \\ S3 & \to & 6 \end{bmatrix}$ | $\{S1, S2, S3\}$ |
| Hardware | Glove | $\begin{bmatrix} S1 & \to & 9 \\ S2 & \to & 9 \end{bmatrix}$ | $\{S1, S2\}$ |
| Linen | Glove | $\begin{bmatrix} S2 & \to & 2 \end{bmatrix}$ | $\{S2\}$ |

Figure 4.4: Relation salesrel

## Domain Value Constants (DVCs)

Recall that the union of all of the domains of the database attributes is the set UD. Corresponding to UD we define the set of individual constants in $IL_s$, $C_e = \{d'|d \in UD\}$, so that we can refer in the logic to any value that might appear in any state of the database.

## Time Constants (TCs)

The domain of times in the database is the set $T$. Corresponding to this set we define the set of state constants in $IL_s$, $C_s = T$. It will also prove useful to allow constants that refer to sets of states, in particular to contiguous states or **intervals**; for example, a constant 1978 of type $< s, t >$ would denote the set of all moments of time in the year 1978. We will therefore allow in $IL_s$ a set of constants of this type, viz. $C_{<s,t>}$. These latter are not determined by the database instance or by the database schema, but rather by the kinds of users and queries that the database system is intended to support.

The general picture of the historical database as encoded in the $IL_s$ model is provided by the denotations of the remaining four sorts of constants. Before stating formally the rules for deriving their denotations from the database, we give the following overview.

1. The set of entities (e.g. EMPloyees) in any state is given by the denotation of the corresponding entity constant (e.g. $EMP'_*$) for that entity set;

2. The set of $n$-tuples participating in any $n$-ary relationship in any state is given by the denotation of the relationship constant $REL_n$. All $n$-ary relationships can be combined into a single function because of our constraint that the entity sets of the participants uniquely determine the relationship.

3. For each role (e.g. SALary), the set of ICs that fill that role in any state is given by the denotation of the corresponding role constant (e.g. $SAL'$.) An IC fills a role only in those states in which its associated object exists.

4. $n$-ary objects are bound *permanently* to all of their role ICs by the denotation of the non-indexical constant $AS_n$. Thus, e.g., each EMPloyee is permanently bound to three ICs which, in those states in which the employee exists, are its SAL-, MGR-, and DEPT- picking-out functions.

## Entity Existence Constants (EECs)

For each historical entity relation with entity key K we use a non-logical constant $K'_*$ in $IL_s$ of type $< s, < e, t >>$ which denotes, at each state, the set of individuals (subset of $E$) which exist as $K$-entities in that state. For example, the historical entity relation DEPTREL with entity key DEPT induces in the logic the constant

$DEPT'_*$ of type $< s, < e, t >>$. $DEPT'_*$ denotes at any state the set of entities which are departments in that state. $C_{<s,<e,t>>}$ is the set of all these entity-key constants.

## Relationship Existence Constants (RECs)

For each $n$ for which there exists one or more $n$-ary historical relationship relations the set $C_{<s,<e^n,t>>}$ consists of the single non-logical constant $REL_n$, which denotes at each state the set of logical $n$-tuples (subset of $E^n$) which exist as $n$-ary relationships in that state. For example, SALESREL is a binary historical relationship relation that induces in the logic the constant $REL_2$ of type $< s, < e, < e, t >>>$. $REL_2$ denotes at any state the set of binary relationships (in this example, this is just the set of DEPT-ITEM pairs) that exist in that state.

## Role Constants (RCs)

For each role attribute $A$ in the historical database scheme we use a non-logical constant $A'$ of type $< s, << s, e >, t >>$ in $IL_s$, which denotes, at each state, the set of $A$-ICs which exist in that state. $C_{<s,<<s,e>,t>>}$ is the set of all of these role constants. For example, the role attributes DEPT (from EMPREL) and VOL (from SALESREL) induce in the logic the constants $DEPT'$ and $VOL'$ of type $< s, << s, e >, t >>$. $DEPT'$, for example, denotes in any state the set of DEPT-ICs (i.e., department-of-some-employee roles) that exist in that state. Notice that $DEPT'$ and $DEPT'_*$ are two different constants of different types, induced by two different *occurrences* (and two different *uses*) of the single database attribute DEPT. This distinction between *object* (entity or relationship) attributes and *role* attributes is an important one. The values of object attributes are entities, while the values of role attributes are functions (ICs.) If, as in the case of departments in this example, an attribute is considered in one case (EMPREL) as a role attribute (an attribute of the entity EMP) and in another as an object attribute (the entity department), two different constants denoting two different functions are induced in the logic. Attributes of a department are attributes of the department as an entity and not as a role.

## Association Constants (ACs)

For each $n$ for which there is an object in the database the set $C_{<e^n,<<s,e>,t>>}$ consists of the single non-logical constant $AS_n$ which denotes the permanent association (i.e., time-independent, or non-indexical) between each object of arity n and each of its role attributes. For example, the constant $AS_1$ of type $< e, << s, e >, t >>$ in the logic represents the association between each entity (object of arity 1) and its role IC's; it associates each department with its floor IC, each employee with its manager, department and salary ICs, etc. The constant $AS_2$ of type $< e, < e, << s, e > , t >>>$ represents the association between each binary relationship and its role IC's; it associates each DEPT-ITEM relationship with its sales-VOLume.

We have been able to use the general constants $REL_n$ and $AS_n$ instead of database-specific constants such as $SALESREL'$ (of type $<s,<e,<e,t>>>$) or $EMP-ASSOC'$ (of type $<e,<<s,e>,t>>$) for the RECs and ACs, respectively, because of the historical entity-relationship constraints on the database. Specifically, we have allowed the EECs (e.g. $EMP'_*$) and RCs (e.g. $SAL'$) to carry the bulk of the semantics. This decision is based on the belief that the attribute names, rather than the relation names, are generally more meaningful. This view is an outgrowth of research in relational database theory involving what has come to be known as the Universal Relation Scheme Assumption, which also assumes that the attribute names bear the database semantics. (See [Ull82] for a general discussion of this and related assumptions. [MW82] presents a particular database model based on this assumption.) Although this assumption has been made here to simplify the logical translations of the QE-III language, it is in no way essential to our approach. If the historical entity-relationship constraints were relaxed, specific constants for each sort of object in the database could be used.

Any given $HRDB$ scheme thus determines a set $C_{HRDB}$ of constants in $IL_{s,HRDB}$ from among these six categories of non-logical constants. (These constants are *uniquely* determined except for the constants of type $<s,t>$, for which many choices can be made. In the case of the department-store database, the following set of constants is determined.

$$C_{dept-store} \;=\; C_e \cup C_s \cup C_{<s,t>} \cup C_{<s,<e,t>>} \cup C_{<s,<e,<e,t>>>} \cup$$
$$C_{<s,<<s,e>,t>>} \cup C_{<e,<<s,e>,t>>} \cup C_{<e,<e,<<s,e>,t>>>}$$

where:

1. $C_e$ is the set of domain value constants

2. $C_s$ is the set of time (or state) constants

3. $C_{<s,t>}$ is some set of state-set constants

4. $C_{<s,<e,t>>} = \{EMP'_*, DEPT'_*, ITEM'_*\}$ is the set of EECs

5. $C_{<s,<e,<e,t>>>} = \{REL_2\}$ is the set of RECs

6. $C_{<s,<<s,e>,t>>} = \{MGR', DEPT', SAL', FLOOR', TYPE'\}$ is the set of RCs

7. the set of ACs $= \{AS_1\} \cup \{AS_2\}$, where $\{AS_1\}$ is $C_{<e,<<s,e>,t>>}$ and $\{AS_2\}$ is $C_{<e,<e,<<s,e>,t>>>}$.

In the following section we will give formal definitions of an $HRDB$ scheme and an instance *hrdb* on this scheme, and show how the interpretation of the constants determined by a given historical database scheme $HRDB$ is induced by an instance *hrdb* over that scheme.

# 4.2    The Intensional Model Induced by a Database

# Instance

Before proceeding to define how a given instance on an $HRDB$ induces the definition of the interpretation-of-constants function $F$, we need to define some preliminary notions.

The view of a relational $hrdb$ as a three-dimensional cube composed of a sequence of static relations has served a useful purpose in guiding our intuition as to how time interacts with the other attributes in the database. It was this view which caused us to look at key attributes as constant ICs, functions from times to individuals, and at role attributes as unconstrained ICs. We will now argue that this view is inadequate in the face of the generally accepted notion of *dense* time, and the English language constructs which refer to time. We will therefore fortify this view with two additional assumptions, the Comprehension Principle and the Continuity Assumption. These will enable us to view an $hrdb$ as modelling an enterprise completely over an interval of the *real time line*, and to answer such crucial questions as what objects exist in any state s, and what are the values of their Ai-ICs in these states.

<u>Definition:</u> A **closed interval** $[t_1, t_2]$ on the real time line is defined, as usual, as the infinite set of all states in $\mathcal{R}$ between and including $t_1$ and $t_2$, i.e.

$$[t_1, t_2] = \{t | t \in \mathcal{R} \land t_1 \leq t \leq t_2\}$$

The appropriately modified definitions for $[t_1, t_2)$, $(t_1, t_2]$, and $(t_1, t_2)$ are assumed, and the general term **interval** will sometimes be used to refer to any of these.

For purposes of illustration let us consider again the historical entity relation scheme EMPREL(<u>EMP</u> DEPT MGR SAL), and assume that we have an instance that is defined over this scheme for a relation lifespan consisting of the sequence of times $< S_1, S_2, \ldots, S_7 >$ . The first assumption which we shall make about any such a relation is that it is intended to model EMPloyee entities over the entire closed interval of time $[S_1, S_7]$. Since under most people's intuitive views of time this interval is assumed to be *dense*, the best that any finite relation can do is to provide a simulation of this infinite set of moments of time. If a relation is modelling contingent data, it simulates this dense interval by means of a a sequence of **snapshots**, or **still photos**, in this case taken at each moment in the sequence $< S_1, \ldots, S_7 >$. (Some relations model non-contingent data and can be computed, as described by [MW80]; we will not consider such relations here.) Because we take this idea as basic, that is, because it seems to be the only reasonable interpretation to place on *any* historical database that records facts over some interval of time, we state it as the following principle.

<u>Definition:</u> The **Comprehension Principle** states that under any reasonable interpretation a historical database defined over a sequence of times $< S_1, S_2, \ldots, S_n >$

should be considered as modelling an enterprise *completely* over the entire closed interval $[S_1, S_n]$. Any and all information about the objects of interest to the enterprise can be assumed to be contained in or implied by the historical database for the entire interval $[S_1, S_n]$. Moreover, for any state $S$ not in the interval $[S_1, S_n]$, as far as the database is *concerned no* entities or relationships exist, and the value of *all* ICs is *undefined*.

One area for further research would be the relaxation of the second part of this principle, which is closely related to the Closed World Assumption of [Rei78b], perhaps with the introduction of a many-valued logic. In our model, the set $TV$ of truth values is the set $\{0, 1\}$, and we use 0 (False) as the obvious choice to mean *does not exist*. It is because no such obvious choice exists from the set $E$ of entities that we have chosen to view IC's as *partial* functions from the set of times $T$ to values in some value domain. We have accomplished this through the use of our auxiliary notion of a *lifespan* for each database object. We do not thereby pretend to be offering anything more than a practical solution to the interesting philosophical problems of existence, properties of nonexistent but possible entities, etc., which are of considerable philosophical and logical interest (Quine in particular [Qui53] and [Qui60], has contributed a great deal to the understanding of these issues from both points of view.) Other researchers have explored the use of so-called *null values* and have developed various proposals for a formal null-value semantics ([Gol81] discusses the entire issue of null values in relational databases.)

It remains only to make an assumption about what the database *means to say* about all those other moments of time (real, or simply *imagined* by the user) which fall in the interval $[S_1, S_7]$ but which are not included in the sequence $< S_1, S_2, \ldots, S_7 >$ specifically mentioned in the database.

The problem stated in simple terms is this. If the lifespan of a tuple includes the interval $S = [S_1, S_7]$, we know that the database samples the values of the ICs of interest for only some *finite* subset of times in $[S_1, S_7]$, yet we want to be able to consider that the database implicitly defines each IC as a *total* function from $S$ into $E$. How are we to interpret the database, i.e., what functions are we to assume that the ICs represent?

Definition: Any assumption which extends a mapping from a finite set of moments $\{S_1, S_2, \ldots, S_n\}$ (ordered as in the sequence $< S_1, S_2, \ldots, S_n >$) into a set of individuals, into a mapping from all moments in the closed, dense interval $[S_1, S_n]$ into that set of individuals, will in general be called a **Continuity Assumption**.

One could in principle, of course, adopt any proposal one wanted for interpolating these role functions in the database, but for the sake of this exposition we will only discuss the following simple assumption. For all role attributes that record non-numeric data (e.g., MGR, DEPT), and for some that record numeric data (e.g., SAL), it is clear that the IC intended by the discrete points recorded in the database in Figure 4.5 is step-function shown in Figure 4.6.

In other words, under the Step-Function Continuity Assumption the value of an IC for any state $s$ within the database cube is given by the value of the function

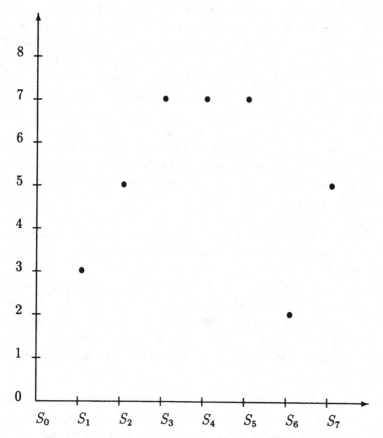

**Figure 4.5: Attribute Values Specified at Points in TIme**

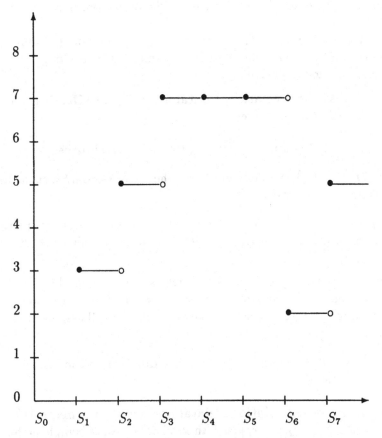

Figure 4.6: Attribute Value as a Step Function

recorded in the database at the greatest state $s'$ less than or equal to $s$. We assume that the *hrdb* initially records information about an object $X$ when it becomes of interest to the enterprise, say at state $s_i$. We then assume that a new tuple for $X$ is added to the database at some subsequent state $s_j > s_i$ *when and only when* one or more of its $A_i$-ICs has changed value, or when it ceases to be an object of interest to the enterprise (EXISTS? becomes 0.) In the interest of keeping our initial model simple, we will commit ourselves here to this view of the temporal semantics of an *hrdb*. That is, for the remainder of this work we assume that *all* role attributes model step-functions. We further assume that when an object ceases to be of interest its current *incarnation* (i.e., interval in its lifespan) is **closed** by some database operation ([CC88a]).

We proceed now to formalize these notions, first by providing definitions of a database scheme $HRDB$ and a database *hrdb*, and then specifying the (logical) model $M$ induced by such a scheme and database.

<u>Definition:</u> A **historical relational database scheme HRDB** is an ordered 5-tuple $< U, D, R, T, DOM >$, where:

1. $U = \{A_1, A_2, .., A_m\}$ is a non-empty set, the set of **attributes**.

2. $D = \{D_1, D_2, \ldots, D_n\}$ is a non-empty set, the set of **domains**, such that each $D_i \in D$ is itself a non-empty set.

3. $R = \{R_1, R_2, \ldots, R_p\}$ is a set of historical-entity and historical- relationship **relation schemes**, where each $R_i \in R$ is an ordered pair $< A_i, K_i >$, such that $\bigcup_{i=1}^{p} A_i = U$.

   Let $T = \{\ldots, t_0, t_1, \ldots\}$ be a set of **times**, at most countably infinite, over which is defined the linear (total) order $<_T$, where $t_i <_T t_j$ means $t_i$ occurs before (is earlier than) $t_j$. (For the sake of clarity we will assume that $t_i <_T t_j$ if and only if $i < j$.)

4. $DOM : A \to HD$ is a function assigning a **domain** to each attribute in $R$, with the restrictions that

<u>Definition:</u> A **historical relational database hrdb on scheme HRDB** is a set of relations, $hrdb = \{r_1, r_2, \ldots, r_p\}$ such that: *hrdb* is a set of completed historical-entity and historical-relationship relations such that for each relation scheme $R_i = < A_i, K_i >$ in $HRDB$, $r_i$ is a relation on $R_i$ that satisfies the appropriate historical entity-relationship constraints.

<u>Definition:</u> The **Model** $M_{hrdb}$ **induced by database** *hrdb* **on scheme** $HRDB$ is an ordered 5-tuple $M_{hrdb} = < E, S, <, <_E, F >$, where:

1. $E = UD$, i.e. the set of all individuals in the domain of $HRDB$

2. $S = \mathcal{R}$, i.e. the set of all times is just the set of real numbers.

3. $<$ is the linear ordering on the real numbers.

4. $<_E = <_D$ (given by $HRDB$.)

5. $F$ is a function from the set of constants $C_{HRDB}$ into objects in $M_{hrdb}$ such that $F(c_a) \in D_a$. The exact specification of $F$ is given in the following section.

## 4.2.1 The Interpretation of the Non-Logical Constants

We will now define precisely what we mean by saying that a given instance *hrdb* on a scheme $HRDB$ induces the definition of $F_{hrdb}$, the function from the set of constants of our $IL_s$-language to the function spaces in our model. We will discuss in turn the interpretation of the six sorts of constants we introduced in the previous section as being induced by a particular $HRDB$ scheme: DVCs (domain value constants), TCs (time constants), EECs (Entity Existence Constants), RECs (Relationship Existence Constants), RCs (Role Constants), and ACs(Association Constants).

### Interpretation of DVCs

For any DVC $d' \in C_e$, $F_{hrdb}(d') = d \in UD$.

### Interpretation of TCs

For any constant $c \in C_s$, $F(c) = f(c)$, i.e. the interpretation given by the embedding of the states in the real numbers. For any set-of-states constant $c \in C_{<s,t>}$, we insist that $F(c)$ defines an interval of time.

### Interpretation of EECs

Let r be a historical entity relation on scheme $R(\underline{K}\ A_1 \ldots A_n)$. Then $F_{hrdb}(K'_*)$, the interpretation of the EEC $K'_*$, of type $< s, < e, t >>$, is that function $f$ in $< s, < e, t >>$ whose value for any state $s \in S$ and individual $x \in E$ is given as follows:

$$f(s, x) = \left| \begin{array}{l} 1 \quad \text{if } s \in t.l \text{ where} \\ \qquad t = \sigma_{K=x}(r) \\ 0 \quad \text{otherwise} \end{array} \right|$$

Thus under our interpretation of the historical database the only $K$-entities that exist are those that the database historical entity relation r with entity key $K$ says exist.

As an example, let us consider the interpretation of the constant $EMP'_*$, and evaluate it for some elements in its domain.

<u>Example 1.</u> "Is Peter an employee in state $S_1$?"

$$f(< S_1, Peter >)$$
$$= S_1 \in (\sigma_{EMP=Peter}(emprel)).l$$
$$= S_1 \in \{S2, S3\}$$
$$= 0$$

i.e., Peter is not an employee in $S_1$.

### Example 2. "Is Liz an employee in state $S_3$?"

$$f(< S_3, Liz >)$$
$$= S_3 \in (\sigma_{EMP=Liz}(emprel)).l$$
$$= S_1 \in \{S2, S3\}$$
$$= 1$$

i.e., Liz is an employee in $S_3$.

### Example 3. "Is entity 50 an employee in state $S_3$?"

$$f(< S_3, 50 >)$$
$$= S_3 \in (\sigma_{EMP=50}(emprel)).l$$
$$= S_3 \in undefined$$
$$= 0$$

i.e., 50 is not an employee in $S_3$.

## Interpretation of RECs

Unlike the case of EECs, in which a single historical entity relation r over a scheme R represented all of the information about the existence of entities of a given sort in the database, in the case of RECs there may be any number of historical relationship relations of a given arity that must together be considered to determine which n-ary relationships exist. Our definition of the interpretation of the constants $REL_n$, therefore, must be given in terms of the entire database and not just of a single relation.

Let $n-rels = \{r_1, \ldots, r_k\}$ be the set of all the n-ary historical relationship relations in the database, i.e. all relations in the database over schemes $R_i$ of the form $R_i(K_{i_1} \ldots K_{i_n} \ldots A_{i_1} \ldots A_{i_m})$. Since these k relations are all defined over the same Logical Domains for the set of attributes $\{K_{i_1}, \ldots, K_{i_n}\}$, we can conceptually take the union of these k projections considered as relations over these Logical Domains. (In other words, in our logical model the domain of $K_{i_j} =$ for all $K_{i_j}$ is E.) In order to do this conveniently we can define a new relation r over the scheme $R(\underline{E_1 \ldots E_n})$ where r is the union of these k relations over these *common* attributes:

$$r = \cup_{i=1}^{k} \pi_{K_{i_1}, \ldots K_{i_n}}(r_i)$$

Then the interpretation of the constant $REL_n$ induced by the database, $F_{hrdb}(REL_n)$, is that function f in $< s, < e^n, t >>$ whose value for any state $s \in S$ and n-tuple $< x_1, x_2, \ldots x_n >\in E^n$ is given as follows:

$$f(s, x) = \begin{vmatrix} 1 & \text{if } s \in t.l \text{ where} \\ & t = \sigma_{<K_1,\ldots,K_n>=<x_1,\ldots,x_n>}(r) \\ 0 & \text{otherwise} \end{vmatrix}$$

which is completely analogous to our definition of the interpretation of the EECs, or 1-ary relationships.

For example, in our department-store database the only binary relationship is the one between DEPTs and ITEMs. We evaluate $f$ for various 2-tuples in various states.

**Example 4.** "Is there a relationship between the Hardware Department and Item Glove in State $S_3$?"

$f(< S_3, Hardware, Glove >)$
$\quad = S_3 \in (\sigma_{DEPT=Hardware,ITEM=Glove}(emprel)).l$
$\quad = S_3 \in \{S1, S2\}$
$\quad = 0$

i.e., the relationship Hardware – Glove does not exist in $S_3$.

**Example 5.** "Is there a relationship between the Toy Dept. and Item Game in state $S_1$?"

$f(< S_1, Toy, Game >)$
$\quad = S_3 \in (\sigma_{DEPT=Toy,ITEM=Game}(emprel)).l$
$\quad = S_3 \in \{S1, S2, S3\}$
$\quad = 1$

i.e., the relationship Toy – Game does exist in $S_3$.

**Example 6.** "Is there a relationship between the Toy Dept. and Peter in state $S_1$?"

$f(< S_1, Toy, Peter >)$
$\quad = S_3 \in (\sigma_{DEPT=Toy,ITEM=Peter}(emprel)).l$
$\quad = S_3 \in undefined$
$\quad = 0$

i.e., the relationship Toy – Peter does not exist in $S_3$.

In order to define the interpretation of the remaining two kinds of non-logical constants that we have defined, we shall need a preliminary definition to handle the role-attribute ICs.

<u>Definition:</u> Let r be a historical relation on scheme $R(\underline{K_1 \ldots K_n} \, A_1 \ldots A_m)$, and let X be a $< K_1, \ldots, K_n >$-value, i.e. $X \in E^n$. Then the $A_i$-**IC associated with the object** X **in** r **on** R, denoted $F1_{A_i,X,r,R}$, is that function of type $< s, e >$ whose interpretation induced by r is given as follows:

$$F1_{A_i,X,r,R}(s) = \pi_{A_i}(\sigma_{<K_1 \ldots K_n>=X}(r))(s)$$

**Definition:** The **set of** $A_i - ICs$ **associated with the object** $X$ **in** $r$ **on** $R$ **in state** $s$, denoted $F2_{A_i,X,r,R}$, is a function of type $< s, << s, e >, t >>$, whose interpretation induced by $r$ is given as follows:

$$F2_{A_i,X,r,R}(s) = \left| \begin{array}{ll} \{F1_{A_i,X,r,R}\} & \text{if } \sigma_{<K_1,...,K_n>=X}(r)(s) \text{ is defined} \\ \emptyset & \text{otherwise} \end{array} \right|$$

In other words, in any state $s$ we associate an object $X$ with its role-attribute ICs *only if* the object $X$ exists in state $s$, otherwise it is not associated with any ICs. (Note that in any state the set given by $F2$ is either a singleton set (containing one IC) or the empty set.) This definition enables us to simplify the types of many of our constants (as compared to Montague's treatment in PTQ) while at the same time avoiding assigning a role to any IC associated with an object that is nonexistent in a given state.

## Interpretation of RCs

Let r be a historical relation on scheme $R(\underline{K_1 \ldots K_n}\ A_1 \ldots A_m)$. Then the interpretation induced by $r$ of the RC $A_i'$ is simply the union of all of the sets of $A_i$-ICs associated with any objects $X$. In other words, $F_{hrdb}(A_i')$ is that function $f$ in $< s, << s, e >, t >>$ whose value for any state $s \in S$ is given as follows:

$$f(s) = \cup_{X \in E^n}\ F2_{A_i,X,r,R}(s)$$

For example, $SAL'$ for any state $s$ denotes the set of all ICs which are the *salary-picking-out* functions of any employee.

## Interpretation of ACs

As in the case of the $REL_n$'s, for any given $n$ we use a single non-logical constant to represent information about all objects of arity $n$, information that may be located in an arbitrary number of database relations. An AC $AS_n$ represents the association between any object of arity $n$ and each of its role ICs. We must therefore define the interpretation of these constants in terms of the entire database and not just of a single relation. We would like to take all of the functions given by $F2$, i.e., the set of all of the ICs associated with any object $X$, and *merge* them all together to yield a single function which, for any object $X$, gives all of the role ICs associated with $X$. In order to do this we need to make this notion of merging precise.

**Definition:** We say that a relation $r$ on $R =< A, K >$ is **defined** for the object $x \in K$ if $x \in \pi_K(r)$.

As before we let $n-rels = \{r_1, \ldots, r_k\}$ be the set of all relations $r_i$ in the database over schemes $R_i$ of the form $R_i(\underline{K_{i_1} \ldots K_{i_n}}\ A_{i_1} \ldots A_{i_m})$. By the historical entity-relationship constraint (2), an entity $X$ can belong to only one entity set, and by constraint (6) only one relationship can exist for any set of entity sets. Together these constraints mean that any $n$-ary object $< x_1, x_2, \ldots, x_n >$ is defined by *at most* one relation in $hrdb$, i.e.

$$\pi_{<K_{1_i}, \ldots, K_{n_i}>}(r_i) \cap \pi_{<K_{1_j}, \ldots, K_{n_j}>}(r_j) = \emptyset$$

for any two distinct relations $r_i, r_j \in n{-}rels$. From this it follows that for any $X \in E^n$ and any role attribute $A$, the function $F1_{A,X,r_i,R_i}$ is defined for at most one $r_i \in n{-}rels$; this is thus also the case for the function $F2_{A,X,r_i,R_i}$.

Then the interpretation of $AS_n$ induced by the database is that function $f$ in $< e^n, << s, e >, t >>$ whose value for any $X \in E^n$ is given as follows:

$$f(X) \;=\; \left| \begin{array}{ll} \cup_{s \in S} \cup_{A_i \in R} F2_{A_i,X,r,R}(s) & \text{if for some } r \in n{-}rels \\ & \text{the object } X \text{ is defined in } r \\ \emptyset & \text{otherwise} \end{array} \right|$$

In other words the interpretation of $AS_n$ gives, for any $n$-ary object $X$, the set of *all* IC's (of any role) associated with $X$ in any state.

After this more formal presentation of the logical model induced by an $hrdb$ instance, it will be informative to take a look at each of the elements in the historical database in turn to see how it is reflected in the model.

# 4.3   Informal Discussion of IL$_s$ and HRDB

## 4.3.1   Domains and values

In the definition of the $HRDB$ the set $UD$ consists of the names of all of the individuals that may possibly be referenced in any stage of the database history. The database itself can be viewed as a collection of sentences in an implied logic, and we have just presented a translation from this language into IL$_s$. The domains correspond in the following way: the set $C_e$ of constants of type $e$ in IL$_s$ is defined to be $\{d | d \in UD\}$. Correspondingly, the set $E$ of individuals in the model for IL$_s$ is defined to be $\{\mathbf{d} | d \in D\}$. Moreover we have specified the interpretation of these constants in the obvious way:

$$F_{hrdb}(d) = \mathbf{d}.$$

## 4.3.2   Attributes

It is convenient in the HRDM model – particularly when looking at the problem of natural-language querying, as we are shortly to do – to identify two different kinds of attributes: attributes that are keys whose values are **rigid designators** of entities, and role attributes which are unconstrained functions (ICs) which in any state give some property of either an entity or a relationship. Montague describes this distinction between constant and unconstrained ICs in this manner: "'Ordinary' common nouns (for example **horse**) will denote sets of constant individual concepts (for example, the set of constant functions on worlds and moments having horses as their values; from an intuitive viewpoint, this is no different from the set of horses.) It would be unacceptable to impose this condition on such 'extraordinary' common nouns as **price** or **temperature**; the individual concepts in their extensions would in the most natural cases be functions whose values vary with their temporal arguments." [Mon73, p.264] . We have made the same claim here in the $HRDB$ realm; in particular we have argued that key attributes (like **EMP**) and role attributes (like **SAL**) are to be identified with Montague's "ordinary" and "extraordinary" common nouns, respectively.

It is, of course, the set of times $T$ – and the semantics with which it is provided in the operators of HRDM – which bears the burden of providing the model's temporal semantics. We believe that it is best to define the model in terms of a very general temporal semantics, and allow the user to specify (via Meaning Postulates) further properties of the temporal dimension of the application and its data . We have described here our Step-Function Continuity Assumption as a means of interpolating the partial function given by the historical database. The lifespan concept enables objects to come in and out of focus at will as objects of interest to the enterprise. When an object is of interest, a new *incarnation* in its lifespan is created, and all of the role attributes for that object are defined; for any times outside of an object's lifespan, the value of all of its attributes is undefined.

### 4.3.3   Tuples

A tuple in the $HRDB$ model, as in the entity-relationship model, is viewed as a collection of facts about a single object, an entity or a relationship. In either case it has seemed more natural to us to view the association between an object and its attributes as essentially binary. The theory could easily have treated n-ary tuples as n-ary associations among the various ICs involved. With the choice of semantic primitives that we have made, a tuple in a historical relation representing an object of arity $n$ with $m$ role attributes and a lifespan consisting of $p$ states is reflected in the logic IL$_s$ by a simple sentence composed of three parts:

1. $n$ entity existence terms and, if $n > 1$, an additional relationship existence term

2. $m \times p$ terms identifying the sorts of the $m$ role attributes in each of the $p$ states

3. $m \times p$ terms giving the value of each of the $m$ role attributes in each of the $p$ states

4. $m$ terms associating the $n$-ary object with each of its $m$ attributes

For example, the first tuple in deptrel is completely represented in $IL_s$ by the following formula in $IL_s$ (assume that the variable $x$ is of type $< s, e >$):

$\exists x[DEPT'_*(S_1, Toy) \wedge$
$\quad FLOOR'(S_1, x) \wedge FLOOR'(S_2, x) \wedge FLOOR'(S_3, x) \wedge$
$\quad\quad x(S_1) = F1 \wedge x(S_2) = F2 \wedge x(S_3) = F2 \wedge$
$\quad\quad AS_1(Toy, x)]$

The third tuple in salesrel is completely represented in $IL_s$ by the following:

$\exists x[DEPT'_*(S_1, Hardware) \wedge ITEM'_*(S_1, Glove) \wedge$
$\quad\quad VOL'(S_1, x) \wedge VOL'(S_2, x) \wedge$
$\quad\quad x(S_1) = 9 \wedge x(S_2) = 9 \wedge$
$\quad\quad AS_2(Toy, Ball, x)]$

## 4.3.4   Data Dependencies and Constraints

The inclusion of an explicit time component in the $HRDB$ model allows us to express the semantics of a wide class of database constraints in the *same* language, something not possible in a first-order logic without some extra apparatus. We divide these database constraints into two categories, and make the following definitions:

<u>Definition:</u> An **extensional database constraint** is a constraint on *individual* valid states of the database. It can be said to hold (or not to hold) simply on the basis of the extension of the database with respect to a *single state*.

<u>Definition:</u> An **intensional database constraint** is a constraint which defines valid *state transitions* in the database. It can be said to hold (or not to hold) only by examining *at least two* states of the $HRDB$.

Current theoretical relational database research has been primarily concerned (without itself using the term) only with extensional constraints, such as FDs or MVDs. The relationship between the FDs and MVDs of the relational model, and axioms expressed as formulas in a first-order logic, is one which is well understood (see, e.g., [Nic78] and [NG79].) The FD $EMP \rightarrow SAL$, e.g., is an abbreviation for the first-order formula:

$$\forall x \forall y \forall z[EMP(x) \wedge SAL(y) \wedge SAL(z) \wedge AS_1(x, y) \wedge AS_1(x, z) \rightarrow y = z]$$

in the domain relational calculus (i.e., with variables having individuals as their domain), or for the formula:

$$\forall t_1 \forall t_2[t_1(EMP) = t_2(EMP) \rightarrow t_1(SAL) = t_2(SAL)]$$

in the tuple relational calculus (i.e., with variables having tuples as their domain.) [Ull80] contains a discussion of these two calculi and a demonstration of their equivalence. An intensional logic allows us to easily express more fully the full intent of these FDs: we can specify explicitly that they must hold over all states of the database. Moreover, we can make the more explicit statement that there is only one function (IC) that picks out a given attribute (e.g., the SALary) of any object (e.g., EMP) that has that attribute:

$$\forall x \forall y \forall z \forall i [EMP'(i,x) \wedge SAL'(i,y) \wedge SAL'(i,z) \wedge AS_1(x,y) \wedge AS_1(x,z) \rightarrow y = z]$$

Here we have quantified over all states of the database with the state variable $i$ (type $s$), and have equated, not merely the *value* (extension) of the two SALaries, but the SALary-ICs (functions) themselves. (We note in passing that the comparable axiom in $IL_s$ using *tuple* variables would require a different approach than we have taken: we would have to have tuple variables of the appropriate *type*, since $IL_s$ is a typed logic.) Similar intensional axioms for MVDs would constrain the acceptable models for our *HRDB*.

Intensional constraints have not received much attention in the database literature. Where they have been examined (e.g. by [SS77], [NY78], and [CB79]) as *dynamic constraints* or constraints upon update operations), they have been considered as different in kind from extensional (or *static*) constraints. We have shown here how $IL_s$, as a higher-order language with a temporal dimension, allows us to consider different types of objects (e.g. states, individuals, ICs, and other arbitrarily-defined functions) and to make statements about any of these objects with the full power of quantified logic and lambda calculus. We can thus express both types of constraints in $IL_s$ in the same natural way, i.e., as axioms about *objects* (of the appropriate type), without having to invent a new technique for expressing the dynamic constraints.

Consider the following kind of constraint that might hold in an enterprise keeping a relation on *EMPREL*:

*No employee can ever be given a cut in pay.*

This is an intensional constraint: it constrains the kind of *function* that can serve as a SAL-IC for any EMPloyee, in particular to those functions from states to dollar values that have everywhere non-negative derivative. It is not expressible as a first-order database axiom because it does not refer simply to the *extension* of the SALary function in any one state, but rather to the entire function considered as an intensional object, viz. an IC. In $IL_s$ this constraint is expressible quite naturally and directly as:

$$\forall i_1 \forall u \forall x [EMP' * (i_1, u) \wedge SAL'(i_1, x) \wedge AS_1(u, x) \rightarrow \forall i_2 [i_1 < i_2 \rightarrow x(i_1) <= x(i_2)]]$$

This ability to consider both intensional and extensional constraints as essentially the same kind of constraints, and to express them in the *same language*, is a good example of the power that an intensional logic has to provide a *unified theory of database semantics*. In the section on queries to follow we give examples of the *definition* in $IL_s$ of English words such as "rehire" (an EMPloyee) or "raise" (a SALary) or "transfer" (a DEPT assignment), definitions which use the same concept of explicit quantification over states of the *HRDB*.

## 4.3.5 Queries

As with database constraints, the inclusion of the state component in the historical database model allows us to consider a much broader class of database queries in a consistent manner. We are similarly motivated, therefore, to make the following distinction.

<u>Definition:</u> An **extensional database query** is a query whose evaluation depends only on the values in the database with respect to a *single index* or state.

<u>Definition:</u> An **intensional database query** is a query whose evaluation depends on the *intensions* of at least one attribute, i.e. on the function from states to individuals (ICs) that represents that attribute.

It should be apparent that extensional queries are precisely those that static databases have been concerned with handling, and moreover that these queries are handled just as well by a historical database. We note, however, that since the *HRDB* contains, as it were, many static databases indexed by state, it is possible to ask the same extensional queries *with respect to different states*, and thus to get potentially different answers. For example, the answer to "What is Peter's salary?" with respect to state $S_2$ yields the answer "30K," but with respect to state $S_3$ what appears to be the *same query* of the *same database* yields the equally correct (but *different*) answer "35K." Thus we see that in order to utilize the power of the *HRDB*, extensional queries must be more fully specified to indicate the *state* at which evaluation is to be performed. In Chapter 5 this process is explained more fully, and the concept of a variable **now**, whose interpretation is always the *latest state* of the *HRDB*, is discussed.

It is the class of intensional queries in which we are most interested, because these queries utilize the full power of the *HRDB*, and show it to be a much closer model of the real world than a one-dimensional static database. We suggest that within the context of an *HRDB* we have the potential to answer all of the queries which were mentioned at the beginning of Section III. We repeat them here.

- "Has Peter's salary risen?"

- "When was Peter rehired?"

- "Did Elsie work for the toy department last year?"

- "Has Liz ever earned the same as Peter?"

- "Will the average salary in the linen department surpass 30K within the next 5 years?"

How, for instance, might we handle the query "Has Peter's salary risen?" Let us assume a mechanism for translating this query into the following formula in $IL_s$:

$$\exists x[SAL'(now, x) \land EMP'_*(now, Peter) \land AS_1(Peter, x) \land RISE'(now, x)]$$

In order to evaluate this query, we need some mechanism for providing a meaning to the predicate $RISE'$. There are two ways that we could do this: either by providing the denotation of $RISE'$ via a direct translation from the database, analogous to the way we defined our primitives (like $SAL'$), or by providing its denotation indirectly, essentially making $RISE'$ a predicate whose meaning is *derived* from the denotations of the basic predicates induced by the database. This is the course we shall take, as the former method is impractical – it would have to be updated with each database update. Before we can provide any definition we must, of course, *decide* upon an appropriate meaning for the English word "rise." We suggest the following: $RISE'$ is true of a SALary IC at a given state $i$ *iff* there is a preceding interval of time culminating in state $i$ during which the SAL-IC has an everywhere non-negative derivative (or, equivalently, is monotonically non-decreasing.) Of course we could quibble about this definition for a while, but that is not the point: the point is that given *any* such well-defined semantics for the word we could express its meaning in $IL_s$. The suggested definition translates into the $IL_s$ Meaning Postulate:

$$\forall x \forall i [RISE'(i, x) \leftrightarrow [SAL'(i, x) \wedge \exists i_1 \forall i_2 \forall i_3 [i_1 <= i_2 < i_3 <= i \rightarrow x(i_2) <= x(i_3)]]]]$$

We hasten to point out that there is nothing sacred in this definition about the attribute SAL. In the context of other attributes (e.g., the BALance of a bank account, the BATting-AVErage of a baseball player, etc.) that in English might meaningfully be said to "rise," the above Meaning Postulate could easily be generalized.

Given this MP, we evaluate the predicate $RISE'(i, x)$ as follows. From emprel we see that the SAL-IC associated with Peter is an IC defined over the domain $\{S2, S3\}$ and whose value is:

$$\begin{bmatrix} S_2 & \rightarrow & 30 \\ S_3 & \rightarrow & 35 \end{bmatrix}$$

The value of this IC for all other states is *undefined*. Let us call this function $SJ$. Then $RISE'(i, SJ)$ evaluated for $i = S_3$ is true (pick $S_2$ as the $i_1$ which the MP asserts must exist).

As another example, we could define the English verb "rehire" as follows:

$\forall u \forall i [REHIRE(i, x) \leftrightarrow$
$\qquad [EMP' * (i, u) \wedge \exists i_1 \exists i_2 [i_1 < i_2 < i \wedge EMP' * (i_1, u) \wedge \neg EMP' * (i_2, u)]]]$

i.e., it is true at state $i$ that the individual $u$ has been rehired if $u$ is an EMPloyee at time $i$, and at some earlier time $i_1$ was also an EMP, while at some third time $i_2$ between $i$ and $i_1$ was *not* an EMP.

# CHAPTER FIVE

# OVERVIEW OF ENGLISH QUERY LANGUAGE QE-III

## 5.1   Introduction

In the previous chapters of this book we have presented the historical relational database model HRDM as a means of formally incorporating a temporal semantics into the relational database model. We now turn our attention to the problem of providing a semantics for querying an hrdb using natural language, specifically English. Our method will be to define the semantics of queries expressed in English in terms of the semantics of the HRDM model already presented by defining a small query fragment as a Montague Grammar (as in [Mon73], henceforth PTQ.) The correlation between the database semantics we have already defined and this query language will be made explicit by providing the semantics of the query fragment via an indirect translation into the intensional logic $IL_s$. The translations will provide for a completely extensional treatment of verbs, (i.e., there will be no verbs like "seek" which can be nonextensional in object position in the PTQ treatment). This treatment is dictated by the application of the Montague Semantics approach to a database environment, in which existence is tantamount to existence in the database. Through these translations, then, the model for $IL_s$ that we defined as induced by the database will also serve as the model for a formal definition of the semantics of the English queries. In addition to providing a semantic interpretation, which in model-theoretic terms is called its denotation, we also provide for each expression a pragmatic interpretation in a manner to be explained.

Our goal in this effort has not been to define an English database query language that is, in any sense of the term, complete. Rather we have been motivated by two complementary goals. First, we have wanted to investigate the possibility of defining both the syntax and the semantics of a database query language in a completely formal, model-theoretic way. This led (somewhat) naturally to our interest in Montague Semantics and to our second goal, demonstrating that Montague's theories of natural language semantics are applicable to such a practical task. Along the way we discovered that it was simpler and more natural to define the interpretation of this query language in two components, one semantic and the other pragmatic.

As we shall point out, we imposed a number of criteria that had to be met by any theory that we would ultimately accept as a reasonable groundwork for this task. In adopting these criteria we were guided by two overriding principles. First was that whatever interpretation or *meaning* our theory would give to a natural language database query should be as close as possible to the interpretation given to database queries in, say, the relational algebra or calculus. This meant that the interpretation of a query should somehow encompass its *answer* – or a method to compute that answer – as represented in the underlying database. Second, we wanted to present a theory that made sense from a computer science viewpoint. This meant taking into account what had already been learned about parsing strategies for Montague Grammars, as well as what database theory had to say about the semantics of the modelled enterprise. This led to our interest in adopting systematic simplifications to the PTQ translations from English to logic wherever these were suggested by the simplified view of the semantics of the enterprise provided by the database model. Moreover, since we were not attempting to develop a semantic theory of questions for English in general, these simplifications have been introduced into the translation process as early as possible. We believe that this strategy has the dual effect of making some of the PTQ theory a little more accessible, and eliminating the need to resort to the less computationally attractive technique of introducing a large number of Meaning Postulates and using logical equivalences to perform the reductions at a later stage.

A word about the syntax of the fragment is in order. We have made little attempt to develop a sophisticated syntax for our fragment. Numerous extensions to the syntax of the PTQ fragment have been investigated by researchers in the past decade that we have not incorporated into our fragment. Since our primary concern has been *getting the meaning right*, we felt that a too broad syntactic coverage might obscure our major points. For this reason we have extended the PTQ fragment only slightly. The treatment of questions that we present is syntactically naive, although in its favor we might point out that, unlike most work on questions in Montague Grammar QE-III makes a stab at direct questions. We believe that the semantic theory of questions that we present, and particularly our proposal to capture the answer in a pragmatic component, are an important contribution to the formalization of the interpretive component of natural language understanding systems. Naturally the true test of a *natural language* query facility is in how useable it is; certainly the syntax of QE-III will have to be extended before anyone would think of using it.

In this section we will discuss the major issues of the query fragment that we have defined. These issues fall roughly into two broad categories: aspects of the process of database querying that we have incorporated into the fragment, and modifications and additions to the PTQ fragment that these, and the database semantics, have occasioned. As in much of the work that has been done in the area of Montague

Semantics since Montague's death in 1970, we have allowed the PTQ fragment to stand pretty much intact as the heart of QE-III. However we have redefined this fragment in terms of the language $IL_s$, for the reasons outlined in Chapter 4.

## 5.2   Preliminaries

### 5.2.1   Individual Concepts vs. Entities

Most recent research in the field of Montague Semantics has incorporated the suggestion, first made by Bennett [Ben74], that Montague's treatment of common nouns (CNs) and intransitive verbs (IVs) as denoting sets of individual concepts (ICs) is unduly complicated. Under Bennett's suggestion both CNs and IVs are treated as denoting sets of simple individuals, with the result that the entire typing scheme of the English categories in these fragments is considerably simplified. In Chapter 4 we argued for the notion that key attributes and role attributes are to be identified, respectively, with *ordinary* CNs (which reduce to sets of entities in PTQ by means of *Meaning Postulate 1*) and *extraordinary* CNs (which do not so reduce.) Accordingly we have not adopted the Bennett type system, but have instead maintained the treatment of PTQ.

### 5.2.2   Verbs

Montague's semantic treatment of verbs leaves them completely unanalyzed; thus, for example, the English verb "walk" translates into the constant "*walk'*" in IL, "love" into "*love'*", etc. The interpretation of these constants is some function in the model for the language, a function about which Montague says nothing except to specify its logical type (and in certain cases to specify an extensional Meaning Postulate). Because we are using a database as a representation of the logical model we are in a position to provide an analysis of English verbs that takes into account the meaning of the verbs as encoded in the database. This analysis is given in terms of the semantic primitives into which we have shown how the database can be encoded. For example, instead of translating the verb "manage" into the unanalyzed predicate "*manage'*", we take advantage of the database semantics to incorporate directly into its translation the information that its subject must be an IC in the role of a MGR, and that its object must be an entity that is an EMP. We do not change the logical type of the translation, i.e. a transitive verb in our fragment denotes the same kind of function as it does in Montague's treatment; we simply analyze its meaning in terms of the database primitives. This analysis in terms of a small set of primitive meaning units is not very different from some approaches taken in AI work in natural language understanding (e.g. [Sha72]), or to the linguistic theory of deep cases [Fil68]. The difference, of course, is that our primitives or cases are different, motivated by the

HRDM model and by the schema design of the particular application, and are no more absolute than any well-chosen database design.

As an example, the translation of "manage" in our fragment is given as:

$$\lambda W \lambda x W(i)(\lambda y AS{-}1(y(i), x) \wedge EMP'_*(i)(y(i)) \wedge MGR'(i)(x))$$

This expression is of the same logical type as *manage'* in a PTQ-like treatment, and will combine with Terms in the same way, but it does not leave "managing" unanalyzed. Instead it specifies what attribute class(es) its subject and object must belong to in the database, and how they must be related. In general the translation of any verb in our theory will so specify the attribute of its subject (or the disjunction of alternatives, if any). The translation of a TV will further specify the attribute(s) of its direct object, and of a DTV of its indirect object. Moreover any relationship(s) among these attributes will also be specified, using the ACs or RECs defined by the HRDB scheme.

## 5.3   The Problems of Tense and Time

### 5.3.1   Intervals or States?

David Dowty in [Dow79] presents a discussion of a broad spectrum of semantic and syntactic issues relevant to the understanding of English, and in particular to providing a Montague-Semantic analysis of these issues. In the final chapter of this book he formalizes many of the ideas he has discussed by defining a Montague fragment of English that includes such features as temporal adverbs, dative-taking verbs, a theory of word formation, and a treatment of several compound tense structures. In order to provide a semantics for this expansion of the PTQ fragment Dowty argues for the necessity of several significant extensions to the logic IL: a radically different treatment of the phenomenon of tense is one of his contributions. Because we are concerned with many of the same issues as Dowty – in particular tenses and direct temporal references – it seems appropriate to discuss his work and to contrast two different solutions to some of the same issues.

A major section of the book is concerned with developing a rigorous taxonomy of verbs in English based upon several syntactic and semantic criteria. The problems with a number of different classification schemes that have been proposed over the years are discussed, in particular Vendler's scheme [Ven67] which divides verbs into the four categories of statives, activities, accomplishments, and achievements. Dowty judges all of these proposals by the two criteria of syntactic and semantic uniformity: can all of the verbs assigned to a given class appear in the same syntactic constructs, and are the same inferences in meaning justified for all like-classified verbs? Dowty's final taxonomy, offered with many reservations, defines eight different verb categories.

Dowty proceeds to develop a semantic theory of these verbs by first defining the semantics of a number of stative predicates directly in terms of a logical model. He then provides a formal apparatus for defining the semantics of non-stative verbs in terms of the statives by means of a small number of logical connectives (DO, BE-COME, etc.) which are given a fixed interpretation. For example, "kill" is defined in terms of the connectives CAUSE and BECOME, whose *meanings* are defined model-theoretically, and the predicate "alive", a non-logical constant. (Again this goal is reminiscent of the work of the *primitivists* in AI natural language understanding.) His tentative solution of eight verb classes depends on two orthogonal criteria: four temporal properties of verbs (related, but not entirely equivalent, to Vendler's four classes), and the agentive/non-agentive distinction.

These *aspectual* verb distinctions, and particularly the semantics of the progressive tenses, lead Dowty to espouse a theory of interval semantics, earlier proposed by Bennett and Partee [BP72], wherein truth conditions are given relative to an interval, rather than to a moment, of time. Unlike other proposed changes to Montague's PTQ analysis of English, this proposal causes major modifications to the most basic semantic notion of IL, and indeed of most other temporal logics that have been studied (e.g. [RU71].) We are not convinced of the necessity of taking this step (indeed Dowty himself says that "it results in a system that is really too powerful for natural language semantics" [Dow79, p.138]). Certainly from the perspective of database querying the complications that it introduces into the logic seem unnecessary.

The existence of an actual historical database as the heart of our logical model is the major constraint within which all of our work must be undertaken. This *given*, which in essence already takes a stand on the semantics of the real world, stands as the major difference between Dowty's enterprise and ours. The semantic theory that we present is a theory of the semantics of English when used as a database query language for an HRDB, and not when used in *ordinary discourse*, whatever that might be. If these two theories diverge, it should be neither surprising nor disturbing, and it should be of interest to compare and contrast them.

It is apparent that an HRDB is a gross abstraction of the real world: entities are represented by unique identifiers, complex relationships are reduced to simple tuples in relations, time is rather crudely represented as a set of states of gross, perhaps even somewhat amorphous, granularity. And yet in spite of these limitations these databases are found to be useful to a large and growing number of people. What kind of constraints does the abstraction of *real-world* semantics embodied in the HRDB impose upon our enterprise? Precisely this: the historical database embodies a semantics that is based upon the notion of truth with respect to a state. Every fact in the database is recorded with respect to a state which *time-stamps* it; this is interpreted as asserting that the fact is true *at that state*. To be sure, intervals come into play: the Continuity Assumption asserts that the fact is to be interpreted as true from the time of its recording in the database until such time as a different fact of the same sort is recorded with a later time stamp (or until the current incarnation in the object's lifespan is closed) and throughout that interval. But these intervals are therein defined entirely with respect to discrete states and state changes. Therefore the semantics of any predicates that describe situations recorded in the database must be expressed in terms of truth with respect to states and state changes. Since intervals are not a primitive time unit in the HRDM, any properties that need to be defined with respect to an interval (e.g. "rise") will be defined from properties that are defined with respect to the moments of time that define that interval.

Dowty proposed an interval semantics in order to distinguish between the entailments of stative verbs on the one hand and of achievement and accomplishment verbs on the other. The sentence "John was working for the shoe department for three years", it is argued, intuitively should entail that "John works for the shoe department" is true at each moment during that three-year period. On the other hand, "John was falling asleep for ten minutes" does not so entail that "John falls asleep" is true at every moment of those ten minutes. As Dowty puts it:

> When we say 'It took John an hour to draw that circle,' we clearly do not mean that the tenseless atomic sentence 'John draws that circle' was true at all moments during some interval of one hour's duration; on the contrary, the tenseless sentence is clearly not true of any interval of LESS than one hour's duration. It is this independence of the truth of a tensed sentence at an interval from the truth of its constituent sentence(s) at all moments within the interval that traditional tense logic is not equipped to deal with. ([Dow79, p.138]).

The differences that Dowty examines certainly exist; they do not, however, seem relevant in most database applications. Our analysis would treat the progressive tenses synonymously with their simple counterparts:

> Did John earn 30K last week? *and*
> Was John earning 30K last week?

> Does Peter work for the Hardware Department? *and*
> Is Peter working for the Hardware Department?

Perhaps it is the case that database applications do not lend themselves to handling achievements or accomplishments, but instead record stative information. In any case it is difficult to conceive of many real database examples where distinctions of the sort that Dowty's analysis is concerned with actually make a difference.

Our analysis of the interaction of tenses and temporal expressions, on the other hand, accords exactly with Dowty's. Sentences with such interaction, such as "John worked yesterday," cannot be analyzed as resulting from two separate temporal operators ("-ed" and "yesterday") acting on the proposition that John works, as the following example should make clear:

**Example 5.1** *John worked yesterday.*

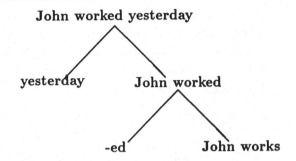

**Figure 5.1: Derivation of "John worked yesterday."**

| | | |
|---|---|---|
| John works | $\longrightarrow$ | $work'(i)(John)$ |
| -ed | $\Longrightarrow$ | $\lambda p \exists i_1[[i_1 < i] \wedge p(i_1)]$ |
| John worked | $\Longrightarrow$ | $\lambda p \exists i_1[[i_1 < i] \wedge p(i_1)](\lambda i\ work'(i)(John))$ |
| | $\longrightarrow$ | $\exists i_1[i_1 < i] \wedge work'(i_1)(John)]$ |
| yesterday | $\Longrightarrow$ | $\lambda p \exists i_2[yesterday'(i_2) \wedge p(i_2)]$ |
| John worked yesterday | $\Longrightarrow$ | $\lambda p \exists i_2[yesterday'(i_2) \wedge p(i_2)]$ |
| | | $(\lambda i \exists i_1[[i_1 < i] \wedge work'(i_1)(John)])$ |
| | $\longrightarrow$ | $\exists i_2 \exists i_1[yesterday'(i_2) \wedge [i_1 < i_2]$ |
| | | $\wedge work'(i_1)(John)]$ |

**Figure 5.2: Translation of "John worked yesterday."**

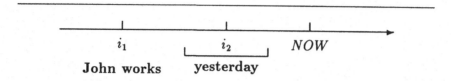

**Figure 5.3: Time Line Consistent with Logical Translation**

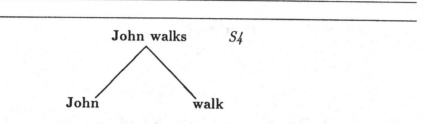

**Figure 5.4: PTQ Derivation of "John walks."**

The derivation is given in Figure 5.1, and its translation in Figure 5.2.

This analysis (or the reverse which would first apply "yesterday" and then "-ed") causes the two time operators to compete with each other, placing the event in the wrong time frame. For example, the time line in Figure 5.3 is consistent with this logical analysis, but inconsistent with the intended meaning of the English.

Instead the two temporal operators must be treated as operating *in conjunction*; the English -ed is, in a sense, semantically superfluous in the presence of the other time indicator. Thus the fragment has rules for applying tense operators, and separate rules for applying tense operators in conjunction with other temporal adverbials. These rules differ slightly from Dowty's in that we treat all temporal operators as operating on entire clauses, rather than simply on verb phrases. The next section will explore some of the reasons for this decision.

## 5.3.2  Sentential vs. Verb-phrasal Temporal Operators

Our analysis of tense differs from the PTQ analysis and the one in Dowty in the manner in which tense is incorporated into an English sentence. In PTQ, the rule S4 combines a Term with an IV to from a present-tensed sentence, as in:

**Example 5.2** *John walks.*

whose derivation is shown in Figure 5.4.

The past and future tenses are accommodated in rule S17, which similarly combines the subject and predicate to form a sentence in either of these tenses.

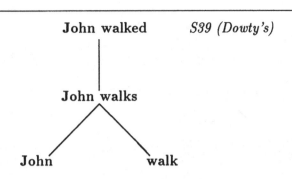

**Figure 5.5: Dowty's Derivation of "John walked."**

Dowty's analysis is somewhat different. In his fragment a sentence is always formed first by using S4; if the tense is other than present, he introduces this with an additional rule which takes the present-tensed sentence as input and forms its past-tense counterpart, as in the following example derived as in Figure 5.5:

**Example 5.3** *John walked.*

Extensions to the PTQ fragment have had to deal with this issue of tense and how it interacts with the other components of a sentence. We agree with Dowty's basic premise that tense is really a property of the sentence (actually, clause) as a whole. This is particularly important when, as in our fragment, there are different kinds of sentences: declarative, WH-questions, Yes-No-questions, and When-questions. For under a straightforward extension of the PTQ treatment the number of rules would proliferate, since separate rules would be needed for each kind and tense of the sentence formed by conjoining a Term and a VP. However under Dowty's treatment, the tense rules applied after S4 in most cases must undo the syntactic work that it has done, viz. the inflection of the verb as third person singular present tense. (Semantically the treatment is the same, i.e., the untensed version denotes exactly what the present-tensed version does.) This syntactic undoing is both inelegant and computationally unattractive. For this reason, we have incorporated into QE-III the additional categories of Tensed sentences of each variety, and have modified S4 so that it creates an untensed sentence from a Term and an IV. The strings of ultimate interest in the fragment, then, are the tensed sentences (categories $T - t$, $T - WHQ$, $T - YNQ$, and $WHENQ$). The following example from QE-III illustrates this for a simple declarative sentence derived as in Figure 5.6:

**Example 5.4** *John worked.*

In Chapter 7, when we discuss further examples of tensed sentences, particularly tensed questions and when-questions, we will discuss this issue further.

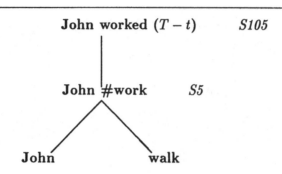

**Figure 5.6: QE-III Derivation of "John worked."**

# 5.4  Questions

## 5.4.1  Introduction

Questions are perhaps our most basic form of gaining knowledge of the world around us. Throughout our lives we rely upon our ability to ask others for information, upon their understanding the meaning of what we ask, and (hopefully) their ability to provide us with an answer. It is therefore interesting that in analyzing language and our use of language, both linguists and philosophers have considered interrogative sentences the *poor relation* of the declaratives, to which they have paid the bulk of their attention. Among linguists there is no generally accepted theory about the syntactic generation of English questions ([KR72], [Pop76]), and philosophers and logicians have until recently given little attention to the question of questions. Formal logic from its inception directed its attention to languages based upon the notion of formulas, abstractions of declarative sentences in natural languages. Only recently have logicians begun to investigate the semantics of questions in any depth, and to develop formal languages powerful enough to express questions in order to carry out these investigations. Hintikka [Hin74] discusses a number of recent linguistic and philosophical attempts to provide an analysis of questions.

It is one of the great tributes to the work of Richard Montague that it has attracted the attention and enthusiasm not only of other philosophers and logicians, but of linguists and computer scientists as well. Although Montague, too, focussed his attention on a formal treatment of the syntax and semantics of declarative sentences in natural language, the framework of using a lambda-calculus and the model-theory of intensional logic, developed in PTQ, is rich enough to incorporate a view of natural language questions as well. In what seems to be his only published remark on the issue of questions he says: "In connection with imperatives and interrogatives truth and entailment conditions are of course inappropriate, and would be replaced by fulfilment conditions and a characterization of the semantic content of a correct answer." ([Mon73], footnote 3.)

Perhaps inspired by this comment, a number of researchers have begun investigating ways to incorporate a formal account of the syntax and semantics of questions within the framework of Montague Semantics. [Ham73], [Kar77], [Ben77] and [Ben79], [HZ78], [Gun81], [Bel82], and [Sch83] are perhaps the most important of these investigations, and we will discuss their work in relation to ours in the following section. Many of the aspects of the solution that we propose have been adapted from or influenced by the work of these researchers.

Others not working within the MG framework have also made important contributions to our understanding of the issues involved. Approaching this issue from an entirely different perspective, researchers in Artificial Intelligence (AI) have over the years developed and implemented automatic question-answering theories and systems to varying degrees of success. These have ranged from some early experimental programs [GWCL63] to database querying programs bound to a particular database domain ([WKN81] and [Wal78]) to some rather sophisticated DBQ systems today that are designed to be general and easily portable ([Har78], [HSSS78].) The research behind these systems seems to share a goal common to most of the work in AI (excluding that branch (separate field?) that calls itself Cognitive Science), i.e. an interest more in getting a system to "work" than in developing a formal theory that explains its behavior. This is said not in criticism of such work, but merely in order to differentiate the goals of such work from our own goals.

Earlier we mentioned that among the researchers working within the MG framework were computer scientists. The work described in [FW78], [War79], and [Lan81], among others, has shown that not only are Montague's ideas important from a theoretical point of view, but that they are in addition computationally tractable. What this means or should mean to the computer science community is both that MG has something to say to those interested in doing language analysis within the CS discipline, but also that, as Barbara Partee has pointed out [PBW81], the computer is a useful tool for testing linguistic theories in MG.

In the previous section we attempted to show that a formal semantics can be given to the concept of a historical relational database. The semantics given was shown to be analogous to the semantics given to the relational database model by viewing it as an applied first order theory; extending the relational model to a historical database prompted a move to the higher-order language $IL_s$ (with its built-in concept of denotation with respect to an index) in order to provide a formal semantics for such databases in a natural way.

In this section we attempt to show that a successful formal treatment can be given to a Natural Language querying facility for an HRDB, again through the medium of the logic $IL_s$. We view this work as important for two very different reasons. First it represents one of the first attempts to adapt the ideas of MG to a practical problem. ([Jan86] discusses computer applications of the Montague Semantic approach.) The research that has been done since the PTQ paper has generally either been in the form of extensions or modifications to its linguistic or logical theory, or of implementations of the theory on the computer. We will attempt to show that this theory of language can serve as the formal foundation of a useable computer system for querying actual databases.

Second, it represents a change in emphasis in approaching the NLQ problem from the engineering approach – get as much coverage as possible and get the system to work – to a more formal approach – proceed in small steps and develop a formal theory of what you do with each step that you take. This work represents only a first step in this direction within a Montague-Semantics framework. The fragment of English which we define herein is certainly not adequate to express all of the queries that one would want to present to an HRDB. It is intended only to lay the groundwork for a formal theory of database querying that is both extendible and implementable.

## 5.4.2  Database Questions

As guidelines to help us judge any proposed theory of questions we have adopted a number of self-imposed criteria that any solution acceptable to us should meet:

1. It must fall within the general confines of Montague's framework. This means that the syntax and semantics of our language must be defined in parallel, with the semantics of a phrase defined compositionally in terms of the semantics of its components.

2. The interpretation of questions should be closely analogous to the interpretation of queries in the relational database model. This means that their interpretation should be objects in the logical model which have direct analogs in the HRDM developed in the previous section.

3. The theory should be computationally tractable. While this work does not discuss a computer implementation of its results, an extension of Warren's PTQ parser [War79] to the QE-III fragment has been implemented [Has82].

4. Proper treatment must be given to the interaction of questions and quantifiers. The PTQ treatment successfully accounts for multiple readings of sentences with interacting quantifiers ("A woman loves every man.") Our solution should likewise allow for all of the readings of questions involving quantified terms ("Who manages every employee?")

5. Y/N questions, WH-questions involving "who" and "what," and temporal questions ("when") should be provided for. This means that we do not treat indirect questions ("Tell me whether ..."), since these do not generally arise within the database framework and could nevertheless easily be paraphrased as direct YNQs.

6. The theory should account for multiple WH-questions, ("Who sells what to whom?" as these seem indispensable in a database context.

In the relational database model "a query is a computation upon relations to yield other relations" [Mai83]. This is an operational view of a database query; a denotational semantics view (which after all is the view of formal logic) would hold that a query denotes a relation that is its answer, and would define just how, in fact, the query so denoted. In order to provide for the closest possible parallel between the interpretation of questions that our theory defines and the query semantics of our (essentially relational) database model, we hoped to define the semantics of our English query language in just such a way, viz., such that each query would denote the relation that is its answer with respect to the database. In other words, if a query in the relational database context denoted an n-ary relation over entities (i.e., a set of n-tuples), we felt that its expression as a question in our fragment should be defined to denote a function of type $< e^n, t >$. As we shall see we were able to accomplish this easily and naturally not in the semantics, but by extending the framework of Montague Semantics to include a pragmatic component.

Computational tractability is another criterion for an acceptable solution to the problem of question semantics. Because we are interested in developing a theory for natural language query systems that are ultimately implementable, this criterion lead us to direct our attention to solutions that within the general framework of the PTQ program. This is because there have been successful results [War79] and [Lan81] implementing parsers and semantic interpretation routines for fragments defined within this framework, and we wanted to build upon this work as much as possible. A grammar for the QE-III fragment has been implemented [Has82] as an extension to Warren's implementation.

The problem of providing a correct analysis of questions that involve quantified terms is another one that we have considered in our theory. An analysis of queries like "Who manages every employee?" should only be considered adequate if it is able to find such a query ambiguous between an interpretation of "every" as "all" and also as "each." In PTQ Montague provided a solution to the familiar problem of the multiple readings of such sentences as "A woman loves every man." Under one reading there is a single woman who (magnanimously) loves each and every man, while under the other reading there is, for each man, some woman or other who loves him. A similar problem arises with respect to the interaction between *ordinary* and question Terms:

"Who manages every employee?"

Under one reading the questioner wishes to know what individual(s) manage all of the employees, whereas under the other reading what is wanted is really a set of ordered pairs, viz., for each employee, the set of individuals who manage him/her. Our interpretation of English questions must permit both readings, since either one is possible; the problem of disambiguating between the two is best left, as in PTQ, to a later stage that has access to domain-dependent Meaning Postulates.

In order to get these readings, we propose making a change in the standard interpretation of the English word "every.". It is well known that this word is ambiguous –

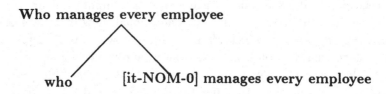

**Who manages every employee**

who          [it-NOM-0] manages every employee

**Figure 5.7: One Possible Derivation of "Who manages every employee?"**

[it-NOM-O] manages every    $\implies$    $\forall x[EMP'(i)(x) \longrightarrow MGR'(i)(x_0)$
    employee                                                     $\wedge manage'(i)(x_0, x)]$

who                                          $\implies$    $\lambda P \exists y[y(i) = u \wedge P(i)(y)]$

who manages every employee    $\longrightarrow$    $\exists y[y(i) = u \wedge \forall x[EMP'(i)(x) \longrightarrow$
                                  $MGR'(i)(y) \wedge manage'(i)(y, x)]]$

**Figure 5.8: A Possible Translation of "Who manages every employee?"**

in some cases it means "all" and in others "for each." This is precisely the ambiguity in this case, and we must provide for both readings.

The first reading, where "who" has wider scope than "every," presents no problems:

**Example 5.5** *Who manages every employee?*

With the derivation shown in Figure 5.7, this question would receive the translation in Figure 5.8.

The other reading, derived in Figure 5.9, requires the opposite scoping, as well as a different meaning for "every employee." The desired reading is accomplished by allowing "every" to be ambiguous between its standard meaning "for all" and its interrogative meaning of "for each" in which it is essentially synonymous with "which."

With this reading, the translation becomes that in Figure 5.10. This treatment of "every" yields the desired second (and more likely) reading, the one that denotes a

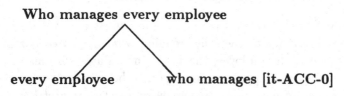

**Who manages every employee**

every employee          who manages [it-ACC-0]

**Figure 5.9: Another Possible Derivation of "Who manages every employee?"**

| | | |
|---|---|---|
| who manages [it-ACC-O] | $\longrightarrow$ | $\exists y[y(i) = u \wedge MGR'(i)(y) \wedge EMP'(i)(x_0)$ |
| | | $\wedge manage'(i)(y, x_0)]$ |
| every employee | $\longrightarrow$ | $\lambda P \exists z[z(i) = v \wedge EMP'(i)(z) \wedge P(i)(z)]$ |
| who manages every | $\longrightarrow$ | $\lambda P \exists z[z(i) = v \wedge EMP'(i)(z) \wedge P(i)(z)]$ |
| employee? | | $(\lambda i \lambda x_0 \exists y[y(i) = u \wedge MGR'(i)(y) \wedge$ |
| | | $EMP'(i)(x_0 \wedge manage'(i)(y, x_0)])$ |
| | $\longrightarrow$ | $\exists z \exists y[z(i) = v \wedge EMP'(i)(z) \wedge y(i) = u$ |
| | | $\wedge MGR'(i)(y) \wedge manage'(i)(y, z)]$ |

**Figure 5.10: A Possible Translation of "Who manages every employee?"**

set of ordered pairs $< u, v >$ such that $u$ manages $v$.

Another criterion for our work has been a successful solution to the problem of multiple WH-questions. There is a rather simple solution to the question-semantics problem that meets these criteria if one is willing to restrict one's attention to questions that involve only one WH-word; it is well known, however, that multiple-WH words require a considerably more complex treatment if the semantics is to be defined compositionally, as in a Montague framework it must [KR72]. Furthermore, within the database context a restriction to single WH-questions would be too severe a constraint – it would limit the language to queries that return relations over only a single attribute.

In the next section we discuss a number of different possible solutions to this issue of multiple WH-questions, and ultimately adopt one as our solution. We will see, however, in the course of this presentation, that there are considerable technical difficulties in defining the semantics in such a way as to get it all to come out right for both single- and multiple-WH questions. The solution that we adopt, involving the addition of a formally specified pragmatics for the fragment, does have this property in addition to meeting our other criteria; moreover, the simplicity of our solution, as contrasted with the considerable complexity in other proposals for a question semantics, e.g. [Ben77], [Ben79] and [HZ78], makes it especially attractive. However, it is clear that many researchers have found the same kinds of difficulties in extending Montague's work in the direction of interpreting questions, and that further work in this area is needed. We hope that our proposal to treat the answering of a question as a component of a formally-specified pragmatics of the language, apart from its semantics, is a step in the proper direction.

## 5.5   The QE-III Theory of Questions

### 5.5.1   Introduction

We will first present a general view of the substance of our theory of the interpretation of questions and then discuss how this theory is carried out technically for the various types of questions that we consider. As we have said, our goal is a formal interpretation of questions as the set of their correct answers with respect to an index and a model (state and database.) This viewpoint is inspired by the relational database querying paradigm, wherein a query *denotes* the relation that is its answer with respect to the current state of the database. In order to understand some of the points we will make in this section, we should keep in mind the distinction between objects in a model for $IL_s$ that we may consider as an interpretation for a question, and objects in the relational database model. In the relational model, particularly when dealing with the relational algebra, one tends to think of all relations as being the same kind of object. One projects and joins relations at will, since these relational operators are defined *generically*. However, models for $IL_s$ are strongly typed; considerations of the domains and ranges of functions are of critical importance. Within $IL_s$, e.g., a one-place relation of individuals is a function from $D_e$ to $D_t$ (denoted by expressions of type $< e, t >$), a two-place relation of individuals a function from $D_e$ to functions from $D_e$ to $D_t$ (denoted by expressions of type $< e, < e, t >>$), etc. Thus under our theory a question such as "Who manages Peter?" is pragmatically interpreted (in a sense to be made clear below) as an object of a *completely different type* from the interpretation of a question such as "Who manages whom?" Later on we will see that this theory does not fall within the mainstream of the logical theories for question semantics that have been proposed.

### 5.5.2   Yes-No Questions

A semantic analysis of Yes-No questions (YNQs) that meets the criteria set forth in the introduction to this section is not difficult to obtain. Since we want to interpret YNQs as either "Yes" or "No" (or equivalently T or F, or 1 or 0), they can be defined to denote objects in $\{0, 1\}$. But this is just the denotation set of the corresponding declarative sentence that expresses the proposition that the YNQ asks. Thus we easily meet our criteria by providing that a YNQ denote the same proposition as that denoted by the declarative sentence from which it was derived. For example,

> John manages the shoe department

would be (roughly) translated as:

$$manage'(i)(John, ShoeDept)$$

This formula is true with respect to any state $s$ just in case John manages the shoe department in that state. Our analysis of the corresponding question "Does John manage the shoe department?" provides that it is derived syntactically from "John manages the shoe department" and that semantically it denotes the same object in the model. Under this view, then, a formula in the logic essentially *questions* the model as to its truth or falsity in the same way that a YNQ questions the database for the response "yes" or "no." This analysis is provided by the following pair of syntactic and semantic rules for our fragment:

**S101. [YNQ Formation]**

$< F_{101a}, < t >, YNQ >$  and  $< F_{101b}, < t >, YNQ >$

$F_{101a}(\phi) = \#\text{AUX } \phi^*$ where $\phi^*$ is $\phi$ with the *first verbs* unmarked.

$F_{101b}(\phi) = $ "Is it the case that" $\phi$

**T101.** $F_{101a}(\phi)$ and $F_{101b}(\phi) \Longrightarrow \phi'$

This "$\Longrightarrow$" notation is used in each translation rule that is not an instance of the general rule of function application. In this case it indicates that the translation of the expression formed by performing the operation $F_{101a}$ (or $F_{101b}$) on the input string $\phi$ is exactly the same as the translation which has already been assigned to $\phi$, which we denote with the notation $\phi'$. The particular operation in question, say $F_{101b}$, is defined in terms of various string manipulations; here the operation is to prepose the string "Is it the case that" onto the input string "$\phi$". The semantic account in this example works, since we want the interpretation of the Yes-No question to be the same as the interpretation of the declarative sentence from which it is derived.

In what follows we examine the more difficult problem of defining compositionally a model-theoretic semantics for general WH-questions.

## 5.5.3  WH-Questions

Let us now begin to develop the solution that we are ultimately to propose, by proceeding in stages. We first present a semantic solution that does provide for a successful interpretation for questions that involve only one WH-word, e.g. "Who manages Peter?" This solution has its simplicity to recommend it, but is unfortunately unable to accommodate multiple WH-questions. We will then examine a number of alternative solutions to illustrate some of the many problems involved in attempting to accommodate these multiple questions.

It is an obvious linguistic fact that question words like "who," "what," "whom," etc. behave syntactically in much the same way as Terms like "Peter" or "an employee" (e.g. see [Ham73].) In subject position there is virtually no difference, as seen in Figure 5.11, while in object position, seen in Figure 5.12, there is what linguists call WH-Q-Movement.

Nonetheless in both cases the question word takes the role of a Term syntactically. Semantically, however, there is a difference. Whereas ordinary terms refer to an

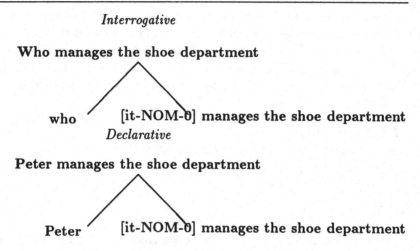

Figure 5.11: Similarity of Question Terms and Terms in Subject Position

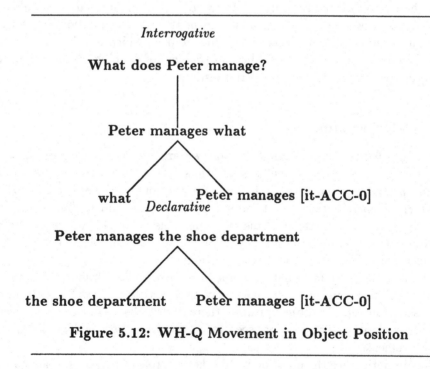

Figure 5.12: WH-Q Movement in Object Position

| Term | Logical Translation | Logical Type |
|------|---------------------|--------------|
| Peter | $\lambda P \exists x [x(i) = Peter \wedge P(i)(x)]$ | $<< s, << s, e >, t >>, t >$ |
| an employee | $\lambda P \exists x [EMP(i)(x) \wedge P(i)(x)]$ | " |
| who | $\lambda P \lambda u \exists x [x(i) = u \wedge P(i)(x)]$ | $<< s, << s, e >, t >>, < e, t >>$ |

**Figure 5.13: Similarity of Semantics of Terms and WH-Terms**

Peter $\implies \lambda P \exists x [x(i) = Peter \wedge P(i)(x)]$

[it-NOM-O] manages the $\implies$ $manage'(i)(x_0, shoe - dept)$
shoe department

Peter manages the $\implies \lambda P \exists x [x(i) = Peter \wedge P(i)(x)]$
shoe department $\qquad (\lambda i \lambda x_0 \; manage'(i)(x_0, shoe - dept))$

$\longrightarrow \exists x [x(i) = Peter \wedge$
$\qquad manage'(i)(x, shoe - dept)$

**Figure 5.14: Translation of "Peter manages the shoe department."**

individual or a set of individuals in the model (actually in PTQ to the set of properties of these individuals, but this point need not concern us here), question terms seem in some way to refer to the set of all possible individuals that, when substituted for the individual variable in a matrix, make the resulting formula true. This observation leads to the consideration that question words should denote, not sets of properties or sets of individuals, but rather functions from sets of properties to sets of individuals that have those properties. The table in Figure 5.13 makes this analogy clearer.

Because of the similarity of these WH-words to ordinary Terms, both syntactically and semantically, we shall refer to them as WH-Terms. The schematic essentials of the translations of two of the above examples will show how this analysis of the semantics of WH-Terms provides the desired analysis of the WH-question. In this presentation we follow Partee in using a double arrow "$\implies$" to indicate the immediate result of applying a Translation rule of the fragment, and a single arrow "$\longrightarrow$" to indicate the result of any of a number of logical simplifications (principally $\lambda$-reduction.) The two translations are shown in Figures 5.14 and 5.15.

The first example (Figure 5.14) demonstrates the PTQ-like analysis of a declarative sentence translating into a formula whose interpretation in the model with respect to a given state is a truth value.

The second example (Figure 5.15) provides an analysis of an interrogative sentence containing a single WH-Term, using an analogous substitution rule. We obtain an

| who | $\Longrightarrow$ | $\lambda P \lambda u \exists x [x(i) = u \wedge P(i)(x)]$ |
| who manages the | $\Longrightarrow$ | $\lambda P \lambda u \exists x [x(i) = u \wedge P(i)(x)]$ |
| shoe department | | $(\lambda i \lambda x_0 \, manage'(i)(x_0, shoe - dept))$ |
| | $\longrightarrow$ | $\lambda u \exists x [x(i) = u \wedge$ |
| | | $manage'(i)(x, shoe - dept)$ |

**Figure 5.15: Translation of "Who manages the shoe department."**

expression of type $< e, t >$ whose denotation with respect to an index is a set of entities, viz. the set of entities who manage the shoe department in that state.

This analysis, unfortunately, cannot be generalized. Although it can also be made to provide the desired analysis for single WH-Terms in direct or indirect object position, it will not allow for multiple WH-Questions. To see why this is the case, consider what the S and T rules for the above analysis might look like.

**S$_{WH}$.**

If $\alpha$ is a WH-Term and $\phi$ is a formula, then $F_{WH-n}(\alpha, \phi)$ is a WH1-?, where $F_{WH-n}(\alpha, \phi)$ would be defined as some sort of substitution of $\alpha$ for the first occurrence of $x_n$, and the appropriate pronoun for each subsequent occurrence, as in the PTQ substitution rules.

**T$_{WH}$.**

$F_{S-WH-n}(\alpha, \phi) \Longrightarrow \alpha'(\lambda i \lambda x_n [\phi'])$.

Notice that this rule, unlike the analogous substitution rules in the PTQ fragment, cannot be applied recursively to its output. This is because the PTQ substitution rules are of the form

$$P_\alpha + Q_\beta \Longrightarrow R_\beta$$

(i.e. an expression of type $\alpha$ combines with an expression of type $\beta$ to yield another expression of type $\beta$) whereas this rule is of the form

$$P_\alpha + Q_\beta \Longrightarrow R_\gamma$$

(i.e., the output is of a different type from either of the inputs.)

A number of alternatives present themselves at this point to allow for an analysis of multiple WH-questions within this framework. The first requires that WH-Terms have different *flavors* ($who_0$, $who_1$, $who_2$,...) depending on the meaning of the expression into which they are substituted for a free variable. The second requires subcategorizing the category Term, and substituting all Terms in for free variables at one time. The third, and the one we shall adopt, achieves the same semantic

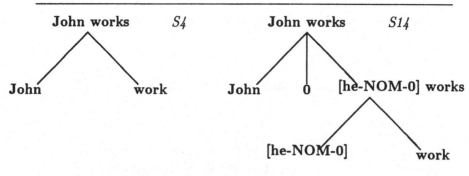

**Figure 5.16: Two PTQ Derivations of "John walks."**

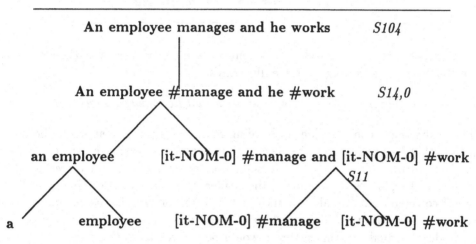

**Figure 5.17: Pronominal Co-reference**

effect as the rule T-WH, but in a two-stage process involving a separate pragmatic component. We will examine each of these ideas in turn. First, however, we need to say a word about substitution.

In the PTQ analysis, a Term can become a constituent part of a sentence either by directly combining with some other constituent, or indirectly by means of substitution for a free variable that has been so directly combined. For example, consider the two PTQ-like derivations of the sentence "John works" in Figure 5.16.

Under the semantic analysis of PTQ it turns out that these two derivations receive the same translation, and hence the same *meaning*. But the substitution rules are not gratuitous. They are introduced as a theory to account for pronominal co-reference and quantifier scoping. The derivation in Figure 5.17 illustrates how pronominal co-reference is handled by means of one of the substitution rules.

In this derivation, the substitution rule S14,0 provides for the reading in which the same individual is the referent of the terms "an employee" and "he." The same

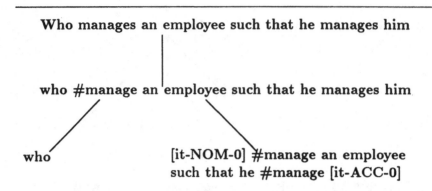

**Figure 5.18: Co-reference in Questions**

problem of accounting for co-reference occurs in the consideration of the semantics of questions, as the following example illustrates:

**Example 5.6** *Who manages an employee such that he manages him?*

(The "such that" construction for heading relative clauses is a syntactic holdover from the PTQ fragment which, because our concern is primarily semantic, we have not attempted to replace with a more sophisticated treatment. For a treatment of more *normal* English relative clauses, the reader is referred to [Coo79].) The PTQ theory of co-reference, extended to allow substitution of WH-Terms, is equally able to capture the fact that "who" and "him" are co-referent, as are "an employee" and "he." Under our analysis, this sentence would be derived as in Figure 5.18.

This idea of extending the PTQ theory of co-reference to the case of interrogatives is not ours. It is used in most of the work on question semantics in the Montague Semantic tradition (including [Kar77], [Ben77] and [Ben79], and [Bel82].) It is that theory which we have incorporated into our fragment. Because question words in our fragment are always assumed to have the entire sentence as their scope (i.e., there are no embedded question-clauses), and because of the extensional nature of our theory as dictated by the database, question words can always be brought in indirectly by means of substitution rules. The difference in our respective treatments lies in our attempts to formalize the *meaning* given to questions.

Let us take a look now at why the analysis we have presented so far cannot be extended to multiple WH-questions. According to that analysis, the derivation of a question like "Who manages what?" is blocked after the first WH-Term is brought in, as shown in Figure 5.19.The lower constituents of this derivation are translated as seen in Figure 5.20.

Syntactically the derivation is blocked because the proposed rule S-WH only allows a WH-Term to combine with a string in the category sentence, and under the analysis "[it-NOM-0] manages what" is not a sentence. More to the point is the semantics.

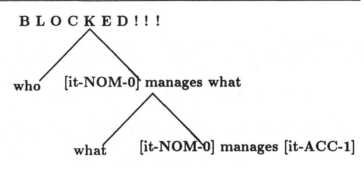

**Figure 5.19: Blocked Analysis**

$$
\begin{aligned}
\text{[it-NOM-0] manages [it-ACC-1]} &\implies manage'(i)(x_0, x_1) \ \textbf{(PTQ-rules)} \\
\text{what} &\implies \lambda P \lambda u \exists x [x(i) = u \wedge P(i)(x)] \\
\text{[it-NOM-0] manages what} &\implies \lambda P \lambda u \exists x [x(i) = u \wedge P(i)(x)] \\
&\longrightarrow \lambda u \exists x [x(i) = u \wedge manage'(i)(x_0, x)]
\end{aligned}
$$

**Figure 5.20: Translation of Lower Constituents in Blocked Analysis**

"Who" denotes a function from sets of properties to sets of individuals (having those properties), and the meaning of "[it-NOM-0] manages what" is not an appropriate argument for such a function.

But suppose that the "who" which combined with formulas to form expressions denoting sets of individuals were a different function from the "who" that combined with expressions denoting sets of individuals to form expressions denoting sets of ordered pairs of individuals, etc.? Suppose, that is, that the English "who" were really a syntactic realization of a number of different meanings, $who_0$, $who_1$, etc., as in Figure 5.21.

These different functions of the English "who" would be captured by their different translations into the logic (reflecting their interpretation as different semantic functions), as seen in Figure 5.21. With this analysis we could complete the above derivation, previously blocked, as in Figure 5.22.

In theory there would be an infinite number of such (related) meanings to the word "who," one for each natural number $n$, and we could even give a rule for generating these meanings inductively from the single meaning of $who_0$. In practice (and computationally), since English allows for Terms in only a relatively small number of places (Subject, Direct and Indirect Objects, Object of Preposition, etc.) only three or four would actually ever be used in any normal English question. The S and T rules for this analysis would be something like the following:

$S_{WH-n}.$

---

*Who*$_0$   combines with propositions to form a set of individuals

*Who*$_1$   combines with sets of individuals to form a set of ordered pairs

*and in general*                                                    ,

*Who*$_i$   combines with sets of ordered $i$-tuples to form sets of ordered $i + 1$-tuples

| who-word | Translation | Type |
|----------|-------------|------|
| $who_0$ | $\lambda P \lambda u \exists x[x(i) = u \wedge P(i)(x)]$ | $<< s, < s, e >, t >, < e, t >>$ |
| $who_1$ | $\lambda R \lambda v \lambda w \exists z[z(i) \;\; = \;\; v \;\; \wedge \;\; R(i)(z, w)]$ | $<< s, << s, e >, < e, >>>, < e, < e, t >>>$ |

**Figure 5.21: Multiple "who" Semantics**

---

$$
\begin{aligned}
&\text{[it-NOM-0] manages what} &\Longrightarrow\quad& \lambda u \exists x[x(i) = u \wedge manage'(i)(x_0, x)] \\
&\text{who } (as\ who_1) &\Longrightarrow\quad& \lambda R \lambda v \lambda w \exists z[z(i) = v \wedge R(i)(z, w)] \\
&\text{who manages what} &\Longrightarrow\quad& \lambda R \lambda v \lambda w \exists z[z(i) = v \wedge R(i)(z, w)] \\
& & & (\lambda i \lambda x_0 \lambda u \exists x[x(i) = u \wedge manage'(i)(x_0, x)]) \\
& &\longrightarrow\quad& \lambda v \lambda w \exists z[z(i) = v \wedge \\
& & & \exists x[x(i) = w \wedge manage'(i)(z, x)] \\
& &\longrightarrow\quad& \lambda v \lambda w \exists z \exists x[z(i) = v \wedge x(i) = w \wedge \\
& & & manage'(i)(z, x)]
\end{aligned}
$$

**Figure 5.22: A Multiple "who" Semantics Treatment of "Who manages what?"**

---

If $\alpha \in P_{WH-Term-i}$ and $\beta \in P_{?i?}$ (i.e. $\beta$ denotes a set of $i$-tuples), then $F_{WH,n}(\alpha, \beta) \in P_{?i+1?}$, where $F_{WH,n}(\alpha, \beta)$ is the result of replacing the first occurrence of [it-CASE-n] in $\beta$ with $\alpha$, and replacing all subsequent occurrences of [it-CASE-n] in $\beta$ with he/she/it or him/her/it, respectively, according to the gender of $\alpha$ and the CASE of [it-CASE-n].

$\mathbf{T}_{Wh-n}.$

$$F_{WH,n}(\alpha, \beta) \Longrightarrow \alpha'(\lambda i \lambda x_n \beta')$$

Moreover, to account for derived WH-Terms like "which employee" in "which employee sells shoes?", we could extend this analysis to the interrogative determiners "which" and "what." This would dictate that $which_0$ combined with employee to form $[which\ employee]_0$, $which_1$ with employee to form $[which\ employee]_1$, etc., of the appropriate types.

Upon reflection this analysis did not seem too farfetched. After all, in asking "Who manages John?" the word "who" is in some way asking for a set of individuals, viz. those that manage John. In asking "Who manages whom?" however, rather than asking for a set of individuals, "who" is asking in conjunction with "whom" for a set of ordered pairs such that the first component manages the second component. A theory such as this that we have sketched would claim that English allows for these many semantic functions of interrogative terms to be performed by the same surface words like "who."

We might also point out here a closely related alternative to this approach. Instead of having an infinite number of meanings for each WH-Term, we could suffice with one and allow an infinite number of syntactic and semantic rules for performing the substitutions. These rules would perform the necessary conversions of the meanings, not of the WH-Term, but of the sentential form into which it is being substituted. Thus, e.g., the T-WH-1 rule for combining "who" with "[it-NOM-0] manages whom" would form the following expression (where $WHO*$ stands for the translation of "who"):

$$\lambda w[WHO * [\lambda i \lambda x_0 \beta * (w)]]$$

For example, combining "who" with "[it-NOM-0] manages what", would give us the translation in Figure 5.23.

Notice that this rule schema essentially converts the 1-place relation denoted by one of its arguments ("[it-NOM-0] manages what" in the example) into a formula (by function application to the new individual variable $w$) in order to allow the single meaning of "who" to apply. Lastly, it $\lambda$-abstracts this variable $w$ over the result in order to obtain a 2-place relation. A slightly unfortunate result of this rule is that the order of the individuals in the relation is exactly opposite from the order in which the WH-Terms were quantified in.

A second possible approach that would handle multiple WH-questions would dispense with this essentially inductive treatment of $i$-place questions and attack the

who                          $\Longrightarrow$   $\lambda P \lambda v \exists y[y(i) = v \wedge P(i)(y)]$
[it-NOM-0] manages          $\Longrightarrow$   $\lambda u \exists x[x(i) = u \wedge manage'(i)(x_0, x)]$
   what
who manages what            $\Longrightarrow$   $\lambda w[\lambda P \lambda v \exists y[y(i) = v \wedge P(i)(y)]]$
                               $([\lambda i \lambda x_0[\lambda u \exists x[x(i) = u \wedge manage'(i)(x_0, x)](w)])$
                       $\longrightarrow$   $\lambda w[\lambda P \lambda v \exists y[y(i) = v \wedge P(i)(y)]]$
                               $([\lambda i \lambda x_0[\exists x[x(i) = w \wedge manage'(i)(x_0, x)]]])$
                       $\longrightarrow$   $\lambda w \lambda v \exists y \exists x[y(i) = v \wedge x(i) = w$
                               $\wedge \, manage'(i)(y, x)]$

**Figure 5.23: An Infinite WH-Rule Semantics Treatment of "Who manages what?"**

**Who supplies what to which departments such that they sell shoes**

who:0
what:1
which department:2

[it-NOM-0] supplies [it-ACC-1] to [it-DAT-2]
such that [it-NOM-0] sells shoes

**Figure 5.24: Simultaneous Substitution of WH-Terms**

problem all at once. Such a theory would derive all questions in the same manner, by simultaneously substituting all WH-Terms into the matrix sentence, keeping track of which terms were substituted for which variables. For example, the question "Who supplies what to which departments such that they sell shoes?" would be analyzed as in Figure 5.24.

Either of these two theories is possible; indeed, at one time or another during the course of this research we have worked with both of them. In the end, however, we were led to reject them both for a number of reasons. First, if we were unhappy with the necessity for an infinite number of meanings for WH-Terms and WH-Determiners, or for an infinite number of rules schemas for their substitution, we were even more unhappy by the need that it occasioned to use the same technique for each of the tense rules, and for each of the tense rules with time-adverbials, and for each of the "when"-question rules, the rules for "when"-questions with tenses, for "when"-questions with tenses and time-adverbials, etc. In other words, accepting a solution which types all questions differently depending upon what they ask for forces the inclusion of rule schemas for all of the other semantic functions that in a simple theory would operate only on one type, the type given to sentences. Later we will discuss how the solutions of Bennett and Belnap and of Hausser and Zaefferer entail a similar rippling effect of complexity throughout the rest of the semantic theory already developed for declarative sentences.

For an example of this effect in the theory under consideration, consider what the rule for adding past tense to a sentence would look like. (Recall our arguments for the necessity of treating tense as a property of the entire sentence.) Such a rule would have to be of the form:

$$P_\alpha + -ED \Longrightarrow Q_\alpha$$

where $\alpha$ could be the category declarative sentence (type $t$), 1-term question (type $< e, t >$), 2-term question (type $< e, < e, t >>$), etc. Because of the strict typing system of $IL_s$ (and of the categorial grammar of the PTQ theory of English syntax), this would require an infinite number of such rules, one for each of the possible input categories. While such a scheme is possible, it seems to violate a concern for simplicity and elegance.

An additional problem with a theory dependent upon simultaneous substitution is a difficulty of conceiving of it in semantic terms. Having worked within such a framework for a while, we believe that the translation rules for such a theory can be described (although they are somewhat complicated.) However they easily lead to the trap of thinking that the translation rules themselves are the semantics, when in fact they are nothing more than syntactic operations on strings of logical symbols. (This is a common problem for people working with Montague Semantics, occasioned by the indirect way that the semantics for English is specified. Dowty refers to this problem [Dow78] when he reminds us that "the translation is a completely dispensable part of the [PTQ] theory. The 'real' semantic interpretation of an English sentence is the model-theoretic interpretation of its translation and nothing but the model-theoretic interpretation of that translation."). When examined in terms of the semantic space of functions in the model, it was not at all clear what simultaneous substitution in the syntax *denoted* model-theoretically.

## 5.5.4  Temporal Questions

A major claim of this work is that a database model that incorporates a temporal semantics is more useful in that it captures more of the *meaning* of the enterprise being modelled. The temporal component of the database has of course been involved in every query type that we have considered, since a query is evaluated with respect to a state in the real time interval covered by the database. However it should also be possible to provide an interpretation for queries of the sort that directly ask the system about when a particular state of affairs holds in the database enterprise.

"When" questions are different from any of the questions we have considered so far for three reasons. First they ask about an entity of a different type: all of the questions we have considered have been treated as in some way referring to sets of

---

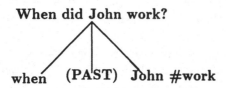

**When did John work?**

when    (PAST)    John #work

Figure 5.25: Wide Scope of "when"

---

$n$-tuples of individuals (of type $e$); "when" questions, on the other hand, refer to states (of type $s$).

Second, although sentences can and do make reference to more than one time ("I know that John was here"), multiple when-questions are very infrequent. In most situations "when" in English can generally only be asked once in a given sentence. "When and when ...?" does not make sense, and questions like "when did John come and when did he leave?" are really two conjoined questions. (Although David Warren suggests considering the following sort of exchange:

   [SHE]:   "There are several Fire Island ferries each day."

   [HE]:    "Oh, really! When do they arrive and when do they leave?"

It is natural to interpret this as a request for the set of ordered pairs $< t_1, t_2 >$ representing the arrival and departure times of particular ferry runs. Other sorts of multiple when-questions that ask for a range ("Between when and when ...") seem to be of this same type.) We have not accounted for multiple when-questions of this sort in our theory. An interpretation for them could be formulated in a manner analogously to our treatment of multiple WH-questions, but this would require modifying the treatment of time (modelled after Montague's) in the semantics. We will have more to say about this in our discussion of pragmatics.

Finally, when combining with WH-Terms "when" must be brought in last to have the widest scope, for essentially the same reasons that led to the recognition that tense must have widest scope. Moreover, some account must be given of how "when" interacts with our treatment of tenses, the other major temporal indicator in the surface structure of English. The example derivation in Figure 5.25 indicates how "when" is introduced into a sentence and *captures* the variable $i$ in all of its free occurrences.

The question is interpreted as asking for the set of times in the past at which John was an employee, as seen in the translation of Figure 5.26

## 5.5.5   Pragmatics or Semantics?

In considering which of the various possible theories for a question semantics to adopt, we found ourselves unhappy with all of them. All of the theories sketched

$$John \; \#work \qquad \longrightarrow \quad EMP'_*(i)(John)$$
$$When \; did \; John \; work? \quad \longrightarrow \quad \lambda p \lambda i_1 [[i_1 < i] \wedge p(i_1)](\lambda i \, EMP'_*(i)(John))$$
$$\longrightarrow \quad \lambda i_1 [[i_1 < i] \wedge (\lambda i \, EMP'_*(i)(John)(i_1)]$$
$$\longrightarrow \quad \lambda i_1 [[i_1 < i] \wedge EMP'_*(i_1)(John)]$$

**Figure 5.26: Translation of "When did John work?"**

above, and also those of a number of other researchers in the Montague framework to be discussed shortly, made significant complications to the semantics of other parts of the PTQ analysis in order to incorporate these new sentences. We began to feel that we might all be overtaxing the semantic component of our language theories, asking it to do for us more than it was intended to do. For example, most theories of question semantics have attempted to include some representation of the answer of the question as part of its denotation. Even though we were trying to accomplish this as well, it grated on our intuition, which feels that there is something odd in a theory that holds that a question denotes its answer, especially if one has tried (or tried not) to think of *denoting* as a formal counterpart to the intuitive notion of *meaning*. Yet in one form or another (denoting the set of possible answers (Hamblin), the set of correct answers (Karttunen), functions from sequences of individuals to propositions (Bennett and Belnap), and our sets of *n*-tuples of individuals) many researchers have been investigating ways to accomplish this in a formal semantics. Moreover, the similarity between WH-Terms and unbound pronouns ("who loves whom?" versus "he loves him") kept appearing as something important. We began to feel that the right approach was to have questions denote as declarative sentences (with unbound pronouns) do, and to allow some other component of the language theory account for their *question-ness* and encompass their answers.

Pragmatics is the least understood branch of the tripartite division of the study of language that Morris proposed in his theory of semiotics [Mor38]. This century has seen tremendous successes in the development of formal logical syntax and model-theoretic semantics, but very little in the way of formal pragmatics ([Mar59] is an early attempt in this direction.) "As for pragmatics, the almost commonly held opinion is that it may be only a descriptive science" says Marciszewski [Mar71] in a survey of the field. "There is no well-established body of literature that can be identified as work in (pure) pragmatics" says Donald Kalish [Kal72] in the entry on "Semantics" in the *The Encyclopedia of Philosophy*. This seems to be because there has been less agreement as to the scope of this branch of the field. Morris originally defined pragmatics as the study of "the relation of signs to interpreters" [Mor38]. Later, at least partly in response to Carnap's proposal that "if in an investigation explicit reference is made to the ... user of a language, then we assign it to the field of pragmatics" [Car42], Morris felt the need to expand upon this definition. In [Mor46] he says that pragmatics is "that portion of semiotic which deals with the origins, uses, and effects of signs within the behavior in which they occur."

Montague's conception of pragmatics [Mon68,Mon70b,Mon73], based upon Bar-Hillel's discussion of indexical expressions [Bar54] , represents a departure from the traditional view. Hamblin [Ham73] felt that Montague's incorporation of a pragmatic component directly in the syntax and semantics was unconventional, and felt the need "to defend pragmatics from this weakened interpretation ... Pragmatics is the study of the *use* (not just reference) of language of all kinds; or, if it is not, we need a new name for the study that complements syntax and semantics. Montague's 'pragmatics' would be better classed as a special part of semantics." [Dow78], while admitting that "the linguist's use of the term pragmatics is far from standardized," adopts the view that it should encompass direct and indirect speech acts, presuppositions, and implicatures, and explicitly rejects Montague's use of the term to encompass a treatment of indexical expressions.

Asa Kasher discusses this issue at some length [Kas77]. "Bar-Hillel focussed his attention on the context of use, paving the way for Montague's attempt to see through his brilliant formal lenses just indices – time of utterance, place of utterance, addressee or addressees, etc. Saturated with indexicality, intoxicated with excessive formal powers, Montague's theory left most parts of Pragmatics of natural languages, such as the studies of speech acts and implicatures, out of focus, blurred." The goal of pragmatics, he goes on to say, should be the "specification and explanation of the constitutive rules of the human competence to use linguistic means for effecting literal purposes."

What we propose in our theory of questions is that the proper place for considering the answer(s) to a question is in a separate theory of pragmatics for the language. We do not propose a completely general theory of pragmatics. But we believe that incorporating a formal pragmatic component to our fragment that treats the notion of a response to a question is defensible as at least one component of a theory of language use. In the first place, Montague notwithstanding, it falls within the confines of pragmatics as that term is generally understood. For whether one speaks of "the use and effects" of language [Mor46], the "relation of signs to their interpreters" [Mor38], the notion of "speech acts" [Dow78], or of the "linguistic means for effecting literal purposes" [Kas77], it is clear that the notion of responding to a question is encompassed. Our attempt to formalize a pragmatic component to our theory of QE-III accords well with what Stalnaker sees as the goals of "a formal semiotics no less rigorous than present day logical syntax and semantics." [Sta72]. Those goals, he goes on to say, include an analysis of such linguistic acts as "assertions, commands, ...., requests ... to find necessary and sufficient conditions for the successful (or perhaps in some cases normal) completion of the act."

A second argument in favor of this approach comes from looking at the way that linguists have described the concept of a question. Linguists have traditionally classified sentences into four distinct types: declarative, interrogative, imperative, and exclamatory. A glance through some standard text or reference books on English grammar reveals two separate approaches to the rationale behind this scheme. According to one school, as in [Rob54] it is based upon the "different kinds of meaning" a sentence may have. The other school, as in [QG74] considers that the distinction is based upon such criteria as word order in the sentence, presence or absence of a subject, the presence of an interjection, etc. Clearly the disagreement is over whether to consider this a syntactic or a semantic distinction. Is it wrong to suggest that in some sense it is mainly a pragmatic one, reflecting both the use and effects of the utterance?

Finally this approach in its technical details is both simple and elegant. It removes from the semantics the burden of providing an account of the response to a question, and allows it to do what semantics theories have always done best, account for reference. Then, just as the semantics of a language is based upon its syntax, the pragmatics is based upon both the syntactic ann semantic analyses (or, in Hamblin's phrase, it "complements syntax and semantics."). The simplicity with which we can state the formal pragmatic rules for our fragment, which take into account the notion of the answer to a question, is based upon this ability to have both the syntax and the semantics at hand upon which to build a theory of pragmatics.

We believe that a general theory of natural language pragmatics for a language L would involve a definition something like the following:

$$PI(\alpha) = f(Sy(\alpha), Se(\alpha), C_1, C_2, \ldots, C_n)$$

where $PI(\alpha)$, the **Pragmatic Interpretation of** $\alpha$ in the language $L$, is a function with the following arguments:

1. $Sy(\alpha)$ is the Syntactic derivation of the utterance $\alpha$, i.e. "how" the utterance was phrased in $L$

2. $Se(\alpha)$ is the Semantics of the utterance $\alpha$, its *denotation* with respect to a model $M$; essentially this indicates the objects referred to by the utterance

3. Each of the $C_i$'s would represent various aspects, yet to be formalized, of the *context* in which the utterance was made, including discourse elements, objects in view of the speaker and the hearer, participants in the discussion, belief models, etc. [Lew76] discusses many of these issues and their importance to formal semantics.

In this work we make only a modest beginning towards such a theory. In QE-III the pragmatic interpretation PI is defined as a function of two arguments, $Sy(\alpha)$ and $Se(\alpha)$. An example should make this clear.

Under the theory of QE-III, questions denote (a semantic concept) just as declarative sentences do. Thus the following two semantic analyses for "Who manages whom?" in the syntactic category WH-Question, and "He manages him" in the category declarative sentence:

who manages whom? $\rightarrow$ $\exists x[x(i) = u_2 \wedge EMP'_*(i)(u_1) \wedge AS{-}1(u_1, x)]$
he manages him $\rightarrow$ $\exists x[x(i) = u_2 \wedge EMP'_*(i)(u_1) \wedge AS{-}1(u_1, x)]$

Both are treated as denoting the same object with respect to an index, a variable assignment, and a model. But they are interpreted differently in the pragmatics. We define our pragmatics as a function that, given a derivation for an expression of QE-III together with its syntactic category and its (semantic) denotation, returns a (possibly) new object in the same model as its pragmatic interpretation. Thus, although we view pragmatics as a separate component of a language theory, it is closely allied to the semantics – both provide interpretations of linguistic expressions within the context of the same logical model. The formal definition of the pragmatic component in Chapter 6 will effect that these two sentences, interpreted pragmatically, denote what the following expressions of $IL_s$ denote:

$$
\begin{aligned}
\text{who manages whom?} \quad &\longrightarrow \quad \lambda u_2 \lambda u_1 \exists x [x(i) = u_2 \wedge EMP'_*(i)(u_1) \\
&\qquad\qquad \wedge MGR'(i)(x) \wedge AS\text{--}1(u_1, x)] \\
\text{he manages him} \quad &\longrightarrow \quad \exists x [x(i) = u_2 \wedge EMP'_*(i)(u_1) \wedge MGR'(i)(x) \\
&\qquad\qquad \wedge AS\text{--}1(u_1, x)]
\end{aligned}
$$

The pragmatic interpretation of the question is the set of $n$-tuples that answer it, while of the declarative sentence is the same as its denotation.

### 5.5.6   Conclusions

The QE-III theory that we present in Chapter 6 defines the denotation of a question in exactly the same way as the denotation of the corresponding declarative sentence that has pronouns in place of the interrogatives, but defines its pragmatic interpretation as the set of $n$-tuples that *answer* it. We have discussed our initial attempts to accomplish this result directly, by having WH-Terms denote functions from sets of properties to sets of individuals that had those properties. Technically, we discovered that to accomplish this directly required a considerable complication of the semantics throughout the structure of our fragment. And we discovered, as we shall see, that others with similar goals had also been forced to introduce more complexity into their logical model in order to accomplish these goals in the semantic component of their theory. Finally we realized that by eliminating as a goal of the semantics the capturing of the answer(s) of questions, we could leave the basic semantic theory of PTQ intact, and moreover we could easily accomplish this goal in the pragmatics.

This concludes our informal discussion of the syntax, semantics, and pragmatics of the language QE-III. We now proceed to discuss the theory in relation to some of the other work in the field of Montague Semantics that has attempted to extend the PTQ fragment to include a theoretical account of the syntax and semantics of questions.

# 5.6  Related Work

## 5.6.1  Introduction

Two common threads run through much of the recent work on formalizing a theory of questions. The first is the idea that all questions should be defined so as to denote objects of the same type. Generally this has meant propositions or sets of propositions, but it seems that even before the choice of just what questions denote was made, this *single semantics* viewpoint had been adopted. The other, as we have already pointed out, is that some account of the answer(s) to a question should be included at least as a component of its semantics. When combined with other factors these two biases have led to somewhat different results. Thus Hamblin [Ham73] suggests that a question denotes the set of all "propositions that count as answers to it;" [Kar77] "the set of propositions expressed by[its] true answers;" Bennett [Ben77, Ben79] (and also Belnap [Bel82], who worked with Bennett on the theory) "sets of open propositions: functions from sequences of individuals to propositions."

Our initial bias was against the single-semantics goal, motivated as we were by the database view of query semantics. This is ultimately reflected in our theory in the way that different questions are pragmatically interpreted to different sorts of objects, related to our intuitive notions of what the question is asking for. As we discuss a number of other approaches to the inclusion of the answer in the semantics, we shall again find motivation for the independent pragmatic component of our theory.

## 5.6.2  Karttunen

As we have said [Kar77] presents an analysis of the semantics of questions that falls within the single-semantics tradition. ([Ham73] earlier proposed a treatment similar to Karttunen's, but his theory was not worked out in as much detail.) In Karttunen's theory, for example, the question "Who manages John?" would be translated roughly as:

$$\lambda p \exists x [p(i) \wedge p = \lambda i [manage'(i)(x(i), John)]]$$

Within the semantic component this expression, when interpreted with respect to a model and a state, would have the question denotes the set which contains, for each person $x$ that manages John, the proposition that $x$ manages John.

Such a treatment of the semantics of questions seems inappropriate to us for two related reasons. First it seems to confuse propositions with the sentence s that express them. Whatever a proposition might be in our informal use of the term, it is in the formal system defined by IL, a function from indices to truth values, or equivalently a set of indices. In order to see why this seems an inappropriate choice for the semantic object denoted by a question, consider a model in which the constants *manage'* and *love'* are interpreted as follows:

$$F(manage') = \begin{bmatrix} 1978 & \rightarrow & \{< \text{Mary}, \text{John} >, < \text{Susan}, \text{John} >\} \\ 1979 & \rightarrow & \{< \text{Mary}, \text{John} >, < \text{Bill}, \text{John} >\} \\ 1980 & \rightarrow & \{< \text{Bill}, \text{John} >\} \end{bmatrix}$$

$$F(love') = \begin{bmatrix} 1978 & \rightarrow & \{< \text{Bill}, \text{John} >, < \text{Susan}, \text{John} >\} \\ 1979 & \rightarrow & \{< \text{Bill}, \text{John} >\} \\ 1980 & \rightarrow & \phi \end{bmatrix}$$

Now consider the two queries:

**Q1** $=$ Who manages John 1n 1978?

$\rightarrow$ $\lambda p \exists x [manage'(1978)(x(i), John) \wedge p = \lambda i\, manage'(i)(x(i), John)]$

**Q1** $=$ Who loves John 1n 1978?

$\rightarrow$ $\lambda p \exists x [love'(1978)(x(i), John) \wedge p = \lambda i\, love'(i)(x(i), John)]$

What is the interpretation of these two queries in this model given these translations, i.e. what is [Q1] and [Q2]?

[Q1] $=$ {{1978, 1979}   /* **Mary manages John** */
        {1978}}          /* **Susan manages John** */

[Q2] $=$ {{1978, 1979}   /* **Bill loves John** */
        {1978}}          /* **Susan loves John** */

Under this interpretation both queries, which are obviously quite distinct, denote exactly the same set of propositions in the model, the set containing the proposition {1978,1979} and the proposition {1978}. Thus under this interpretation we cannot distinguish between these two questions – they are semantically equivalent under this theory in the database.

The second and related objection is that under this interpretation all direct mention of the entities (Mary, Susan, John, ... ) involved disappears. Instead the theory claims that the question denotes a set that contains sets of states (years). What this implies is that there is no obvious way of going backwards from these objects in the model (the sets of propositions) to some *useful* expression in a language (for example, English) that names them. Since in this theory the denotation of questions *loses* the people involved, we have no simple way to recover their names and report them to the questioner. The theory neglects considering the use and effects of the question. Moreover there seems to be no way even to add a pragmatic component to such a theory in order to account for a question's answer(s), for on the one hand the syntax has no mention of the *names* of the individuals involved, nor on the other hand does the denotation involve any *individuals* at all. In the pragmatics of our theory the two queries would instead be interpreted, with respect to a given database, as follows (where [Q$i$] means the pragmatic interpretation of Q$i$):

[Q1] = {Mary,Susan}

[Q2] = {Bill,Susan}

With these interpretations we have not lost the people involved, and there is an obvious relationship between these objects and English expressions for them ("Mary and Susan" and "Bill and Susan") as well as the relations in the database that express the same information:

| Q1 |
| --- |
| Mary |
| Susan |

| Q2 |
| --- |
| Bill |
| Susan |

([Tic78] makes many of the same points that we make here regarding the proposition idea. )

## 5.6.3 Bennett and Belnap

As noted earlier, Bennett discussed the issue of the logic of questions in two separate papers, and collaborated with Belnap in the development. Their theory is presented cumulatively in [Ben77,Ben79] and in [Bel82]. Motivated again by the goal of a single semantics, and even more strongly by a desire to account for the individuals that answer the question, Belnap and Bennett (apparently acting on a suggestion made by Thomason) develop a theory that incorporates sequences of individuals into the model theory. Thus a question like "Whom does John love?" is treated as denoting a set of functions from sequences of individuals to propositions. Essentially all and only those sequences that close the open proposition "John loves [it-ACC-0]" and make it True are included in this denotation. What this is tantamount to is incorporating the standard (Tarskian) notion of a variable assignment into the model theory, instead of leaving it in the meta-theory of the logic. For technical reasons the entire system must be altered to include these sequences, so that even sentences are no longer translated into formulas, but rather into expressions denoting sets of such sequences. This rippling effect of the complications to the semantics is extraordinarily reminiscent of the problems we had in formulating a theory with inductive WH-Terms!

In order to accomplish this result, the set of types of the IL is expanded to include as a basic type $n$, expressions of type $n$ denoting a natural number. Thus the natural numbers must be included as objects in the model, as well as functions constructed from them. Of particular interest in their theory are the functions from $\aleph$ to individuals, i.e. sequences. The ripple effect necessitates that "all expressions of English [denote] functions from sequences of individuals to their usual extensions" [Ben79].

| Variable symbols | Type of variable symbol |
|---|---|
| $P$ | $< e, t >$ : sets of individuals |
| $r, s$ | $< n, e >$ : sequences of individuals |
| $O$ | $<< n, e >, < s, t >>$ : open propositions |

**Figure 5.27: Variables in Bennett/Belnap Theory**

Even sentences are no longer translated into formulas, but rather into expressions of type $<< n, e >, t >$ that denote sets of sequences. Unfortunately the results of this complication to the logic and the English translations do not seem to justify the cost. Certainly this theory represents a step closer to the goal of capturing explicitly in the denotation the individuals that answer the question, so it is an improvement over the proposition proposal. But these individuals are hidden somewhere inside *infinite* sequences of individuals, with no indication of their position within those sequences.

An example should clarify this point. In order to understand it, the table in Figure 5.27 shows the types of the variables used. In the Bennett/Belnap theory, for example, an *open* sentence like "John loves him" is translated as :

$$[\lambda s[love'([^{\wedge}\lambda P \, P(s(1))])(John')]]$$

which denotes (ignoring intensions) the set of sequences such that John loves the first member of each of them. The corresponding question "Whom does John love?" (actually their syntax does not cover direct questions, and so this is really their treatment of "John loves him" in the category of Basic Question; it seems clear, however, that they intend the semantics of the corresponding direct question to be the same) would be:

$$[\lambda O[O = [\lambda s[love'([^{\wedge}\lambda P \, P(s(1))])(John')]] \wedge \exists r[^{\vee}O(r)]]]$$

which denotes a set of open propositions. But these again involve infinite sequences of individuals, and there is no indication of which projection of these sequences represents the individuals that John loves.

This problem, of having the individuals that constitute the answer embedded in infinite sequences without knowing how to project them out is the same one that we have in our semantic theory. For our semantics translates questions into open formulas, which denote the set of variable assignments that satisfy the formula. Our relegating to pragmatics the task of projecting these variable assignments could also be used to solve this problem here. But if this is the case, then what is gained by paying the price for the complication to the model theory and the translation rules? This use of sequences in effect duplicates the variable assignment of their Tarskian meta-theory (albeit restricted to the domain $D_e$) in the object language and in the logical model with no noticeable advantages.

### 5.6.4 Hausser and Zaefferer

The proposal of Hausser and Zaefferer ([HZ78] and hereafter H-Z) is quite different from the other theories we have discussed, and makes a number of interesting points. The theory is motivated early in the paper by a discussion of the range of answers that are possible to any given question, and a classification of these possibilities as ranging from *minimal* to *redundant*. For example, in answer to the question "Who dates Mary?" the following list of possibilities is cited:

- (a) Bill.
- (b) Bill does.
- (c) Bill does so.
- (d) Bill dates her.
- (e) Bill dates Mary.

Answer (e), of course, is just what the propositional approach would say that the question denotes (assuming Mary is *going steady* with Bill.) H-Z goes on to say, however, that "the truth value of the answer expression will depend on the question in the context of which it is uttered, except for [the completely redundant answer]. This shows that redundant answers are not very interesting from a semantical point of view since their semantic representation is identical to that of ordinary declarative sentences. Since both redundant and non-redundant answers are possible, and since non-redundant answers are generally much more natural, we hold that no serious theory of questions and answers should restrict itself to a treatment of redundant answers alone, and that it should be able to handle both."

H-Z then proceeds to develop a theory to account for all of these possible answers, by extending the PTQ grammar and the logic IL. This theory replaces the model theory of IL by what they call a *context-model*. In essence this model is an IL-model expanded to include as model-theoretic objects the entire language of IL itself. Minimal answers are then translated into expressions that denote formulas when interpreted within the context of a preceding question. This is accomplished technically by including in the logic a set of context variables, and by including an abstraction over a context variable in the translation of the non-redundant answers. A context variable denotes an expression of IL, viz. the question that has set up the context. This idea of a context allows H-Z to define a semantics not just for questions like "Who dates Mary?" but also for each of the answers (a) through (e) in such a way that each of them is equivalent in extension.

H-Z's concern with the semantics of the answers to the questions, which at first sight seems to be our concern, is in fact another issue. For our theory, while it takes the answers of questions into account, is essentially not a theory of answers but a theory of questions. Of course, in the context of a more complete and user-friendly question-answering system, the ability to keep track formally of the context of the discourse and to express the answer in a number of different ways, is very attractive. Such a system would need the ability to go *backwards* from expressions in the logic to expressions in English with the same interpretation; [Fri81] discusses

| Question class | Our typing | H-Z typing |
|---|---|---|
| yes-no | $t$ | $<< s, << s, t >, t >>, t >$ |
| 1 individual | $< e, t >$ | $<< s, f(T) >, t >$ |
| 2 individual | $< e, < e, t >>$ | $<< s, f(T) >, << s, f(T) >, t >>$ |

Figure 5.28: Questions in QE-III and H-Z

this issue from the point of view of the PTQ fragment. But the development in H-Z of the semantics of the questions themselves, although motivated from this different concern with the equivalence of redundant and non-redundant answers, does also lead them to an analysis of question-semantics outside of the single-semantics framework. Their analysis "lets questions denote different types of sets according to the type of that expression which is the critical one in any kind of answer." In other words, their semantic analysis of answers is quite similar to our pragmatic analysis of questions! The table in Figure 5.28 compares the types assigned to various kinds of questions by their semantics and our pragmatics and should help to make this analogy clearer.

### 5.6.5   Scha and Gunji

The work of Scha on the PHLIQA1 project [Sch83] and Gunji [Gun81], both being developed concurrently with the development of QE-III [Cli82a], are remarkably similar in spirit, though not in detail, to the present work. The close parallels in the motivation of these three works indicate a trend among many researchers toward developing a formal foundation for computer systems that do natural language processing.

The major theoretical difference between QE-III and that of the PHLIQA1 project of Scha are that we make a distinction between the semantics and pragmatics of sentences in QE-III, so that the pragmatic interpretation of questions in QE-III is closely analogous to Scha's semantics for the same question. We continue to believe that this separation between the *denotation* of a sentence (given by the semantic component of the language) and its *interpretation* (given by the pragmatic component) is a simpler and more easily extendible approach to the problem of providing a formal account of *meaning*.

Much of the motivation for the work reported in [Gun81], namely to provide a formal pragmatics to a language specification by means of the computational application of a *super-interpreter* after the completion of the syntactic and semantic interpretation, is the same as ours. Gunji's *super-interpreter*, in fact, is quite clearly the computational realization of what we have termed our pragmatic interpretation. The major difference between these two projects is in the scope of their languages, which reflect Gunji's focus on conversation implicatures and ours on querying historical databases. Whereas Gunji's work covers declarative and imperative sentences, and True-False questions, QE-III resulted from a concentration on WH-questions and an explicit treatment of time-denoting expressions.

This concludes our informal discussion of the goals and philosophy behind the definition of the fragment QE-III, and its relation to other recent work in the area of formal question semantics. Chapter 6 present the formal definition of the syntax, semantics, and pragmatics of the language. This is followed in Chapter 7 by a series of examples and discussions illustrating its major features.

# CHAPTER SIX

# FORMAL DEFINITION OF QE-III

## 6.1   Introduction

In this Chapter we give a formal specification of a simple English Query Fragment, QE-III, for the historical department store database example discussed in earlier chapters. This fragment incorporates all of the features that we discussed in the previous chapter. Towards the end of the chapter we present a Fragment Schema for a QE-III type query language that could be adapted to other domains by defining the relevant vocabulary in the categories of the fragment. The schema and the guidelines for defining such a fragment are intended both to help a database administrator in the process of designing a language for a new domain, and also to show some of the general principles relating aspects of the HRDM model to the query language semantics.

We present the language definition in three parts. First we describe the syntactic component, which consists of defining the categories of the language and the basic expressions of these categories, followed by the rules of formation. Together these constitute an inductive definition of the set of meaningful expressions of QE-III. The semantics of the language is presented next, following Montague's general procedure in PTQ. This consists of giving, for each syntactic rule, a corresponding rule of translation into the logic $IL_s$, for which a direct semantic interpretation has already been specified (in Chapter 2.) Finally, we provide a pragmatics for the language when used in the assumed context of a question-answering system. The pragmatics is presented as a set of rules that together define a function which, for any derivation tree of an expression in the language, provides what we call its pragmatic interpretation.

## 6.2   The Syntax of QE-III

### 6.2.1   The Categories

The set of possible syntactic categories of QE-III is the smallest set CAT such that:

1. $e, t, YNQ, WHQ, WHENQ, T\text{-}t, T\text{-}YNQ, T\text{-}WHQ$, and $Tm$ are in CAT, and

2. whenever $A$ and $B$ are in CAT, then so are $A/B, A//B$, and $A///B$.

This system is based on the *categorial grammar* system of Ajdukiewicz, [Ajd35]. In such a system an expression of category $A/B$ combines with an expression of category $B$ to form an expression of category $A$. Montague adopted the categorial grammar system and extended it by providing a mapping from the syntactic categories of English into *logical* types in IL. Because there are cases where syntactically different categories of English correspond to the same logical type, he introduced the *multiple slash* notation: the categories $A/B$ and $A//B$ are syntactically different categories of English but correspond to the same logical type. [Dow78] and [DWP81] provide an excellent discussion of the many issues involved in Montague's semantic program.

Each of the non-empty categories of this fragment is given below, along with the following information:

1. its categorial definition, if any,

2. its corresponding type in $IL_s$, and

3. the Basic Expressions of the category, if any.

The translation of the Basic Expressions into $IL_s$ is given as rule T1 in the definition of the semantics of QE-III. In general, the type assignment for any category is given by the function $f$, defined by the following recursion on the set CAT:

1. $f(e) = e$

2. $f(t) = f(T\text{-}t) = f(YNQ) = f(T\text{-}YNQ) = f(WHQ) = f(T\text{-}WHQ) = t$

3. $f(WHENQ) = f(Tm) = <s,t>$

4. for all categories $A$ and $B$, $f(A/B) = f(A//B) = f(A///B) = $
   $<<s, f(B)>, f(A)>.$

**T: Terms**
*Categorial Definition:* t/TV
*Type:* $<<s, <<s,e>, t>>, t>$
*Basic Expressions:* for each element in UD, its English name; for each natural number $i$, and each CASE in {NOM,DAT,ACC}, the *variable Terms* [it-CASE-$i$]
**CN: Common Nouns**

*Categorial Definition: t//e*

*Type:* $<< s, e >, t >$

*Basic Expressions:* employee, department, manager, salary, item

**IV: Intransitive Verbs**

*Categorial Definition: t/e*

*Type:* $<< s, e >, t >$

*Basic Expressions:* #work, #manage

**TV: Transitive Verbs**

*Categorial Definition: IV/T*

*Type:* $<< s, << s, << s, e >, t >>, t >>, << s, e >, t >>$

*Basic Expressions:* #earn, #manage, #work-for, #work-in, #have, #be

**DTV: Dative Taking Verbs**

*Categorial Definition: TV/T*

*Type:* $<< s, << s, << s, e >, t >>, t >>,$
$<< s, << s, << s, e >, t >>, t >>, << s, e >, t >>>$

*Basic Expressions:* #supply

**S-TmADV: Sentence Time Adverbial**

*Categorial Definition: t//t*

*Type:* $<< s, t >, t >$

*Basic Expressions:* sometimes, today, yesterday, 3/5/50

**VP-TmADV: Verb Phrase Time Adverbial**

*Categorial Definition: t///t*

*Type:* $<< s, t >, t >$

*Basic Expressions:* always, sometimes, never

**Tm: Time**

*Type:* $< s, t >$

*Basic Expressions:* today, yesterday, 1985, $S_1, \ldots$

**TmPrep: Time-Phrase-Forming Preposition**

*Categorial Definition: (t//t)/t*

*Type:* $<< s, t >, << s, t >, t >>$

*Basic Expressions:* in, during, throughout, before, after

**TmConj: Time-Phrase-Forming Conjunction**

*Categorial Definition: S − TmADV/t*

*Type:* $<< s, t >, << s, t >, t >>$

*Basic Expressions:* while, before, after

**WHT: Interrogative Term**

*Type:* $<< s, << s, e >, t >>, t >$

*Basic Expressions:* who, whom, what

**Tm-Int: Time Interrogative**

*Type:* $<< s, t >, < s, t >>$

*Basic Expressions:* when

**e : entity**

*Type: e*

*Basic Expressions:* (none)

**t: Declarative Sentence**

*Type: t*

*Basic Expressions:* (none)

**$T-t$: Tensed Declarative Sentence**

*Type: t*

*Basic Expressions:* (none)

**WHQ : WH-Question**

*Type: t*

*Basic Expressions:* (none)

**$T-WHQ$ : Tensed WH-Question**

*Type: t*

*Basic Expressions:* (none)

**YNQ : Yes/No Question**

*Type: t*

*Basic Expressions:* (none)

**$T-YNQ$ : Tensed Yes/No Question**

*Type: t*

*Basic Expressions:* (none)

**WHENQ : Tensed When Question**

*Type:* $< s, t >$

*Basic Expressions:* (none)

**I-DET: Interrogative Determiner**

*Categorial Definition:* $T/CN$

*Type:* $<< s, << s, e >, t >>, << s, << s, e >, t >>, t >>$

*Basic Expressions:* which, what, how much, how many, every

**T/T: Common Noun as Term Modifier**

*Type:* $<< s, << s, << s, e >, t >>, t >>, << s, << s, e >, t >>, t >>$

*Basic Expressions:* (same as CN)

**DET: Determiner**

*Categorial Definition:* $T/CN$

*Type:* $<< s, << s, e >, t >>, << s, << s, e >, t >>, t >>$

*Basic Expressions:* a, the, every

## 6.2.2    The Syntactic Rules of Formation

The formation rules for QE-III are given in a format similar to the format used in [Dow78] and [DWP81], an amalgam of the presentation formats used by Montague in PTQ and UG. Each syntactic rule is an ordered triple of the form $< F, < I_1, I_2, \ldots I_n >, O >$, where $F$ is the name of the structural operation performed by the rule, the $I_i$'s are the categories of the inputs to the rule, and $O$ is the category of the output of the rule.

Rules 1 through 16 are basically the rules from the PTQ fragment adapted to $IL_s$, with some minor changes in the notational apparatus. The rules new to QE-III are presented at the end, beginning with rule number 100.

In giving the syntactic rules, we follow [Dow79] and describe at the beginning those common string operations that appear repeatedly, assigning them mnemonic superscripts. All other syntactic operations are described in the rule which uses them. Moreover, we subscript each syntactic operation with the number of the rule in which it appears.

$$F_n^I(\alpha) \quad = \quad \alpha$$
*(Identity operation)*

$$F_n^{RC}(\alpha,\beta) \quad = \quad \alpha\beta$$
*(Right Concatenation)*

$$F_n^{LC}(\alpha,\beta) \quad = \quad \beta\alpha$$
*(Left Concatenation)*

$$F_n^{RCA}(\alpha,\beta) \quad = \quad \alpha \text{ [it-ACC-m] if } \beta = [it - m], \text{ otherwise } \alpha\beta$$
*(Right Concatenation with Accusative Case Marking)*

$$F_n^{RW}(\alpha,\beta) \quad = \quad$$ the result of inserting $\beta'$ after the first word in $\alpha$, where $\beta'$ is [it-ACC-m], $\beta$ is [it-CASE-m] (any CASE), and $\beta'$ is $\beta$ o.w.
*(Right Wrap)*

$$F_{n,m}^{Q}(\alpha,\phi) \quad = \quad$$ the result of replacing the first occurrence of [it-CASE-m] in $\phi$ with $\alpha$, and replacing all subsequent occurrences of [it-NOM-m], [it-ACC-m], or [it-DAT-m] in $\phi$ with "he"/"she"/"it", "him"/"her"/"it" or "to him"/"to her"/"to it" respectively, according to the gender of the first basic CN or T in $\alpha$.
*(Quantification)*

Finally we note that the PTQ fragment makes use of certain auxiliary notions (the gender of a CN or a T, the he/him distinction for case markers, the proper form of verbs in several tenses, etc.) that were not rigorously defined, though they might have been. The present fragment makes use of the following additional such auxiliary notions:

**case** each variable Term is marked as either uncased, or as one of NOM, ACC, or DAT. (this is a generalization of the he/him distinction that in PTQ serves to distinguish the accusative case from all others.)

**plural** the plural form of each CN is required

## S1. [Basic Expressions]
$B_A \in P_A$ for every category $A$.

## S2. [Determiner and Common Noun]
$< F_2^{RC}, < DET, CN >, T >$

**S3. [Relative Clauses]**

$< F_{3,n}, < CN, t >, CN >$ .

$F_{3,n}(\alpha, \beta) = \alpha$ "such that" $\phi^*$

> where $\phi^*$ comes from $\phi$ by replacing each occurrence of [it-NOM-n], [it-ACC-n] or [it-DAT-n] in $\phi$ by "he"/"she"/"it", "him"/"her"/"it" or "to him"/"to her"/"to it" respectively, according to the gender of the first basic CN in $\alpha$.

**S4. [SUBJ + PRED: Untensed]**

$< F_4^{RC}, < T, IV >, t >$ .

If the $T$ is a variable it is marked as being in NOM case.

**S5. [TransVerb + Direct Object]**

$< F_5^{RW}, < TV, T >, IV >$ .

If the $T$ is a variable it is marked as being in ACC case.

**S6. [Preposition + Object]**

$< F_6^{RCA}, < IAV/t, T >, IAV >$ .

**S7. [Sentence Complement]**

$< F_7^{RC}, < IV/t, t >, IV >$ .

**S8. [Infinitive Complement]**

$< F_8^{RC}, < IV//IV, IV >, IV >$ .

**S9.** *(replaced by S103 - S105).*

**S10. [IV-Modifier]**

$< F_{10}^{LC}, < IV/IV, IV >, IV >$ .

**S11. [Sentence Conjunction]**

$< F_{11a}, < t, t >, t >$  and  $< F_{11b}, < t, t >, t >$ .

$F_{11a}(\phi, \psi) = \phi$ "and" $\psi$

$F_{11b}(\phi, \psi) = \phi$ "or" $\psi$

**S12. [IV-Conjunction]**

$< F_{12a}, < IV, IV >, IV >$ and  $< F_{12b}, < IV, IV >, IV >$ .

$F_{12a}(\alpha, \beta) = \alpha$ "and" $\beta$

$F_{12b}(\alpha, \beta) = \alpha$ "or" $\beta$

**S13. [Term Disjunction]**

$< F_{13}, < T, T >, T >$

$F_{13}(\alpha, \beta) = \alpha$ "or" $\beta$

**S14. [Quantification of Term over Declarative Sentence]**

$< F_{14,n}^Q, < T, t >, t >$ .

**S15. [Quantification of Term over CN]**

$$< F_{15,n}^Q, < T, CN >, CN >$$

## S16. [Quantification of Term over IV]
$$< F_{16,n}^Q, < T, IV >, IV >$$

## S17. [Negation]
*(the remaining functions of PTQ Rule 17 are handled by Rules S104 - S109.)*
$$< F_{17}, < t >, t >$$
$$F_{17}(\phi) = \phi^*$$

> the result of replacing the *first verb(s)* in $\phi$ (see [Fri79]) by their negation.

## NEW RULES   S100. [DTV + Indirect Object]
$$< F_{100}^{RCA}, < TV/T, T >, TV >$$

If the $T$ is a variable it is marked as being in DAT case.

## S102. [WHQ Formation]
$$< F_{102,n}, < WHT, t >, WHQ >$$

$F_{102,n}(\alpha, \phi)$ is defined as follows:
Let $\beta$ be the first occurrence of a variable Term [it-CASE-n] with subscript $n$ in $\phi$.

1. If CASE of $\beta$ is NOM, then $F_{102,n}$ is $F_{102,n}^Q$.

2. If CASE of $\beta$ is ACC or DAT, then $F_{102,n}(\alpha, \beta)$ is $\alpha^* \# AUX \phi^*$ or "To" $\alpha^* \# AUX \phi^*$, respectively, where

   (a) $\alpha^*$ is "whom" if $\alpha$ is "who", and $\alpha$ otherwise,
   (b) $\phi^*$ is $\phi$ with
      i. $\beta$ removed,
      ii. each of its *first verbs* unmarked, and
      iii. each subsequent occurrence of [it-CASE-n] replaced by "he"/"him"/"to him" according as the CASE is NOM/ACC/DAT respectively.

## S103. [WHT Quantification]
$$< F_{103,n}, < WHT, WHQ >, WHQ >$$

$F_{103,n}(\alpha, \beta)$ is defined as follows:
Let $\gamma$ be the first variable Term in $\beta$.
Then $F_{103,n}$ is applicable only if $\gamma$ is [it-CASE-n], (i.e., has subscript $n$),

in which case $F_{103,n}(\alpha, \beta) = \beta^*$, where $\beta^*$ is the result of replacing $\gamma$ in $\beta$ as follows:

1. Replace with $\alpha$ if the case of $\gamma$ is NOM, or with "to" $\alpha^*$ otherwise, where $\alpha^*$ is "whom" if $\alpha$ is "who", and $\alpha$ otherwise;

2. Replace all subsequent variable Terms with subscript $n$ with "he"/"she"/"it", "him"/"her"/"it", or "to him"/"to her"/"to it" respectively, according to their case and gender.

The following tense rules, S104 through S109, are perhaps best thought of as rule schemas or meta-rules. The symbol PS (for Proto-Sentence) is not really a category, but is a meta-symbol for the three possible input categories t, YNQ, and WHQ, and T-PS for the three corresponding output categories $T-t$, $T-YNQ$, and $T-WHQ$, respectively. They are stated as one rule for simplicity, since the syntactic operation is the same in each case. Another way of looking at these rules is to think of the category PS as being a super-category for these other three, as in the following tree:

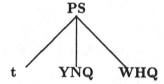

**S104. [Present Tense Sentence]**
$< F_{104}, < PS >, T - PS >$

$F_{104}(\phi) = \phi$ with each word of the form #$\alpha$ replaced by its present tense form.

**S105. [Past Tense Sentence]**
$< F_{105}, < PS >, T - PS >$

$F_{105}(\phi) = \phi$ with each word of the form #$\alpha$ replaced by its past tense form.

**S106. [Future Tense Sentence]**
$< F_{106}, < PS >, T - PS >$

$F_{106}(\phi) = \phi$ with each word of the form #$\alpha$ replaced by its future tense form.

**S107. [Present Tense with Time-Adverbial]**
$< F_{107a}, < S - TmADV, t >, T{-}t >$
$< F_{107b}, < S - TmADV, PS >, T - PS >$
$< F_{107c}, < VP - TmADV, PS >, T - PS >$

$$F_{107a}(\alpha, \phi) \;=\; \alpha\phi^*$$

$$F_{107b}(\alpha, \phi) \;=\; \phi^*\alpha$$

> where $\phi^*$ is $\phi$ with each word of the form $\#\beta$ replaced by its present tense form.

$$F_{107c}(\alpha, \phi) \;=\; \phi^*$$

> where $\phi^*$ is the result of inserting $\alpha$ before the first word in $\phi$ of the form $\#\beta$, and then replacing each word of this form by its present tense form.

## S108. [Past Tense with Time-Adverbial]

$< F_{108a}, < S - TmADV, t >, T\!-\!t >$
$< F_{108b}, < S - TmADV, PS >, T - PS >$
$< F_{108c}, < VP - TmADV, PS >, T - PS >$

$$F_{108a}(\alpha, \phi) \;=\; \alpha\phi^*$$

$$F_{108b}(\alpha, \phi) \;=\; \phi^*\alpha$$

> where $\phi^*$ is $\phi$ with each word of the form $\#\beta$ replaced by its past tense form.

$$F_{108c}(\alpha, \phi) \;=\; \phi^*$$

> where $\phi^*$ is the result of inserting $\alpha$ before the first word in $\phi$ of the form $\#\beta$, and then replacing each word of this form by its past tense form.

## S109. [Future Tense with Time-Adverbial]

$< F_{109a}, < S - TmADV, t >, T\!-\!t >$
$< F_{109b}, < S - TmADV, PS >, T - PS >$
$< F_{109c}, < VP - TmADV, PS >, T - PS >$

$$F_{109a}(\alpha, \phi) \;\; = \;\; \alpha\phi^*$$

$$F_{109b}(\alpha, \phi) \;\; = \;\; \phi^*\alpha$$

where $\phi^*$ is $\phi$ with each word of the form $\#\beta$ replaced by its future tense form.

$$F_{109c}(\alpha, \phi) \;\; = \;\; \phi^*$$

where $\phi^*$ is the result of inserting $\alpha$ before the first word in $\phi$ of the form $\#\beta$, and then replacing each word of this form by its future tense form.

## S110. [Tensed WHENQ Formation]
$< F_{110a}, < Tm - Int, PS >, WHENQ >$
$< F_{110b}, < Tm - Int, PS >, WHENQ >$
$< F_{110c}, < Tm - Int, PS >, WHENQ >$

$$F_{110a}(\alpha, \phi) \;\; = \;\; \alpha \text{ ``does''} \beta^*$$

if $\beta$ does not begin with "To," and otherwise
$\alpha$ "and" $\beta$
where $\beta^*$ is $\beta$ with the *first verbs* unmarked.

$$F_{110b}(\alpha, \phi) \;\; = \;\; \alpha \text{ ``did''} \beta^*$$

if $\beta$ does not begin with "To," and otherwise
$\alpha$ "and" $\beta$
where $\beta^*$ is $\beta$ with the *first verbs* unmarked.

$$F_{110c}(\alpha, \phi) \;\; = \;\; \alpha \text{ ``will''} \beta^*$$

if $\beta$ does not begin with "To," and otherwise
$\alpha$ "and" $\beta$
where $\beta^*$ is $\beta$ with the *first verbs* unmarked.

## S111. [Tensed WHENQ Formation with Specified Time]
$< F_{111a}, < Tm - Int, Tm, PS >, WHENQ >$
$< F_{111b}, < Tm - Int, Tm, PS >, WHENQ >$
$< F_{111c}, < Tm - Int, Tm, PS >, WHENQ >$

$F_{111a}(\alpha, \beta, \phi) \;\; \neq \;\; \alpha\beta \text{ "does" } \phi^*$

> if $\phi$ does not begin with "To," and otherwise
> $\alpha\beta$ "and" $\phi$
>> where $\phi^*$ is $\phi$ with the *first verbs* unmarked.

$F_{111b}(\alpha, \beta, \phi) \;\; = \;\; \alpha\beta \text{ "did" } \phi^*$

> if $\phi$ does not begin with "To," and otherwise
> $\alpha\beta$ "and" $\phi$
>> where $\phi^*$ is $\phi$ with the *first verbs* unmarked.

$F_{111c}(\alpha, \beta, \phi) \;\; = \;\; \alpha\beta \text{ "will" } \phi^*$

> if $\phi$ does not begin with "to," and otherwise
> $\alpha\beta$ "and" $\phi$
>> where $\phi^*$ is $\phi$ with the *first verbs* unmarked.

**S112. [TmCONJ + declarative sentence]**
$< F_{112a}, < TmCONJ, t >, S - TmADV >$
$< F_{112b}, < TmCONJ, t >, S - TmADV >$
$< F_{112c}, < TmCONJ, t >, S - TmADV >$
$F_{112a}(\alpha, \phi) \;\; = \;\; \alpha\phi^*$

> where $\phi^*$ is $\phi$ with each word of the form $\#\beta$ replaced by its present tense form.

$F_{112b}(\alpha, \phi) \;\; = \;\; \alpha\phi^*$

> where $\phi^*$ is $\phi$ with each word of the form $\#\beta$ replaced by its past tense form.

$F_{112c}(\alpha, \phi) \;\; = \;\; \alpha\phi^*$

> where $\phi^*$ is $\phi$ with each word of the form $\#\beta$ replaced by its future tense form.

**S113. [TmPREP + Tm]**
$< F_{113}^{RC}, < TmPREP, Tm >, S - TmADV >$

**S114. [WHT Formation]**
$< F_{114}, < I - DET, CN >, WHT >$

| Variable symbols | Type of variable symbol |
|---|---|
| $x, y, z, x_0, x_1, \ldots$ | $< s, e >$ : individual concepts (ICs) |
| $P, Q, Q_1, Q_2, \ldots$ | $< s, << s, e >, t >>$ : properties of ICs |
| $p, q, q_1, q_2, \ldots$ | $< s, t >$ : propositions |
| $i$ | $s$ : distinguished state variable wrt |
|  | which all expressions are evaluated |
| $i_1, i_2, \ldots$ | $s$ : states |
| $W$ | $< s, << s, << s, e >, t >>, t >>$: |
|  | properties of properties of ICs |

**Figure 6.1: Variables Used in QE-III Translations**

$$F_{114}(\alpha, \beta) \quad = \quad \alpha\beta^*$$

where $\beta^*$ is $\beta$ if $\alpha$ is "every," otherwise $\beta^*$ is the plural form of $\beta$.

**S115. [Possessive Formation]**
$< F_{115}, < T >, DET >$
$F_{115}(\alpha) = \alpha\text{"'s"}$

**S116. [Attributive Phrase Formation]**
$< F_{116}, < CN, T >, CN >$
$F_{116}(\alpha, \beta) = \alpha \text{ "of" } \beta$

**S117. [Role Specification for Term (I)]**
$< F_{117}, < T, CN >, T >$
$F_{117}(\alpha, \beta) = \alpha \text{ "as" } \beta$

**S118. [Role Specification for Term (II)]**
$< F_{118}^{RC}, < T/T, T >, T >$

## 6.3   The Semantics of QE-III

For the sake of clarity we have tried (within the limits of the typeset available to us) to maintain the variable-symbol conventions established by Montague in the PTQ presentation and continued (more or less) by others working within the MG framework. Moreover we have established similar conventions for the relevant new types of $\text{IL}_s$. For easy reference we give all of these conventions in the table in Figure 6.1.

In the translation rules, $\alpha'$ and $\beta'$ (etc.) are used to represent the translations of the inputs $\alpha$ and $\beta$ to the rule. If the translation rule is given simply as "function application," this is to be understood as shorthand for the translation $\alpha'(\lambda i \beta')$ for the inputs $\alpha$ and $\beta$ . (See the presentation in Chapter 2 of the correspondence between IL, and IL for the discussion of the use of the distinguished time variable $i$ and its relation to the *Int* operator (^ in PTQ.)

**T1. Translations or translation schemas for Basic Expressions are as follows, by category:**
**(a) T: Terms**
for each English word $\alpha \in B_T$,

$$\alpha \implies \lambda P \exists x [P(i)(x) \wedge x(i) = \alpha']$$

for example:

$$\text{Peter} \implies \lambda P \exists x [P(i)(x) \wedge x(i) = Peter]$$

and for each variable Term [it-CASE-i],

$$[\text{it-CASE-i}] \implies \lambda P [P(i)(x_i)]$$

**(b) CN: Common Nouns**

| | | |
|---|---|---|
| employee | $\implies$ | $\lambda x EMP'_*(i)(x(i))$ |
| department | $\implies$ | $DEPT'(i)$ |
| manager | $\implies$ | $MGR'(i)$ |
| salary | $\implies$ | $SAL'(i)$ |
| item | $\implies$ | $\lambda x ITEM_*(i)(x(i))$ |

**(c) IV: Intransitive Verbs**

| | | |
|---|---|---|
| #manage | $\implies$ | $MGR'(i)$ |
| #work | $\implies$ | $\lambda x EMP_*(i)(x(i))$ |

**(d) TV: Transitive Verbs**

| | | |
|---|---|---|
| #manage (an employee) | $\implies$ | $\lambda W \lambda x [W(i)(\lambda i \lambda y [AS-1(y(i),x) \wedge EMP_*(i)(y(i)) \wedge MGR'(i)(x)])]$ |
| #earn | $\implies$ | $\lambda W \lambda x [W(i)(\lambda i \lambda y [AS-1(x(i),y) \wedge EMP_*(i)(x(i)) \wedge SAL'(i)(y)])]$ |
| #sell | $\implies$ | $\lambda W \lambda x [W(i)(\lambda i \lambda y [REC-2(x(i),y(i)) \wedge DEPT_*(i)(x(i)) \wedge ITEM_*(i)(y(i))])]$ |
| #manage (a department) | $\implies$ | $\lambda W \lambda x \exists z [W(i)(\lambda i \lambda y [AS-1(z(i),x) \wedge AS-1(z(i),y) \wedge EMP_*(i)(z(i)) \wedge DEPT'(i)(y) \wedge MGR'(i)(x)])]$ |
| #have | $\implies$ | $\lambda W \lambda x [W(i)(\lambda i \lambda y AS-1(x(i),y)]$ |
| #be | $\implies$ | $\lambda W \lambda x W(i)(\lambda i \lambda y [x(i) = y(i)])$ |

**(e) DTV: Dative Taking Verbs**

$$\#\text{supply} \implies \lambda W_0 \lambda W_1 \lambda x [W_0(i)[\lambda i \lambda y [DEPT_*(i)(y(i)) \wedge COMP_*(i)(x(i)) \wedge$$
$$W_1(i)[\lambda i \lambda z [ITEM_*(i)(z(i)) \wedge REC-3(x(i),y(i),z(i))]]]]]]$$

(in the sense of "Company supplies item to department")
## (f) S-TmADV: Sentence Time Adverbial

sometimes $\implies$ $\lambda p \exists i_1 [p(i_1)]$
today $\implies$ $\lambda p \exists i_1 [today'(i)(i_1) \wedge p(i_1)]$
yesterday $\implies$ $\lambda p \exists i_1 [yesterday'(i)(i_1) \wedge p(i_1)]$
3/5/50 $\implies$ $\lambda p \exists i_1 [3/5/50'(i_1) \wedge p(i_1)]$

N.B. *today'* and *yesterday'* are indexical constants (their denotation is relative to the current state, **now**) of type $< s, < s, t >>$; 3/5/50' is a non-indexical constant (its denotation is fixed, regardless of the value of **now**) of type $< s, t >$.

## (g) VP-TmADV: Verb Phrase Time Adverbial

always $\implies$ $\lambda p \forall i_1 [p(i_1)]$
sometimes $\implies$ $\lambda p \exists i_1 [p(i_1)]$
never $\implies$ $\lambda p \forall i_1 [\neg p(i_1)]$

## (h) Tm: Time

if $\alpha$ is an indexical Tm (e.g. "today"),
$\alpha \implies \alpha'(i)$
where $\alpha'$ is a constant of type $< s, < s, t >>$.
Otherwise if $\alpha$ is a non-indexical Tm (e.g. 1978),
$\alpha \implies \alpha'$
where $\alpha'$ is a constant of type $< s, t >$

## (i) TmPrep: Time-Phrase-Forming Preposition

in $\implies$ $\lambda q \lambda p [\exists i_1 [q(i_1) \wedge p(i_1)]]$
during $\implies$ $\lambda q \lambda p [\exists i_1 [q(i_1) \wedge p(i_1)]]$
throughout $\implies$ $\lambda q \lambda p [\forall i_1 [q(i_1) \to p(i_1)]]$
before $\implies$ $\lambda q \lambda p [\exists i_1 [[i_1 << q] \wedge p(i_1)]]$
after $\implies$ $\lambda q \lambda p [\exists i_1 [[q << i_1] \wedge p(i_1)]]$

## (j) TmConj: Time-Phrase-Forming Conjunction

while $\implies$ $\lambda q \lambda p [\exists i_1 [q(i_1) \wedge p(i_1)]]$
before $\implies$ $\lambda q \lambda p [\exists i_1 [[i_1 << q] \wedge p(i_1)]]$
after $\implies$ $\lambda q \lambda p [\exists i_1 [[q << i_1] \wedge p(i_1)]]$

## (k) WHT: Interrogative Term

for any $\alpha \in B_{WHT}$,
$\alpha \implies \lambda P \exists y [y(i) = u \wedge P(i)(y)]$

## (l) Tm-Int: Time Interrogative

when $\implies$ $\lambda p \lambda i_1 [p(i_1)]$

## (m) I-DET: Interrogative Determiner

$\alpha \implies \lambda Q \lambda P \exists y [y(i) = u \wedge Q(i)(y) \wedge P(i)(y)]$
for each $\alpha \in B_{I-DET}$.

## (n) T/T: Common Noun as Term Modifier

for any $\alpha \in B_{T/T}$,

$$\alpha \implies \lambda W \lambda P W(i)[\lambda i \lambda y[P(i)(y) \wedge \alpha'(i)(y)]],$$

if $\alpha$ refers to a role attribute, or

$$\alpha \implies \lambda W \lambda P W(i)[\lambda i \lambda y[P(i)(y) \wedge \alpha_*(i)(y(i))]],$$

if $\alpha$ refers to a key attribute

## (o) DET: Determiner

| | | |
|---|---|---|
| a | $\implies$ | $\lambda P \lambda Q \exists x[P(i)(x) \wedge Q(i)(x)]$ |
| the | $\implies$ | $\lambda P \lambda Q \exists y[\forall x[P(i)(x) <=> x = y] \wedge Q(i)(y)]$ |
| every | $\implies$ | $\lambda P \lambda Q \forall x[P(i)(x) \rightarrow Q(i)(x)]$ |

**T2.** function application

**T3.** $F_{3,n}(\alpha, \phi) \implies \lambda x_n(\alpha'(x_n) \wedge \phi').$

**T4.** function application

**T5.** function application

**T6.** function application

**T7.** function application

**T8.** function application

**T9.** (replaced by T103 - T105).

**T10.** function application

**T11.** $F_{11a}(\phi, \psi) \implies [\phi \wedge \psi]$
$\phantom{T11.}$ $F_{11b}(\phi, \psi) \implies [\phi \vee \psi]$

**T12.** $F_{12a}(\alpha, \beta) \implies \lambda x[\alpha'(x) \wedge \beta'(x)]$
$\phantom{T12.}$ $F_{12b}(\alpha, \beta) \implies \lambda x[\alpha'(x) \vee \beta'(x)]$

**T13.** $F_{13}(\alpha, \beta) \implies \lambda P[\alpha'(P) \vee \beta'(P)]$

**T14.** $F_{14,n}^Q(\alpha, \phi) \implies \alpha'(\lambda i \lambda x_n \phi')$

**T15.** $F_{15,n}^Q(\alpha, \beta) \implies \lambda y \alpha'(\lambda i \lambda x_n \beta'(y)])$

**T16.** $F_{16,n}^Q(\alpha, \beta) \implies \lambda y \alpha'(\lambda i \lambda x_n [\beta'(y)])$

**T17.** $F_{17}(\phi) \implies \neg \phi'$


**NEW RULES.** **T100.** function application.

**T101.** $F_{101a}(\phi)$ and $F_{101b}(\phi) \implies \phi'$

**T102.** $F_{102,n}(\alpha, \phi) \implies \alpha'(\lambda i \lambda x_n \phi')$

**T103.** $F_{103,n}(\alpha, \beta) \implies \alpha'(\lambda i \lambda x_n \beta')$

**T104.** $F_{104}(\phi) \implies \phi'$

**T105.** $F_{105}(\phi) \implies \exists i_1[[i_1 < i] \wedge \lambda i \phi'(i_1)]$

**T106.** $F_{106}(\phi) \implies \exists i_1[[i < i_1] \wedge \lambda i \phi'(i_1)]$

**T107.** $F_{107a}(\alpha, \phi), F_{107b}(\alpha, \phi)$ and $F_{107c}(\alpha, \phi) \implies \alpha'(\lambda i \phi')$

**T108.** $F_{108a}(\alpha, \phi), F_{108b}(\alpha, \phi)$ and $F_{108c}(\alpha, \phi) \implies \alpha'(\lambda i i_1[[i_1 < i] \wedge \lambda i \phi'(i_1)])$

**T109.** $F_{109a}(\alpha, \phi), F_{109b}(\alpha, \phi)$ and $F_{109c}(\alpha, \phi) \implies \alpha'(\lambda i i_1[[i < i_1] \wedge \lambda i \phi'(i_1)])$

**T110.** $F_{110a}(\alpha, \phi) \implies \lambda p \lambda i_1[p(i_1)](\lambda i \phi')$
$\phantom{T110.}$ $F_{110b}(\alpha, \phi) \implies \lambda p \lambda i_1[[i_1 < i] \wedge p(i_1)](\lambda i \phi')$
$\phantom{T110.}$ $F_{110c}(\alpha, \phi) \implies \lambda p \lambda i_1[p(i_1)][i < i_1] \wedge p(i_1)](\lambda i \phi')$

**T111.**  $F_{111a}(\alpha, \beta, \phi) \implies \lambda p \lambda i_1 [\beta'(i_1) \wedge p(i_1)](\lambda i \phi')$

$\quad\quad\; F_{111b}(\alpha, \beta, \phi) \implies \lambda p \lambda i_1 [[i_1 < i] \wedge \beta'(i_1) \wedge p(i_1)](\lambda i \phi')$

$\quad\quad\; F_{111c}(\alpha, \beta, \phi) \implies \lambda p \lambda i_1 [[i < i_1] \wedge \beta'(i_1) \wedge p(i_1)](\lambda i \phi')$

**T112.**  $F_{112a}(\alpha, \phi) \implies \alpha'(\lambda i_2 [\lambda i \phi'(i_2)])$

$\quad\quad\; F_{112b}(\alpha, \phi) \implies \alpha'(\lambda i_2 [[\lambda i \phi'(i_2)] \wedge [i_2 < i]])$

$\quad\quad\; F_{112c}(\alpha, \phi) \implies \alpha'(\lambda i_2 [[\lambda i \phi'(i_2)] \wedge [i < i_2]])$

**T113.**  $F_{113}^{RC}(\alpha, \beta) \implies \alpha(\beta)$

**T114.** function application

**T115.**

$F_{115}(\alpha) \implies \lambda W \lambda P \lambda Q \exists x [P(i)(x) \wedge Q(i)(x) \wedge W(i)[\lambda i \lambda y AS-1(y(i), x)]](\lambda i \alpha')$

**T116.**  $F_{116}(\alpha\beta) \implies \lambda x \beta'(\lambda i \lambda y [\alpha'(x) \wedge AS-1(y(i), x)])$

**T117.**  $F_{117}(\alpha, \beta) \implies \lambda P \alpha'[\lambda i \lambda y [P(i)(y) \wedge \beta'(y)]$

**T118.** function application

# 6.4   The Pragmatics of QE-III

The pragmatics which we give here for QE-III is a simple theory of the effects of producing an expression in that language within the assumed context of a question-answering environment. That is, we assume that a user of QE-III is using the language to produce some effect within this context, and it is this effect which we formalize as the pragmatic component of the language definition. We could, of course, have defined the pragmatics in the same manner as the semantics was defined, i.e. inductively over the syntax. However in doing so we would have seemed to be giving some status or importance to the pragmatic interpretation of expressions in every category of QE-III. Because we had no real intuition about what the **pragmatic interpretation** of, say, the expression "in 1978" represented, we decided upon a different form of the definition. Accordingly our definition provides a pragmatic interpretation for expressions in any of the several sentential categories of the language, namely *T-YNQ*, *T-WHQ*, WHENQ, and *T-t*. Chapter 5 contains a discussion both of some of the issues involved in our decision to present a separate pragmatic component to the formal theory of QE-III, as well as some of the considerations for the present form of this theory. A more general pragmatics, in which the pragmatic interpretation function PI would take into account various other aspects of the context of the utterance besides the syntax (which indicates that a *question* has been asked) and the semantics (which indicates the objects referred to in the utterance) is a subject for more research.

The following preliminary definitions are needed before stating the pragmatic rules of QE-III.

1. By /α\ is meant a derivation tree for the meaningful expression α of QE-III, as informally understood from our inductive definition of the syntax. We further assume that nodes of derivation trees are labelled with ordered triples $< A, B, C >$ such that A is the meaningful expression derived at that node, B

is its syntactic category, and $C$ is the rule of syntax applied at that step in the derivation. For simplicity, we shall refer to component $A$ of the root of $/\alpha\backslash$ as $\alpha$, and to the component $B$ as $\text{CAT}(/\alpha\backslash)$.

2. The translation rules guarantee that corresponding to any derivation tree $/\alpha\backslash$ for $\alpha \in ME_{QE-III}$ there is a unique translation into $IL_s$. By $T(/\alpha\backslash)$ shall be understood this unique translation, and by $[/\alpha\backslash]_M$ the denotation of $/\alpha\backslash$ (provided indirectly via $T(/\alpha\backslash)$) with respect to the model M.

3. There are two standard ways of defining a (Tarskian) model-theoretic semantics. One is to define the notion of denotation with respect to a model $M$ only, in which case formulas, e.g., denote the set of their satisfying variable assignments. The other, and more usual procedure (and the one that we followed in Chapter 2 in defining the semantics of $IL_s$) is to define the denotation with respect to a model $M$ and a variable assignment $g$, in which case a formula always denotes either True or False. The two notions are, for all practical purposes, equivalent. Since for the purposes of pragmatics we shall want to consider that open formulas denote the set of their satisfying variable assignments, we shall in this section refer to the notion of denotation with respect to a model $M$ only.

4. If $[/\alpha\backslash]_M$ is a function whose domain is $As(M)$, i.e. the set of all possible variable assignments over $M$, and if further $V = \{v_1, \ldots, v_k\}$ is a set of variables of $IL_s$, then by $\Pi_V([/\alpha\backslash]_M)$ is understood the restriction of $[/\alpha\backslash]_M$ to the domain $V$. Note that if $V = \phi$, then $\Pi_V([/\alpha\backslash]_M)$ is defined to be just $[/\alpha\backslash]_M$.

5. If $f$ is any function with domain $As(M)$, then $\mathbf{now}(f)$ is the restriction of $f$ to the domain $As_{now}(M)$, where

$$As_{now}(M) = \{g | g \in As(M) \text{ and } g(i) = F(\mathbf{now})\}$$

that is, that subset of the possible variable assignments for $M$ for which the distinguished time variable $i$ is interpreted as denoting that state denoted by the constant $\mathbf{now}$.

6. By $FV(/\alpha\backslash)$ we shall understand the set $\{i_1, i_2, \ldots, i_n\}$ of indices of the *variables* (expressions of the form [it-CASE-i]) occurring free in $\alpha$. This notion will not be defined rigorously here, but would be defined inductively over the structure of $/\alpha\backslash$ in the usual manner, with particular attention paid to which rules bind occurrences of variables (all of the PTQ substitution rules) and which rules leave them free (e.g., the rules that introduce WH-Terms.) This definition would be analogous to the definition of the set $FV_e$ of variables of type $e$ occurring free in a logical expression, in particular in the expression $T(/\alpha\backslash)$. It is clear that if $FV(/\alpha\backslash) = \{i_1, \ldots, i_n\}$, then $FV(T(/\alpha\backslash)) = \{u_{i_1}, \ldots, u_{i_n}\}$.

However we emphasize that $FV(/\alpha\backslash)$ is defined over the derivation tree of $\alpha$ (i.e., over the syntax of QE-III) and makes no reference to the (intermediate) translation of this tree into $IL_s$.

7. Finally, if $\beta$ is a meaningful expression of $IL_s$, and if the free variables of type $e$ in $\beta$, $FV_e(\beta)$, are exactly $\{u_{i_1}, u_{i_2}, \ldots, u_{i_n}\}$, such that $u_{i_1}, u_{i_2}, \ldots, u_{i_n}$ are in alphabetical order, then $LC_{FV_e}(\beta)$ is the unique expression: $\lambda u_{i_n} \ldots \lambda u_1 \beta$ formed by first prefixing $\beta$ with $\lambda u_{i_1}$, then prefixing $\lambda u_{i_2}$ to the result, and so on.

In order to understand the form of some of the following definitions we state the following fact (the proof follows directly from the translation rules of QE-III):

**Fact.** If $\beta$ is the translation of any meaningful expression $\alpha$ of QE-III, then the free variables of $\alpha$ are all of type $e$, except for the possible exception of the distinguished variable $i$ of type $s$.

The rules of pragmatics which we now state constitute a definition of the pragmatic function, in a manner analogous to the way in which the translation rules constitute a translation relation. In particular they constitute a definition of the function PI:

$$PI : /QE - III\backslash \longrightarrow M \cup \{ERROR\}$$

which assigns to any derivation tree of a meaningful expression $\alpha$ of QE-III, either an object in the model $M$ or the distinguished symbol $ERROR$ as its **pragmatic interpretation**.

P1. If $CAT(/\alpha\backslash) \notin \{WHENQ, T-WHQ, T-t, T-YNQ\}$, then $PI(/\alpha\backslash) = ERROR$.

P2. If $CAT(/\alpha\backslash) \in \{WHENQ, T-WHQ, T-t, T-YNQ\}$, then $PI(/\alpha\backslash) = \Pi_{FV_e}(\mathbf{now}([/\alpha\backslash]_M))$.

Rule P1 ensures that only sentences are interpreted pragmatically. P2 ensures that all sentences are interpreted with respect to the *current* state index, and that in the case of questions, the infinite sequences of variables that the question denotes is projected down to include only the questioned variables.

It is clear that the set of sequences given by $\Pi_{FV_e}(\mathbf{now}([/\alpha\backslash]_M))$ is equivalently represented by the denotation of the expression $LC_{FV_e}(\lambda i T(/\alpha\backslash)(\mathbf{now}))$ of $IL_s$ with respect to $M$ and $g$.

P2 is therefore alternatively defined as:

$$PI(/\alpha\backslash) = [LC_{FV_e}(\lambda i T(/\alpha\backslash)(\mathbf{now}))]_{M,g}.$$

What this alternative definition allows us to do is to utilize the semantic notion of denotation to define the pragmatic interpretation of sentences in QE-III. For it allows us to take a translation $T(/\alpha\backslash)$ of any sentence $\alpha$ and determine its pragmatic interpretation as the denotation of the expression:

$$LC_{FV_e}(\lambda i T(/\alpha\backslash)(\mathbf{now}))$$

and thus *evaluate* the pragmatic interpretation of $\alpha$ in terms of the semantics of $IL_s$ by means of this simple syntactic transformation on $T(/\alpha\backslash)$.

# 6.5   A QE-III Fragment Schema

The fragment which we presented in the previous sections, and which we called QE-III, was defined as an inductive language. The basis for the induction was a set of basic expressions in a finite set of categories. The inductive part of the definition consisted of a set of formation rules each of which constructed an expression of a certain category, the output category of the rule, from expressions of certain categories, the input categories of the rule. The semantics for the language was also defined inductively and in parallel with the syntax. Here the basis for the induction was the translations into the logic $IL_s$ of each of the basic expressions of QE-III. Finally a simple pragmatics was defined, essentially for the expressions of QE-III in only the sentential categories.

In this section we provide some guidelines for defining other QE-III-like query fragments for databases other than the department store database which we have used as a running example throughout this book. In defining such a new language, the syntactic, semantic and pragmatic rules of induction remain unchanged. All that is needed is to provide basic expressions in any of the desired categories, and to define their logical translation. As we shall see, the basis for these translations is the database scheme itself. We hasten to point out that the process of defining a query language for a new domain is nontrivial, even for such a syntactically simple language as the QE-III family of languages. (For a discussion of this problem of portability see [GL81].)

We present a discussion of how expressions in the vocabulary of the domain of the database should be defined as basic expressions of the appropriate categories of QE-III. The translation of these expressions into $IL_s$ is given relative to their relationship to the database scheme. Before doing so we recall the definition of the non-logical constants induced by a database scheme:

$$
\begin{aligned}
C_{database} \;=\; & C_e \cup \\
& C_s \cup \\
& C_{<s,t>} \cup \\
& C_{<s,<e,t>>} \cup \\
& C_{<s,<e,<e,t>>>} \cup \\
& C_{<s,<<s,e>,t>>} \cup
\end{aligned}
$$

$$C_{<e,<<s,e>,t>>} \cup$$
$$C_{<e,<e,<<s,e>,t>>>}$$

## T: Terms

*Categorial Definition:* t/TV

*Type:* $<< s, << s, e >, t >>, t >$

*Basic Expressions:* for each element in UD, its English name;
for each natural number $i$, and each CASE in {NOM,DAT,ACC}, the *variable*
*Terms* [it-CASE-i]

*Translation:* for each such English word $\alpha$:

$$\alpha \implies \lambda P \exists x [P(i)(x) \wedge x(i) = \alpha']$$

and for each variable Term [it-CASE-i],

$$[\text{it-CASE-i}] \implies \lambda P[P(i)(x_i)]$$

## CN: Common Nouns

*Categorial Definition:* t//e

*Type:* $<< s, e >, t >$

*Basic Expressions:* for each attribute, the common noun(s) that name(s) it.

*Translation:*

1.  if $\alpha$ is a CN that refers to a role attribute A,

    $$\alpha \implies A'(i)$$

    where $A'$ is the appropriate constant in $C_{RC}$.

2.  otherwise $\alpha$ refers to a key attribute B, and

    $$\alpha \implies \lambda x B'_*(i)(x(i))$$

    where $B'_*$ is the appropriate constant in $C_{EEC}$.

## IV: Intransitive Verbs

*Categorial Definition:* t/e

*Type:* $<< s, e >, t >$

*Basic Expressions:* any intransitive verb relevant to the application.

*Translation:*

1.  if $\alpha$ is an IV that denotes a set of ICs that act as a role attribute A, then

    $$\alpha \implies A'(i)$$

    where $A'$ is the appropriate constant in $C_{RC}$.

2.  otherwise $\alpha$ is an IV that denotes a set of ICs that act as a key attribute B, and

$$\alpha \implies \lambda x B'_*(i)(x(i))$$

where $B'_*$ is the appropriate constant in $C_{EEC}$.

## TV: Transitive Verbs

*Categorial Definition: IV/T*
*Type:* $<< s, << s, << s, e >, t >>, t >>, << s, e >, t >>$
*Basic Expressions:* any transitive verb relevant to the application.
*Translation:* the translation depends upon the attribute types that are assigned to the subject and direct object, respectively, by the semantics of the particular application. Some examples of the more common possibilities are:

1. role attribute A, key attribute B:

    $$\implies \lambda W \lambda x[W(i)(\lambda i \lambda y[AS{-}1(y(i), x) \wedge B'_*(i)(y(i)) \wedge A'(i)(x)])]$$

2. key attribute A, role attribute B:

    $$\implies \lambda W \lambda x[W(i)(\lambda i \lambda y[AS{-}1(x(i), y) \wedge A'_*(i)(x(i)) \wedge B'(i)(y)])]$$

3. key attribute A, key attribute B:

    $$\implies \lambda W \lambda x[W(i)(\lambda i \lambda y[REC{-}2(x(i), y(i)) \wedge A'_*(i)(x(i)) \wedge B'_*(i)(y(i))])]$$

4. role attribute A, role attribute B:

    $$\implies \lambda W \lambda x \exists z[W(i)(\lambda i \lambda y[REC{-}2(x(i), y(i)) \wedge A'_*(i)(x(i)) \wedge B'_*(i)(y(i))])]$$

5. Standard TV's:

    $$\#\text{have} \implies \lambda W \lambda x[W(i)(\lambda i \lambda y AS{-}1(x(i), y)]$$
    $$\#\text{be} \implies \lambda W \lambda x W(i)(\lambda i \lambda y[x(i) = y(i)])$$

## DTV: Dative-Taking Verbs

*Categorial Definition: TV/T*
*Type:* $<< s, << s, << s, e >, t >>, t >>,$
$<< s, << s, << s, e >, t >>, t >>, << s, e >, t >>>$
*Basic Expressions:* any dative-taking verb relevant to the application.
*Translation:* Again, this depends upon the combination of the attribute classes of the three Terms taken by the verb. As an example, consider the DTV "supply" in the sense of Company supplies item to department:

$$\#\text{supply} \implies \lambda W_0 \lambda W_1 \lambda x[W_0(i)[\lambda i \lambda y[DEPT'_*(i)(y(i)) \wedge COMP'_*(i)(x(i)) \wedge$$
$$W_1(i)[\lambda i \lambda z[ITEM'_*(i)(z(i)) \wedge REC{-}3(x(i), y(i), z(i))]]]]]]$$

## S-TmADV: Sentence Time Adverbial

*Categorial Definition: t//t*
*Type:* $<<s,t>,t>$
*Basic Expressions:* always, sometimes, never, today, yesterday, and, in general, time adverbials $\alpha$ and $\beta$.
*Translation:*

| always | $\implies$ | $\lambda p \forall i_1[p(i_1)]$ |
| sometimes | $\implies$ | $\lambda p \exists i_1[p(i_1)]$ |
| never | $\implies$ | $\lambda p \forall i_1[\neg p(i_1)]$ |
| today | $\implies$ | $\lambda p \exists i_1[today'(i)(i_1) \wedge p(i_1)]$ |
| yesterday | $\implies$ | $\lambda p \exists i_1[yesterday'(i)(i_1) \wedge p(i_1)]$ |
| $\alpha$ | $\implies$ | $\lambda p \exists i_1[\alpha'(i)(i_1) \wedge p(i_1)]$ |
| $\beta$ | $\implies$ | $\lambda p \exists i_1[\beta'(i_1) \wedge p(i_1)]$ |

N.B. today', yesterday' and $\alpha'$ are indexical constants (their denotation is relative to the current state, **now** ) of type $<s,<s,t>>$; $\beta'$ is a non-indexical constant (its denotation is fixed, regardless of the value of **now**) of type $<s,t>$.

## VP-TmADV: Verb Phrase Time Adverbial

*Categorial Definition: t///t*
*Type:* $<<s,t>,t>$
*Basic Expressions:* always, sometimes, never
*Translation:*

| always | $\implies$ | $\lambda p \forall i_1[p(i_1)]$ |
| sometimes | $\implies$ | $\lambda p \exists i_1[p(i_1)]$ |
| never | $\implies$ | $\lambda p \forall i_1[\neg p(i_1)]$ |

## Tm: Time

*Type:* $<s,t>$
*Basic Expressions:* any words that name database states
*Translation:*

1. if $\alpha$ is an indexical Tm (e.g. "today")

   $$\alpha \implies \alpha'(i)$$

   where $\alpha'$ is a constant of type $<s,<s,t>>$

2. otherwise if $\alpha$ is a non-indexical Tm (e.g. 1989)

   $$\alpha \implies \alpha'$$

   where $\alpha'$ is a constant of type $<s,t>$.

## TmPrep: Time-Phrase-Forming Preposition

*Categorial Definition: (t//t)/t*
*Type:* $<<s,t>,<<s,t>,t>>$

*Basic Expressions:* in, during, throughout, before, after
*Translation:*

| | | |
|---|---|---|
| in | $\Longrightarrow$ | $\lambda q \lambda p [\exists i_1 [q(i_1) \wedge p(i_1)]]$ |
| during | $\Longrightarrow$ | $\lambda q \lambda p [\exists i_1 [q(i_1) \wedge p(i_1)]]$ |
| throughout | $\Longrightarrow$ | $\lambda q \lambda p [\forall i_1 [q(i_1) \rightarrow p(i_1)]]$ |
| before | $\Longrightarrow$ | $\lambda q \lambda p [\exists i_1 [[i_1 << q] \wedge p(i_1)]]$ |
| after | $\Longrightarrow$ | $\lambda q \lambda p [\exists i_1 [[q << i_1] \wedge p(i_1)]]$ |

## TmConj: Time-Phrase-Forming Conjunction

*Categorial Definition:* $S - TmADV/t$
*Type:* $<< s, t >, << s, t >, t >>$
*Basic Expressions:* while, before, after
*Translation:*

| | | |
|---|---|---|
| while | $\Longrightarrow$ | $\lambda q \lambda p [\exists i_1 [q(i_1) \wedge p(i_1)]]$ |
| before | $\Longrightarrow$ | $\lambda q \lambda p [\exists i_1 [[i_1 << q] \wedge p(i_1)]]$ |
| after | $\Longrightarrow$ | $\lambda q \lambda p [\exists i_1 [[q << i_1] \wedge p(i_1)]]$ |

## WHT: Interrogative Term

*Type:* $<< s, << s, e >, t >>, t >$
*Basic Expressions:* who, whom, what
*Translation:*

$\alpha \implies \lambda P \exists y [y(i) = u \wedge P(i)(y)]$

for any WHT $\alpha$

## Tm-Int: Time Interrogative

*Type:* $<< s, t >, < s, t >>$
*Basic Expressions:* when; any question words or phrases $\alpha$ that can be used to inquire about time
*Translation:*

| | | |
|---|---|---|
| when | $\Longrightarrow$ | $\lambda p \lambda i_1 [p(i_1)]$ |
| $\alpha$ | $\Longrightarrow$ | $\lambda p \lambda i_1 [p(i_1)]$ |

## I-DET: Interrogative Determiner

*Categorial Definition:* $T/CN$
*Type:* $<< s, << s, e >, t >>, << s, << s, e >, t >>, t >>$
*Basic Expressions:* which, what, how much, how many, every
*Translation:*

$\alpha \implies \lambda Q \lambda P \exists y [y(i) = u \wedge Q(i)(y) \wedge P(i)(y)]$

for each $\alpha \in B_{I-DET}$.

## T/T: Common Noun as Term Modifier

*Type:* $<< s, << s, << s, e >, t >>, t >>, << s, << s, e >, t >>, t >>$
*Basic Expressions:* (same as CN)
*Translation:*

for any $\alpha \in B_{T/T}$,

$\quad \alpha \implies \lambda W \lambda P W(i)[\lambda i \lambda y[P(i)(y) \wedge \alpha'(i)(y)]]$

if $\alpha$ refers to a role attribute, or

$\quad \alpha \implies \lambda W \lambda P W(i)[\lambda i \lambda y[P(i)(y) \wedge \alpha_*(i)(y(i))]],$

if $\alpha$ refers to a key attribute

## DET: Determiner

*Categorial Definition:* $T/CN$

*Type:* $<< s, << s, e >, t >>, << s, << s, e >, t >>, t >>$

*Basic Expressions:* a, the, every

*Translation:*

| | | |
|---|---|---|
| a | $\implies$ | $\lambda P \lambda Q \exists x [P(i)(x) \wedge Q(i)(x)]$ |
| the | $\implies$ | $\lambda P \lambda Q \exists y [\forall x [P(i)(x) <=> x = y] \wedge Q(i)(y)]$ |
| every | $\implies$ | $\lambda P \lambda Q \forall x [P(i)(x) \rightarrow Q(i)(x)]$ |

The next chapter gives a sense of the expressive power of QE-III by discussing numerous examples of database queries expressible in the language.

# CHAPTER SEVEN

# EXAMPLES FROM THE QE-III FRAGMENT

## 7.1 Introduction

In this chapter we present and discuss examples of the syntactic and translation rules of the QE-III fragment whose definition was given in Chapter 6. As we pointed out in that presentation, the PTQ fragment stands essentially intact as the core of QE-III. There are, however, certain changes to this core. One major change is our use of the logic IL, as the intermediate translation language; this logic is a modification to Montague's IL, and makes explicit the *hidden* abstraction over indices that is a part of the evaluation process in Montague's PTQ analysis. In defining IL, we have already shown that we evaluate any expression $\alpha$ with respect to a state $s$ by forming the expression: $[\lambda i \alpha](s)$.

Moreover, in presenting the pragmatics of QE-III, we showed how the pragmatic interpretation of any sentential expression was essentially given by the denotation of the expression formed by $\lambda$-abstracting over all of the free individual variables and also evaluating with respect to **now**.

In addition to this change in the underlying logic and method of evaluation, the following additional modifications have been made to the rules of the PTQ fragment:

1. Rule S4 has been modified to perform the single function of combining a Term with an IV to form a sort of proto-sentence. It no longer performs the verb inflection for third person singular present tense. The entire treatment of tense and time adverbials is now performed more systematically by rules S101 through S106. (The tensing functions of S17 have therefore been totally eliminated.)

2. Montague's use of the variables $he_0$ and $him_0$ amounted to a simple technique of case marking in order to choose the appropriate personal pronoun upon substitution of a Term. We have expanded this technique somewhat, using variables of the form [it-CASE-i] where CASE ranges over {NOM,DAT,ACC} and $i$ over the natural numbers.

133

| Variable symbols | Type of variable symbol |
|---|---|
| $x, y, z, x_0, x_1, \ldots$ | $< s, e >$ : individual concepts (ICs) |
| $P, Q, Q_1, Q_2, \ldots$ | $< s, << s, e >, t >>$ : properties of ICs |
| $p, q, q_1, q_2, \ldots$ | $< s, t >$ : propositions |
| $i$ | $s$ : distinguished state variable wrt which all expressions are evaluated |
| $i_1, i_2, \ldots$ | $s$ : states |
| $W$ | $< s, << s, << s, e >, t >>, t >>$: properties of properties of ICs |

**Figure 7.1: Variables Used in QE-III Translations**

3. Rule S9 for combining a sentence adverbial ("Necessarily") with a sentence, has been eliminated. This is because the only sentence adverbials in QE-III are Time Adverbials which are brought in together with the tense marker in rules S104 - S106.

4. It is well known that there are problems with the PTQ treatment of conjunction and disjunction of Terms and IVs (see discussion in [Fri79] and [Ben74]). While Friedman's bracketing solution is ultimately more acceptable (both by virtue of its generality and, of particular interest, its natural correspondence to a LISP implementation), we have for simplicity of presentation adopted Bennett's simple solution of marking all Basic Verbs with a # marker which is removed when the verb is ultimately tensed. (We choose this solution because the points we wish to make have only to do with the verbs, and are easily understood with this technique.)

For ease of understanding the translations to follow, we repeat the table showing the types of the variables used, in Figure 7.1.

## 7.2 PTQ-like Examples from the QE-III Fragment

Before illustrating some of the added features of the QE-III database query fragment, we present some examples that fall syntactically within the range of the PTQ fragment (up to vocabulary differences) in order to contrast the way these two fragments would derive and translate the same example sentences. For example, under one analysis

**Example 7.1** *John manages Mary.*

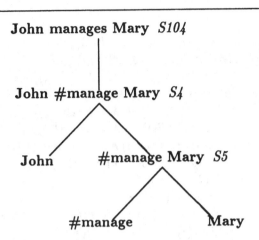

**Figure 7.2: QE-III Derivation of "John manages Mary."**

would have the derivation tree in QE-III that is shown in Figure 7.2.

The syntactic and translation rules illustrated in this example are Rules S4: [SUBJ + PRED: Untensed], S5: [TransVerb + Direct Object], and S104: [Present Tense Sentence].

Several points arise with this example. First we note that this analysis tree presents the derivational history of nonbasic expressions in the language in the obvious way. Each node is labelled with a meaningful expression in QE-III; in case the expression is nonbasic, it is further labelled by the syntactic rule by which it was constructed, and is given children labelled with the expressions from which it was obtained. [Mon70a] provides a more formal definition of analysis trees; it should be sufficient to point out that the language is defined in such a way that to each analysis tree (though not necessarily to each meaningful expression) there corresponds a unique translation into the intermediate logical language.

This analysis of 7.1 illustrates several departures from the corresponding PTQ analysis. First we note that the basic verb is prefixed with #, and this prefix remains even after S4 is applied to combine the Term "John" with the Intransitive Verb Phrase "#manage Mary." Second the rule S104 is new. It takes an untensed sentence as input and gives a (present) tensed sentence as output. Thus we have characterized tense as a property not of verbs but of clauses, although this property in English is realized by the inflection of the main verb of the clause. The importance of this characterization will be made clearer when we consider the interaction of tense with interrogative sentences.

This method of introducing tenses into a sentence obviates the need for undoing the English verb inflections that would be required by a method (such as in PTQ or in [Dow79] that *always* introduced present tense first, subject to possible subsequent modifications. [Dow79] (fn.5, Ch.7)-makes a similar point – though still in terms of

| Mary | $\Longrightarrow$ | $\lambda P \exists x [x(i) = Mary \wedge P(i)(x)]$ |
|---|---|---|
| #manage | $\Longrightarrow$ | $\lambda W \lambda x [W(i)(\lambda i \lambda y [AS\text{--}1(y(i), x) \wedge$ |
| | | $EMP'_*(i)(y(i)) \wedge MGR'(i)(x)])]$ |
| #manage Mary | $\Longrightarrow$ | $\lambda W \lambda x [W(i)(\lambda i \lambda y [AS\text{--}1(y(i), x) \wedge$ |
| | | $EMP'_*(i)(y(i)) \wedge MGR'(i)(x)])]$ |
| | | $(\lambda i \lambda P \exists x [P(i)(x) \wedge x(i) = Mary])$ |
| | $\longrightarrow$ | $\lambda x (\lambda i \lambda P \exists x [P(i)(x) \wedge x(i) = Mary])(i)$ |
| | | $(\lambda i \lambda y [AS\text{--}1(y(i), x) \wedge EMP'_*(i)(y(i)) \wedge$ |
| | | $MGR'(i)(x)])]$ |
| | $\longrightarrow$ | $\lambda x \exists z [AS\text{--}1(z(i), x) \wedge$ |
| | | $EMP'_*(i)(z(i)) \wedge MGR'(i)(x) \wedge z(i) = Mary]$ |
| John | $\Longrightarrow$ | $\lambda P \exists x [x(i) = John \wedge P(i)(x)]$ |
| John #manage Mary | $\Longrightarrow$ | $\lambda P \exists y [P(i)(y) \wedge y(i) = John]$ |
| | | $(\lambda i \lambda x \exists z [AS\text{--}1(z(i), x) \wedge EMP'_*(i)(z(i)) \wedge$ |
| | | $MGR'(i)(x) \wedge z(i) = Mary])$ |
| | $\longrightarrow$ | $\exists y \exists z [AS\text{--}1(z(i), y) \wedge EMP'_*(i)(z(i)) \wedge$ |
| | | $MGR'(i)(y) \wedge z(i) = Mary \wedge y(i) = John]$ |
| | $\longrightarrow$ | $\exists y [AS\text{--}1(Mary, y) \wedge EMP'_*(i)(Mary) \wedge$ |
| | | $MGR'(i)(y) \wedge y(i) = John]$ |
| John manages Mary | $\Longrightarrow$ | $\exists y [EMP'_*(i)(Mary) \wedge$ |
| | | $MGR'(i)(y) \wedge y(i) = John \wedge AS\text{--}1(Mary, y)]$ |

**Figure 7.3: QE-III Translation of "John manages Mary."**

introducing the tense via a SUBJ + PRED rule – but does not incorporate the idea into the fragment presented there.

In a number of the PTQ rules Montague makes use of the auxiliary notions of the gender of a CN or a T, and the third person singular form of a verb. These notions are never defined with the same rigor which Montague demanded of other characteristics of his logic and grammar, presumably because he felt they were obvious and uninteresting. As in [Ben74] we make use of a number of similar auxiliary notions in our rules. This example points out two such notions, viz. that of the tense of a clause and the case of a variable. In our fragment a clause is either untensed or tensed, and belongs to a different category (though of the same logical type) in either case. A variable introduced into a sentence is either uncased, or one of NOM, ACC or DAT.

The translation of 7.1 corresponding to the above analysis tree is given in Figure 7.3. In this presentation we follow Partee in using a double arrow "$\Longrightarrow$" to indicate the immediate result of applying a Translation rule of the fragment, and a single arrow "$\longrightarrow$" to indicate the result of any of a number of logical simplifications (principally $\lambda$-reduction.)

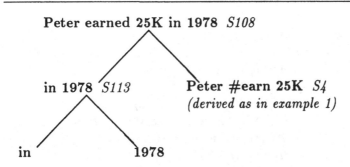

**Peter earned 25K in 1978** *S108*

in 1978 *S113*          Peter #earn 25K *S4*
                        *(derived as in example 1)*

in          1978

Figure 7.4: QE-III Derivation of "Peter earned 25K in 1978."

Our treatment of Proper Terms is slightly different from the PTQ treatment, in that the translations include an individual-concept variable whose extension at the state i is asserted to be the indicated individual. This is done because in HRDM all individuals of interest must be playing a role in the database, and roles can only be filled by individual concepts. Further, as we discussed in Chapter 5, verbs are treated as objects of the same type as in PTQ, but they are analyzed in terms of the database schema.

## 7.3 Temporal Reference in QE-III

In addition to its indication by means of the tense system, temporal reference in English is also indicated by certain time adverbials (today, last year, ...) and also by prepositional phrases (in 1978, on Monday...). Care must be taken in order to analyze properly the semantics of sentences which involve an interaction between tenses and these other temporal indicators. They cannot be applied sequentially as operators to a clause, or the semantics will be incorrect. (David Dowty [Dow79] makes the same observation.)

**Example 7.2** *Peter earned 25K in 1978.*

The derivation for this example, in Figure 7.4, illustrates this aspect of QE-III.
This example illustrates the following two rules:

**S108. [Past Tense with Time-Adverbial]**
$< F_{108a}, < S - TmADV, t >, T\!-\!t >$
$< F_{108b}, < S - TmADV, PS >, T\!-\!PS >$
$< F_{108c}, < VP - TmADV, PS >, T\!-\!PS >$

in $\qquad\Longrightarrow\quad \lambda q\lambda p[\exists i_1[q(i_1) \wedge p(i_1)]]$

1978 $\qquad\Longrightarrow\quad 1978'$

in 1978 $\qquad\Longrightarrow\quad \lambda q\lambda p[\exists i_1[q(i_1) \wedge p(i_1)]](1978')$

$\qquad\qquad\longrightarrow\quad \lambda p[\exists i_1[1978'(i_1) \wedge p(i_1)]]$

Peter earned 25K $\;\Longrightarrow\; \lambda p[\exists i_1[1978'(i_1) \wedge p(i_1)]]\lambda i_2[[i_2 < i]\wedge$
    in 1978 $\qquad\qquad\quad \lambda i \exists y[AS{-}1(Peter, y) \wedge EMP'_*(i)(Peter)\wedge$
$\qquad\qquad\qquad\qquad SAL'(i)(y) \wedge y(i) = 25K](i_2)])$

$\qquad\qquad\longrightarrow\quad \lambda p[\exists i_1[1978'(i_1) \wedge p(i_1)]](\lambda i_2[[i_2 < i]\wedge$
$\qquad\qquad\qquad\quad \exists y[AS{-}1(Peter, y) \wedge EMP'_*(i_2)(Peter)\wedge$
$\qquad\qquad\qquad\qquad SAL'(i_2)(y) \wedge y(i_2) = 25K])$

$\qquad\qquad\longrightarrow\quad \exists i_1[1978'(i_1) \wedge \lambda i_2[[i_2 < i] \wedge \exists y[AS{-}1(Peter, y)\wedge$
$\qquad\qquad\qquad\quad EMP'_*(i_2)(Peter) \wedge SAL'(i_2)(y) \wedge y(i_2) = 25K](i_1)]$

$\qquad\qquad\longrightarrow\quad \exists i_1 \exists y[1978'(i_1) \wedge [i_1 < i] \wedge EMP'_*(i_1)(Peter)\wedge$
$\qquad\qquad\qquad\quad SAL'(i_1)(y) \wedge y(i_1) = 25K \wedge AS{-}1(Peter, y)]$

**Figure 7.5: QE-III Translation of "Peter earned 25K in 1978."**

$F_{108a}(\alpha, \phi) \;=\; \alpha\phi^*$

$F_{108b}(\alpha, \phi) \;=\; \phi^*\alpha$

where $\phi^*$ is $\phi$ with each word of the form $\#\beta$ replaced by its past tense form.

$F_{108c}(\alpha, \phi) \;=\; \phi^*$

where $\phi^*$ is the result of inserting $\alpha$ before the first word in $\phi$ of the form $\#\beta$, and then replacing each word of this form by its past tense form.

**T108.** $F_{108a}(\alpha, \phi), F_{108b}(\alpha, \phi)$ and $F_{108c}(\alpha, \phi) \;\Longrightarrow\; \alpha'(\lambda i_1[[i_1 < i] \wedge \lambda i \phi'(i_1)])$

**S113. [TmPREP + Tm]**
$< F^{RC}_{113}, < TmPREP, Tm >, S - TmADV >$
**T113.** $F^{RC}_{113}(\alpha, \beta) \;\Longrightarrow\; \alpha(\beta)$

The translation in Figure 7.5 correctly indicates that there is some state in the past that is also in the set of states 1978 at which the present tense sentence Peter earns 25K is true.

If we had introduced the two temporal indicators (the tense marker and the adverbial phrase "in 1978") separately, in either order, the resulting translations would be incorrect. Figure 7.6 shows one such derivation; the translation corresponding to that derivation is in Figure 7.7.

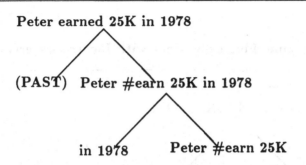

**Figure 7.6: An Incorrect Derivation of "Peter earned 25K in 1978."**

| Peter #earn 25K | $\longrightarrow$ | $\exists y[AS-1(Peter, y) \wedge EMP'_*(i)(Peter) \wedge$ |
|---|---|---|
| | | $SAL'(i)(y) \wedge y(i) = 25K]$ |
| Peter #earn 25K | $\longrightarrow$ | $\exists i_1 \exists y[1978'(i_1) \wedge AS-1(Peter, y) \wedge$ |
| in 1978 | | $EMP'_*(i_1)(Peter) \wedge SAL'(i_1)(y) \wedge y(i_1) = 25K]$ |
| Peter earned 25K | $\longrightarrow$ | $\exists i_2 \exists i_1 \exists y[[i_2 < i] \wedge 1978'(i_1) \wedge EMP'_*(i_1)(Peter)$ |
| in 1978 | | $\wedge SAL'(i_1)(y) \wedge y(i_1) = 25K \wedge AS-1(Peter, y)]$ |

**Figure 7.7: Translation Corresponding to Incorrect Derivation of "Peter earned 25K in 1978."**

**Figure 7.8: Time Line Consistent with Incorrect Derivation**

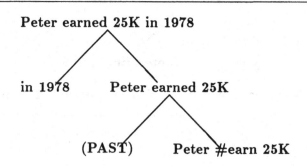

**Figure 7.9: Another Incorrect Derivation of "Peter earned 25K in 1978."**

This derivation places the three times $i_1, i_2$ and **now** on the time line as in Figure 7.8, with $i_1$ *anywhere* on the time line in 1978.

The reverse order of sequential introduction, as seen in Figure 7.9, is also incorrect, for with this derivation, translated as in Figure 7.10, the two times are located as in Figure 7.11. The properties of Peter are asserted to be true in state $i_1$, but $i_1$ may or may not be in 1978, and may or may not be in the past (with respect to **now**.) Only the simultaneous introduction of these temporal operators provides the correct translation.

The following example illustrates how tense is treated as a property of clauses in compound sentences, and how these tenses are independent of one another. The example also illustrates how relative clauses are maintained in the QE-III fragment:

**Example 7.3** *Peter manages an employee such that he earned 30K.*

Its derivation tree is shown in Figure 7.12, and illustrates the rule S105 which introduces the past tense in a manner analogous to S104's introduction of the present. (The future is introduced by the comparable rule S106.)

**S105. [Past Tense Sentence]**
$< F_{105}, < PS >, T\text{--}PS >$
$F_{105}(\phi) = \phi$, with each word of the form $\#\alpha$ replaced by its past tense form.

Peter #earn 25K $\longrightarrow$ $\exists y[AS{-}1(Peter, y) \wedge EMP'_*(i)(Peter) \wedge$
$SAL'(i)(y) \wedge y(i) = 25K]$

Peter earned 25K $\longrightarrow$ $\exists i_1 \exists y[[i_1 < i] \wedge AS{-}1(Peter, y) \wedge$
$EMP'_*(i_1)(Peter) \wedge SAL'(i_1)(y) \wedge y(i_1) = 25K]$

Peter earned 25K $\longrightarrow$ $\exists i_2 \exists i_1 \exists y[1978'(i_2) \wedge [i_1 < i_2] \wedge$
in 1978 $EMP'_*(i_1)(Peter) \wedge SAL'(i_1)(y) \wedge y(i_1) = 25K \wedge$
$AS{-}1(Peter, y)$

**Figure 7.10: Translation Corresponding to Another Incorrect Derivation of "Peter earned 25K in 1978."**

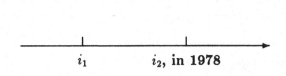

$i_1$      $i_2$, in 1978

**Figure 7.11: Time Line Consistent with Second Incorrect Derivation**

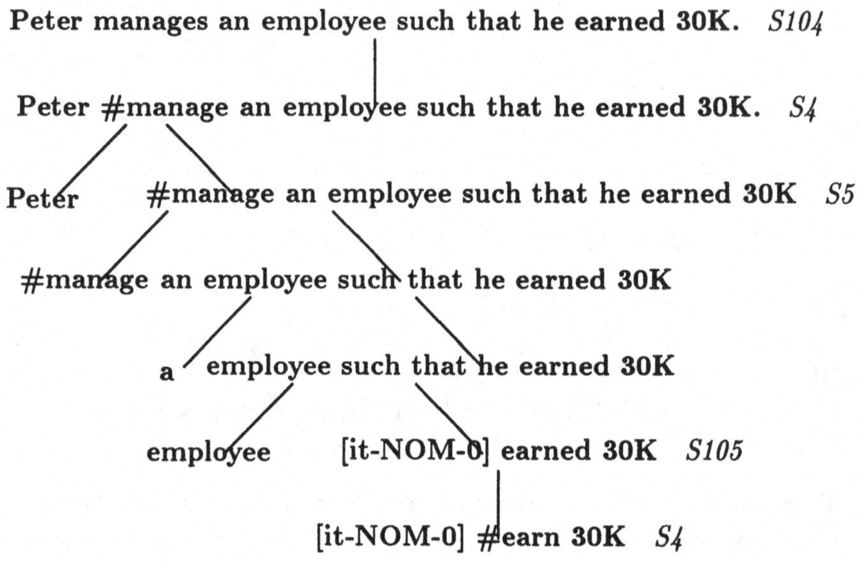

Peter manages an employee such that he earned 30K.  *S104*

Peter #manage an employee such that he earned 30K.  *S4*

Peter        #manage an employee such that he earned 30K   *S5*

#manage an employee such that he earned 30K

a   employee such that he earned 30K

employee        [it-NOM-0] earned 30K   *S105*

[it-NOM-0] #earn 30K   *S4*

**Figure 7.12:** QE-III Derivation of "Peter manages an employee such that he earned 30K."

**T105.**  $F_{105}(\phi) \implies \exists i_1[[i_1 < i] \wedge \lambda i \phi'(i_1)]$

Furthermore, we have dispensed with Montague's treatment of the inflection of pronouns via the technique of the variables $he_i$, $him_i$, etc., and incorporated a more general treatment that uses [it-CASE-i], where CASE is any one of NOMinative, DATive, or ACCusative. This treatment is both more general and more easily extendible to other cases.

The translation for this analysis tree is given in Figure 7.13.

A final example involving tense and a temporal modifier illustrates how propositions can be treated in almost the same way as time constants for denoting sets of states. The sentence

**Example 7.4** *John worked before Mary worked.*

is analyzed as asserting that there was some state $S_1$ before **now** at which John worked, and that $S_1$ was also before some other state $S_2$ before **now** at which Mary worked. An analysis of 7.4 is given by the tree in Figure 7.14.

Rule S112 allows the formation of a time-adverbial phrase from a preposition, a tense, and a sentence:

**S112. [TmCONJ + declarative sentence]**
$< F_{112a}, < TmCONJ, t >, S - TmADV >$
$< F_{112b}, < TmCONJ, t >, S - TmADV >$

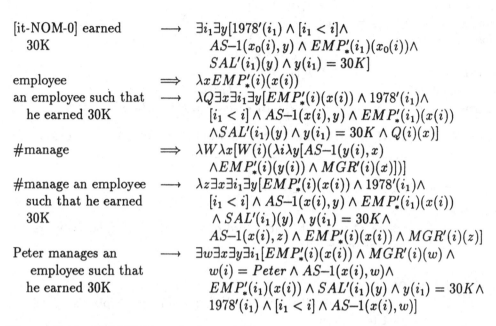

[it-NOM-0] earned $\longrightarrow$ $\exists i_1 \exists y [1978'(i_1) \wedge [i_1 < i] \wedge$
30K $\qquad AS\text{-}1(x_0(i), y) \wedge EMP'_*(i_1)(x_0(i)) \wedge$
$\qquad SAL'(i_1)(y) \wedge y(i_1) = 30K]$

employee $\Longrightarrow$ $\lambda x EMP'_*(i)(x(i))$

an employee such that $\longrightarrow$ $\lambda Q \exists x \exists i_1 \exists y [EMP'_*(i)(x(i)) \wedge 1978'(i_1) \wedge$
he earned 30K $\qquad [i_1 < i] \wedge AS\text{-}1(x(i), y) \wedge EMP'_*(i_1)(x(i))$
$\qquad \wedge SAL'(i_1)(y) \wedge y(i_1) = 30K \wedge Q(i)(x)]$

#manage $\Longrightarrow$ $\lambda W \lambda x [W(i)(\lambda i \lambda y [AS\text{-}1(y(i), x)$
$\qquad \wedge EMP'_*(i)(y(i)) \wedge MGR'(i)(x)])]$

#manage an employee $\longrightarrow$ $\lambda z \exists x \exists i_1 \exists y [EMP'_*(i)(x(i)) \wedge 1978'(i_1) \wedge$
such that he earned $\qquad [i_1 < i] \wedge AS\text{-}1(x(i), y) \wedge EMP'_*(i_1)(x(i))$
30K $\qquad \wedge SAL'(i_1)(y) \wedge y(i_1) = 30K \wedge$
$\qquad AS\text{-}1(x(i), z) \wedge EMP'_*(i)(x(i)) \wedge MGR'(i)(z)]$

Peter manages an $\longrightarrow$ $\exists w \exists x \exists y \exists i_1 [EMP'_*(i)(x(i)) \wedge MGR'(i)(w) \wedge$
employee such that $\qquad w(i) = Peter \wedge AS\text{-}1(x(i), w) \wedge$
he earned 30K $\qquad EMP'_*(i_1)(x(i)) \wedge SAL'(i_1)(y) \wedge y(i_1) = 30K \wedge$
$\qquad 1978'(i_1) \wedge [i_1 < i] \wedge AS\text{-}1(x(i), w)]$

**Figure 7.13: QE-III Translation of "Peter manages an employee such that he earned 30K."**

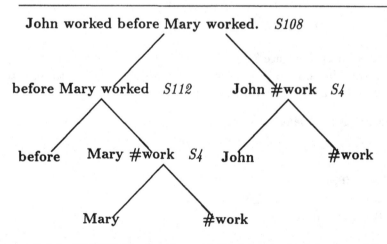

**Figure 7.14: QE-III Derivation of "John worked before Mary worked."**

| | | |
|---|---|---|
| Mary #work | $\longrightarrow$ | $EMP'_*(i)(Mary)$ |
| before | $\Longrightarrow$ | $\lambda q \lambda p [\exists i_1 [[i_1 << q] \wedge p(i_1)]]$ |
| before Mary worked | $\longrightarrow$ | $\lambda p \exists i_1 [[i_1 << (\lambda i_2 EMP'_*(i_2)(Mary))]$ |
| | | $\wedge [i_2 < i] \wedge p(i_1)]$ |
| John #work | $\longrightarrow$ | $EMP'_*(i)(John)$ |
| John worked before | $\longrightarrow$ | $\exists i_1 [[i_1 << (\lambda i_2 EMP'_*(i_2)(Mary))] \wedge$ |
| Mary worked | | $[i_2 < i] \wedge [i_1 < i] \wedge EMP'_*(i_1)(John)]$ |

**Figure 7.15: QE-III Translation of "John worked before Mary worked."**

$< F_{112c}, < TmCONJ, t >, S - TmADV >$

$F_{112a}(\alpha, \phi) \quad = \quad \alpha\phi^*$

   where $\phi^*$ is $\phi$ with each word of the form $\#\beta$ replaced by its present tense form.

$F_{112b}(\alpha, \phi) \quad = \quad \alpha\phi^*$

   where $\phi^*$ is $\phi$ with each word of the form $\#\beta$ replaced by its past tense form.

$F_{112c}(\alpha, \phi) \quad = \quad \alpha\phi^*$

   where $\phi^*$ is $\phi$ with each word of the form $\#\beta$ replaced by its future tense form.

**T112.** $\quad F_{112a}(\alpha, \phi) \quad \Longrightarrow \quad \alpha'(\lambda i_2 [\lambda i \phi'(i_2)])$

$\qquad F_{112b}(\alpha, \phi) \quad \Longrightarrow \quad \alpha'(\lambda i_2 [[\lambda i \phi'(i_2)] \wedge [i_2 < i]])$

$\qquad F_{112c}(\alpha, \phi) \quad \Longrightarrow \quad \alpha'(\lambda i_2 [[\lambda i \phi'(i_2)] \wedge [i < i_2]])$

The translation proceeds as in Figure 7.15.

   Similarly we can combine simple time expressions with prepositions to form temporal adverbials, as in the analysis of 7.5 shown in Figure 7.16.

**Example 7.5** *Rachel worked before yesterday.*

   The new rule that defines this is

**S113. [TmPREP + Tm]**

$< F_{113}^{RC}, < TmPREP, Tm >, S - TmADV >$

**T113.** $\quad F_{113}^{RC}(\alpha, \beta) \quad \Longrightarrow \quad \alpha(\beta)$

The translation for this example is shown in Figure 7.17.

   Notice that there are two restrictions placed upon when the state $i_1$ can occur in time:

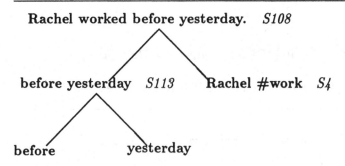

**Figure 7.16: QE-III Derivation of "Rachel worked before yesterday."**

| | | |
|---|---|---|
| Rachel #work | $\longrightarrow$ | $EMP'_*(i)(Rachel)$ |
| before | $\Longrightarrow$ | $\lambda q \lambda p[\exists i_1[[i_1 << q] \wedge p(i_1)]]$ |
| yesterday | $\Longrightarrow$ | $yesterday'(i)$ |
| before yesterday | $\longrightarrow$ | $\lambda p[\exists i_1[[i_1 << yesterday'(i)] \wedge p(i_1)]]$ |
| Rachel worked before yesterday | $\longrightarrow$ | $\exists i_1[[i_1 << yesterday'(i)] \wedge [i_1 < i] \wedge$ |
| | | $\quad EMP'_*(i_1)(Rachel)]$ |

**Figure 7.17: QE-III Translation of "Rachel worked before yesterday."**

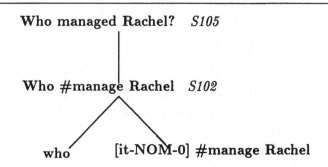

**Figure 7.18: QE-III Derivation of "Who managed Rachel?"**

1. $[i_1 << yesterday'(i)]$ (because of "before yesterday"), and

2. $[i_1 < i]$ (because of the past tense.)

Since a time before yesterday must be before **now** (by the meaning of "yesterday"), a Meaning Postulate for words such as "yesterday" might well be in order here to remove this redundancy and reduce the final translation to:

$$\exists i_1[[i_1 << yesterday'(i)] \wedge EMP'_*(i_1)(Rachel)]$$

We now proceed to discuss the other additional rules of the QE-III fragment. These rules either form expressions that have particular relevance to the database realm (possessives, role specifications, etc.) or form interrogative sentences. We will look first at the questions. A discussion of some of the considerations involved in the framing of these rules for database querying purposes was given in Chapter VI.

## 7.4    Questions in QE-III

Consider the following query:

**Example 7.6** *Who managed Rachel?*

derived as in Figure 7.18.

The rule that introduces a WH-interrogative into a declarative sentence is:

**S102. [WHQ Formation]**
$< F_{102,n}, < WHT, t >, WHQ >$

$F_{102,n}(\alpha, \phi)$ is defined as follows:
Let $\beta$ be the first occurrence of a variable Term [it-CASE-n] with subscript $n$ in $\phi$.

1. If CASE of $\beta$ is NOM, then $F_{102,n}$ is $F_{102,n}^{Q}$.

[it-NOM-0] #manage Rachel $\longrightarrow$ (as above) $[AS{-}1(Rachel, x_0)$
$\wedge EMP'_*(i)(Rachel) \wedge MGR'(i)(x_0)]$

who $\implies \lambda P \exists y[y(i) = u \wedge P(i)(y)]$

Who #manage Rachel? $\implies \lambda P \exists y[y(i) = u \wedge P(i)(y)]$
$(\lambda i \lambda x_0 [AS{-}1(Rachel, x_0) \wedge$
$EMP'_*(i)(Rachel) \wedge MGR'(i)(x_0)])$

$\longrightarrow \exists y[y(i) = u \wedge AS{-}1(Rachel, y)$
$\wedge EMP'_*(i)(Rachel) \wedge MGR'(i)(y)])$

Who managed Rachel? $\implies \exists i_1[[i_1 < i] \wedge \lambda i \exists y[y(i) = u \wedge$
$AS{-}1(Rachel, y) \wedge EMP'_*(i)(Rachel)$
$\wedge MGR'(i)(y)](i_1))$

$\longrightarrow \exists i_1 \exists y[[i_1 < i] \wedge EMP'_*(i_1)(Rachel) \wedge$
$MGR'(i_1)(y) \wedge y(i_1) = u \wedge$
$AS{-}1(Rachel, y)]$

**Figure 7.19: QE-III Translation of "Who managed Rachel?"**

2. If CASE of $\beta$ is ACC or DAT, then $F_{102,n}(\alpha, \beta)$ is $\alpha^* \# AUX \phi^*$ or "To"
$\alpha^* \# AUX \phi^*$, respectively, where

(a) $\alpha^*$ is "whom" if $\alpha$ is "who", and $\alpha$ otherwise,

(b) $\phi^*$ is $\phi$ with

   i. $\beta$ removed,

   ii. each of its *first verbs* unmarked, and

   iii. each subsequent occurrence of [it-CASE-n] replaced by
   "he"/"him"/"to him" according as the CASE is NOM/ACC/DAT
   respectively.

**T102.** $F_{102,n}(\alpha, \phi) \implies \alpha'(\lambda i \lambda x_n \phi')$

The translation is shown in Figure 7.19.

Recall that the pragmatics provides a representation for the answer to questions,
and that the pragmatic interpretation of this query is denoted by the expression

$$\lambda u \exists i_1 \exists y[[i_1 < \mathbf{now}] \wedge EMP'_*(i_1)(Rachel) \wedge MGR'(i_1)(y) \wedge y(i_1) = u \wedge AS{-}1(Rachel, y)]$$

formed by binding all free occurrences of the variable $i$ to the constant **now**, and
$\lambda$-abstracting over all of the free individual variables.

This example illustrates why the tense must be considered a property of the entire
clause, rather than just of the verb phrase, if the interpretation (semantic and pragmatic) of the question is to come out right. For suppose instead that we derived 7.6
as in Figure 7.20.

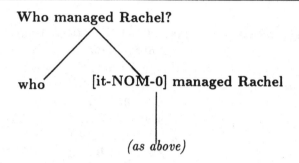

**Who managed Rachel?**

who        [it-NOM-0] managed Rachel

*(as above)*

**Figure 7.20: Incorrect Derivation of "Who managed Rachel?"**

[it-NOM-0] managed Rachel $\implies$ $\exists i_1[[i_1 < i] \land EMP'_*(i_1)(Rachel)$
$\qquad \land MGR'(i_1)(x_0) \land AS-1(Rachel, x_0)]$

who managed Rachel?          $\implies$ $\lambda P \exists y[y(i) = u \land P(i)(y)](\lambda i \lambda x_0 \exists i_1[[i_1 < i]$
$\qquad \land EMP'_*(i_1)(Rachel) \land MGR'(i_1)(x_0) \land$
$\qquad AS-1(Rachel, x_0)])$

$\longrightarrow$ $\exists y \exists i_1[y(i) = u \land [i_1 < i] \land$
$\qquad EMP'_*(i_1)(Rachel) \land MGR'(i_1)(y)$
$\qquad \land AS-1(Rachel, y)]$

**Figure 7.21: Translation Corresponding to Incorrect Derivation of "Who managed Rachel?"**

The corresponding translation would then proceed as in Figure 7.21. The problem with this translation is that the manager-IC y is not *tensed* properly. When evaluated, this query will return the set of individuals u who are the extension of Rachel's manager-IC, not at some time in the past, but **now**. Because "who" has wider scope in this derivation, the past tense operator could not capture the free $i$ of the translation of "who." The question, under our treatment, is correctly analyzed as

**Who (past) managed (past) Rachel?**

rather than as

**Who *now* managed (past) Rachel?**

In order to get this reading, tenses (and tenses + TmADVerbials) must be brought in last over all clauses, including interrogative sentences.

Interrogative Terms (WHT's) can also be derived from common nouns and the interrogative determiners such as "which," as seen in the following example which also illustrates the derivation of a multiple WH-question:

**Example 7.7** *Who manages which employees?*

Its derivation is shown in Figure 7.22.

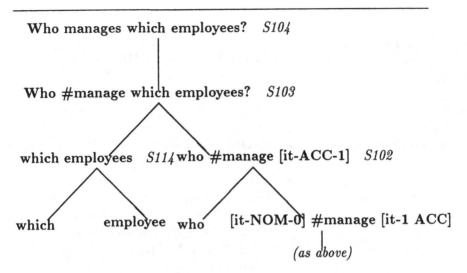

**Figure 7.22: QE-III Derivation of "Who manages which employees?"**

Two rules are illustrated in this example. S114 creates an interrogative term by combining an interrogative determiner with a common noun:

**S114. [WHT Formation]**
$$< F_{114}, < I - DET, CN >, WHT >$$
$$F_{114}(\alpha, \beta) \;=\; \alpha\beta^*$$
where $\beta^*$ is $\beta$ if $\alpha$ is "every," otherwise $\beta^*$ is the plural form of $\beta$.

**T114.** function application

and rule S103 forms multiple WH-questions:

**S103. [WHT Quantification]**
$$< F_{103,n}, < WHT, WHQ >, WHQ >$$

$F_{103,n}(\alpha, \beta)$ is defined as follows:
Let $\gamma$ be the first variable Term in $\beta$.
Then $F_{103,n}$ is applicable only if $\gamma$ is [it-CASE-n], (i.e., has subscript $n$),
in which case $F_{103,n}(\alpha, \beta) = \beta^*$, where $\beta^*$ is the result of replacing $\gamma$ in $\beta$ as follows:

1. Replace with $\alpha$ if the case of $\gamma$ is NOM, or with "to" $\alpha^*$ otherwise, where $\alpha^*$ is "whom" if $\alpha$ is "who", and $\alpha$ otherwise;

2. Replace all subsequent variable Terms with subscript $n$ with "he"/"she"/"it", "him"/"her"/"it", or "to him"/"to her"/"to it" respectively, according to their case and gender.

**T103.** $F_{103,n}(\alpha, \beta) \;\implies\; \alpha'(\lambda i \lambda x_n \beta')$

| | |
|---|---|
| [it-NOM-0] #manage | *(as above)* $AS\text{--}1(x_1(i), x_0)$ |
| [it-ACC-1] | $\wedge EMP'_*(i)(x_1(i)) \wedge MGR'(i)(x_0)$ |
| who #manage [it-ACC-1] $\longrightarrow$ | *(as above)* $\exists y[y(i) = u_1 \wedge AS\text{--}1(x_1(i), y)$ |
| | $\wedge EMP'_*(i)(x_1(i)) \wedge MGR'(i)(y)]$ |
| which $\Longrightarrow$ | $\lambda Q \lambda P \exists z[z(i) = u_2 \wedge Q(i)(z) \wedge P(i)(z)]$ |
| employee $\Longrightarrow$ | $\lambda x EMP'_*(i)(x(i))$ |
| which employees $\Longrightarrow$ | $\lambda Q \lambda P \exists z[z(i) = u_2 \wedge Q(i)(z)$ |
| | $\wedge P(i)(z)](\lambda i \lambda x EMP'_*(i)(x(i)))$ |
| $\longrightarrow$ | $\lambda P \exists z[z(i) = u_2 \wedge EMP'_*(i)(z(i)) \wedge P(i)(z)]$ |
| Who #manage which $\Longrightarrow$ | $\lambda P \exists z[z(i) = u_2 \wedge EMP'_*(i)(z(i)) \wedge P(i)(z)]$ |
| employees? | $(\lambda i \lambda x_1 \exists y[y(i) = u_1 \wedge AS\text{--}1(x_1(i), y) \wedge$ |
| | $EMP'_*(i)(x_1(i)) \wedge MGR'(i)(y)])$ |
| $\longrightarrow$ | $\exists y[EMP'_*(i)(u_2) \wedge y(i) = u_1 \wedge AS\text{--}1(u_2, y)$ |
| | $\wedge MGR'(i)(y)]$ |
| Who manages which $\Longrightarrow$ | $\exists y[EMP'_*(i)(u_2) \wedge MGR'(i)(y) \wedge y(i) = u_1$ |
| employees? | $\wedge AS\text{--}1(u_2, y)]$ |

**Figure 7.23: QE-III Translation of "Who manages which employees?"**

The translation proceeds as in Figure 7.23.

The next example illustrates a 3-Term interrogative:

**Example 7.8** *What does who supply to whom?*

Its derivation is in Figure 7.24.

This example uses the three-place verb "#supply" and a rule for combining such a verb with an indirect object to form a two-place verb. This rule is essentially taken from [Dow79], and is a simple extension of the two-place case.

**S100. [DTV + Indirect Object]**
$< F_{100}^{RCA}, < TV/T, T >, TV >$
If the $T$ is a variable it is marked as being in DAT case.
**T100.** function application.

The corresponding translation is shown in Figure 7.25. Recall that the predicate $REC_3$ indicates a 3-ary relationship among the indicated three individuals.

The next example illustrates a more complicated question that requires, in terms of the database representation, a *join* of two relations:

**Example 7.9** *Who works for a department such that it sells shoes?*

with the derivation in Figure 7.26 and corresponding translation in Figure 7.27.

Yes-No questions can take two forms in the fragment:

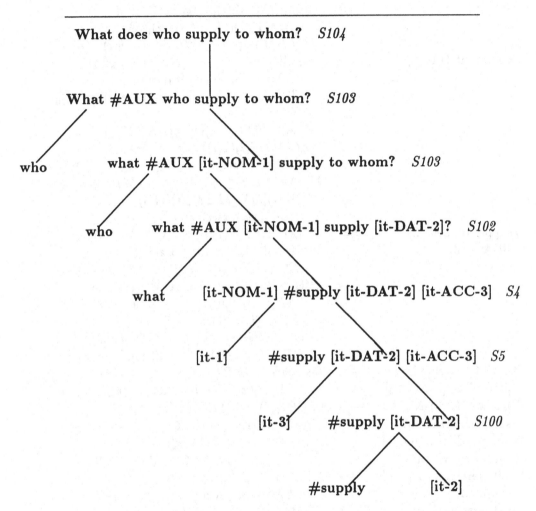

**Figure 7.24:** QE-III Derivation of "What does who supply to whom?"

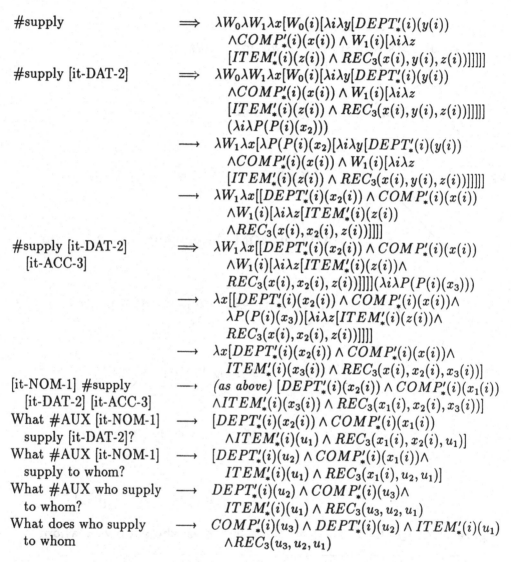

#supply $\implies$ $\lambda W_0\lambda W_1\lambda x[W_0(i)[\lambda i\lambda y[DEPT'_*(i)(y(i))$
$\wedge COMP'_*(i)(x(i))\wedge W_1(i)[\lambda i\lambda z$
$[ITEM'_*(i)(z(i))\wedge REC_3(x(i),y(i),z(i))]]]]]$

#supply [it-DAT-2] $\implies$ $\lambda W_0\lambda W_1\lambda x[W_0(i)[\lambda i\lambda y[DEPT'_*(i)(y(i))$
$\wedge COMP'_*(i)(x(i))\wedge W_1(i)[\lambda i\lambda z$
$[ITEM'_*(i)(z(i))\wedge REC_3(x(i),y(i),z(i))]]]]]$
$(\lambda i\lambda P(P(i)(x_2)))$

$\longrightarrow$ $\lambda W_1\lambda x[\lambda P(P(i)(x_2)[\lambda i\lambda y[DEPT'_*(i)(y(i))$
$\wedge COMP'_*(i)(x(i))\wedge W_1(i)[\lambda i\lambda z$
$[ITEM'_*(i)(z(i))\wedge REC_3(x(i),y(i),z(i))]]]]]$

$\longrightarrow$ $\lambda W_1\lambda x[[DEPT'_*(i)(x_2(i))\wedge COMP'_*(i)(x(i))$
$\wedge W_1(i)[\lambda i\lambda z[ITEM'_*(i)(z(i))$
$\wedge REC_3(x(i),x_2(i),z(i))]]]]$

#supply [it-DAT-2] $\implies$ $\lambda W_1\lambda x[[DEPT'_*(i)(x_2(i))\wedge COMP'_*(i)(x(i))$
[it-ACC-3] $\wedge W_1(i)[\lambda i\lambda z[ITEM'_*(i)(z(i))\wedge$
$REC_3(x(i),x_2(i),z(i))]]]](\lambda i\lambda P(P(i)(x_3)))$

$\longrightarrow$ $\lambda x[[DEPT'_*(i)(x_2(i))\wedge COMP'_*(i)(x(i))\wedge$
$\lambda P(P(i)(x_3))[\lambda i\lambda z[ITEM'_*(i)(z(i))\wedge$
$REC_3(x(i),x_2(i),z(i))]]]]$

$\longrightarrow$ $\lambda x[DEPT'_*(i)(x_2(i))\wedge COMP'_*(i)(x(i))\wedge$
$ITEM'_*(i)(x_3(i))\wedge REC_3(x(i),x_2(i),x_3(i))]$

[it-NOM-1] #supply $\longrightarrow$ *(as above)* $[DEPT'_*(i)(x_2(i))\wedge COMP'_*(i)(x_1(i))$
[it-DAT-2] [it-ACC-3] $\wedge ITEM'_*(i)(x_3(i))\wedge REC_3(x_1(i),x_2(i),x_3(i))]$

What #AUX [it-NOM-1] $\longrightarrow$ $[DEPT'_*(i)(x_2(i))\wedge COMP'_*(i)(x_1(i))$
supply [it-DAT-2]? $\wedge ITEM'_*(i)(u_1)\wedge REC_3(x_1(i),x_2(i),u_1)]$

What #AUX [it-NOM-1] $\longrightarrow$ $[DEPT'_*(i)(u_2)\wedge COMP'_*(i)(x_1(i))\wedge$
supply to whom? $ITEM'_*(i)(u_1)\wedge REC_3(x_1(i),u_2,u_1)]$

What #AUX who supply $\longrightarrow$ $DEPT'_*(i)(u_2)\wedge COMP'_*(i)(u_3)\wedge$
to whom? $ITEM'_*(i)(u_1)\wedge REC_3(u_3,u_2,u_1)$

What does who supply $\longrightarrow$ $COMP'_*(i)(u_3)\wedge DEPT'_*(i)(u_2)\wedge ITEM'_*(i)(u_1)$
to whom $\wedge REC_3(u_3,u_2,u_1)$

**Figure 7.25: QE-III Translation of "What does who supply to whom?"**

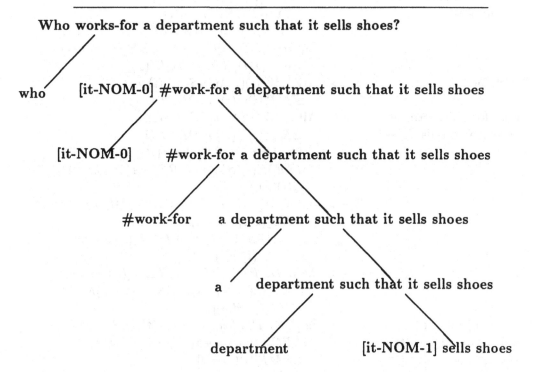

Figure 7.26: QE-III Derivation of "Who works for a department such that it sells shoes?"

| | | |
|---|---|---|
| [it-NOM-1] sells shoes | $\Longrightarrow$ | $DEPT'_*(i)(x_1(i)) \wedge ITEM'_*(i)(Shoes) \wedge$ $REC_2(x_1(i), Shoes)$ |
| department such that it sells shoes | $\Longrightarrow$ | $\lambda x_1(DEPT'_*(i)(x_1(i)) \wedge ITEM'_*(i)(Shoes)$ $\wedge REC_2(x_1(i), Shoes))$ |
| a department such that it sells shoes | $\Longrightarrow$ | $\lambda P\lambda Q \exists x[P(i)(x) \wedge Q(i)(x)]$ $(\lambda i \lambda x_1(DEPT'_*(i)(x_1(i)) \wedge$ $ITEM'_*(i)(Shoes) \wedge REC_2(x_1(i), Shoes)))$ |
| | $\longrightarrow$ | $\lambda Q \exists x[DEPT'_*(i)(x(i)) \wedge ITEM'_*(i)(Shoes) \wedge$ $REC_2(x(i), Shoes) \wedge Q(i)(x)]$ |
| #work-for | $\Longrightarrow$ | $\lambda W \lambda z[W(i)(\lambda i \lambda y[AS\text{--}1(z(i), y) \wedge$ $EMP'_*(i)(z(i)) \wedge DEPT'(i)(y)])]$ |
| #work-for a department such that it sells shoes | $\Longrightarrow$ | $\lambda W \lambda z[W(i)(\lambda i \lambda y[AS\text{--}1(z(i), y) \wedge$ $EMP'_*(i)(z(i)) \wedge DEPT'(i)(y)])]$ $(\lambda i \lambda Q \exists x[DEPT'_*(i)(x(i)) \wedge$ $ITEM'_*(i)(Shoes) \wedge REC_2(x(i), Shoes) \wedge$ $Q(i)(x)])$ |
| | $\longrightarrow$ | $\lambda z[\lambda Q \exists x[DEPT'_*(i)(x(i)) \wedge ITEM'_*(i)(Shoes) \wedge$ $REC_2(x(i), Shoes) \wedge Q(i)(x)]$ $(\lambda i \lambda y[AS\text{--}1(z(i), y) \wedge EMP'_*(i)(z(i)) \wedge$ $DEPT'(i)(y)])$ |
| | $\longrightarrow$ | $\lambda z \exists x[DEPT'_*(i)(x(i)) \wedge ITEM'_*(i)(Shoes) \wedge$ $REC_2(x(i), Shoes) \wedge AS\text{--}1(z(i), x) \wedge$ $EMP'_*(i)(z(i))]$ |
| [it-NOM-0] #work-for a department such that it sells shoes | $\Longrightarrow$ | $\exists x[DEPT'_*(i)(x(i)) \wedge ITEM'_*(i)(Shoes) \wedge$ $REC_2(x(i), Shoes) \wedge AS\text{--}1(x_0(i), x)$ $\wedge EMP'_*(i)(x_0(i))]$ |
| who works-for a department such that it sells shoes | $\Longrightarrow$ | $\lambda P \exists y[y(i) = u \wedge P(i)(y)](\lambda i \lambda x_0 \exists x$ $[DEPT'_*(i)(x(i)) \wedge ITEM'_*(i)(Shoes) \wedge$ $REC_2(x(i), Shoes) \wedge AS\text{--}1(x_0(i), x) \wedge$ $EMP'_*(i)(x_0(i))])$ |
| | $\longrightarrow$ | $\exists x[EMP'_*(i)(u) \wedge DEPT'_*(i)(x(i)) \wedge AS\text{--}1(u, x) \wedge$ $ITEM'_*(i)(Shoes) \wedge REC_2(x(i), Shoes)]$ |

**Figure 7.27: QE-III Translation of "Who works for a department such that it sells shoes?"**

Is it the case that Peter earns 30K?   *S104*

Is it the case that Peter #earn 30K?   *S101*

Peter #earn 30K

**Figure 7.28: QE-III Derivation of "Is it the case that Peter earns 30K?"**

Does Peter earn 30K?   *S104*

#AUX Peter earn 30K?   *S101*

Peter #earn 30K

**Figure 7.29: QE-III Derivation of "Does Peter earn 30K?"**

**Example 7.10** *Is it the case that Peter earns 30K?*

and

**Example 7.11** *Does Peter earn 30K?*

The two derivation trees are shown in Figures 7.28 and 7.29.
   Both of these questions are formed using one of the operations of rule S101:

**S101. [YNQ Formation]**
$< F_{101a}, < t >, YNQ >$ and  $< F_{101b}, < t >, YNQ >$
$F_{101a}(\phi) = $ #AUX $\phi^*$ where $\phi^*$ is $\phi$ with the *first verbs* unmarked.
$F_{101b}(\phi) = $ "Is it the case that" $\phi$
**T101.**  $F_{101a}(\phi)$ and $F_{101b}(\phi) \implies \phi'$

The two translations are given in Figures 7.30 and 7.31.
   "When" questions are illustrated by the following example

**Example 7.12** *When did Peter earn 25K?*

Peter #earn 30K  $\longrightarrow$  *(as above)* $\exists x[AS-1(Peter, x) \wedge EMP'_*(i)(Peter)$
$\wedge SAL'(i)(x) \wedge x(i) = 30K]$

Is it the case that  $\Longrightarrow$  $\exists x[AS-1(Peter, x) \wedge EMP'_*(i)(Peter) \wedge$
Peter #earn 30K?         $SAL'(i)(x) \wedge x(i) = 30K]$

Is it the case that  $\Longrightarrow$  $\exists x[EMP'_*(i)(Peter) \wedge SAL'(i)(x) \wedge$
Peter earns 30K?         $x(i) = 30K \wedge AS-1(Peter, x)]$

**Figure 7.30: QE-III Translation of "Is it the case that Peter earns 30K?"**

Does Peter earn 30K?  $\Longrightarrow$  $\exists x[EMP'_*(i)(Peter) \wedge SAL'(i)(x) \wedge x(i) = 30K$
$\wedge AS-1(Peter, x)]$

**Figure 7.31: QE-III Translation of "Does Peter earn 30K?"**

which makes use of rule S110:

**S110. [Tensed WHENQ Formation]**
$< F_{110a}, < Tm - Int, PS >, WHENQ >$
$< F_{110b}, < Tm - Int, PS >, WHENQ >$
$< F_{110c}, < Tm - Int, PS >, WHENQ >$
$F_{110a}(\alpha, \phi) \;=\; \alpha$ "does" $\beta^*$

if $\beta$ does not begin with "To," and otherwise
$\alpha$ "and" $\beta$
where $\beta^*$ is $\beta$ with the *first verbs* unmarked.

$F_{110b}(\alpha, \phi) \;=\; \alpha$ "did" $\beta^*$

if $\beta$ does not begin with "To," and otherwise
$\alpha$ "and" $\beta$
where $\beta^*$ is $\beta$ with the *first verbs* unmarked.

$F_{110c}(\alpha, \phi) \;=\; \alpha$ "will" $\beta^*$

if $\beta$ does not begin with "To," and otherwise
$\alpha$ "and" $\beta$
where $\beta^*$ is $\beta$ with the *first verbs* unmarked.

**When did Peter earn 25K?** *S110*

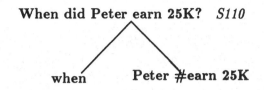

when      Peter #earn 25K

**Figure 7.32: QE-III Derivation of "When did Peter earn 25K?"**

Peter #earn 25K $\qquad \longrightarrow \quad$ *(as above)* $\exists y[AS\text{--}1(Peter,y)\wedge$
$\qquad\qquad\qquad\qquad\qquad\qquad EMP'_*(i)(Peter) \wedge SAL'(i)(y) \wedge y(i) = 25K]$

When did Peter earn $\quad \Longrightarrow \quad \lambda p\lambda i_1[[i_1 < i] \wedge p(i_1)](\lambda i \exists y$
25K? $\qquad\qquad\qquad\qquad [AS\text{--}1(Peter,y) \wedge EMP'_*(i)(Peter)\wedge$
$\qquad\qquad\qquad\qquad SAL'(i)(y) \wedge y(i) = 25K])$

$\qquad\qquad\qquad\quad \longrightarrow \quad \lambda i_1 \exists y[[i_1 < i] \wedge EMP'_*(i_1)(Peter) \wedge SAL'(i_1)(y)$
$\qquad\qquad\qquad\qquad \wedge y(i_1) = 25K \wedge AS\text{--}1(Peter,y)]$

**Figure 7.33: QE-III Translation of "When did Peter earn 25K?"**

**T110.** $\quad F_{110a}(\alpha,\phi) \quad \Longrightarrow \quad \lambda p\lambda i_1[p(i_1)](\lambda i\phi')$
$\qquad\quad F_{110b}(\alpha,\phi) \quad \Longrightarrow \quad \lambda p\lambda i_1[[i_1 < i] \wedge p(i_1)](\lambda i\phi')$
$\qquad\quad F_{110c}(\alpha,\phi) \quad \Longrightarrow \quad \lambda p\lambda i_1[p(i_1)][i < i_1] \wedge p(i_1)](\lambda i\phi')$

The derivation and corresponding translation are given in Figures 7.32 and 7.33.

The next example illustrates the interaction of "when" and an already-formed Term question:

**Example 7.13** *When did who manage whom?*

It is derived as shown in Figure 7.34 and receives the translation shown in Figure 7.35.

Finally, the following example illustrates the introduction of "when" when the first question word is in the dative, and also how "when" questions interact with

**When did who manage whom?** *S110*

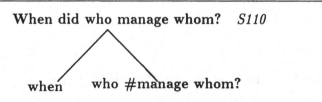

when      who #manage whom?

**Figure 7.34: QE-III Derivation of "When did who manage whom?"**

Who #manage whom?   $\longrightarrow$   $\exists y[EMP'_*(i)(u_2) \wedge y(i) = u_1 \wedge$
$AS\text{--}1(u_2, y) \wedge MGR'(i)(y)]$

When did who manage   $\Longrightarrow$   $\lambda p \lambda i_1[[i_1 < i] \wedge p(i_1)](\lambda i \exists y[EMP'_*(i)(u_2)$
whom?   $\wedge y(i) = u_1 \wedge AS\text{--}1(u_2, y) \wedge MGR'(i)(y)])$
$\longrightarrow$   $\lambda i_1 \exists y[[i_1 < i] \wedge EMP'_*(i_1)(u_2) \wedge MGR'(i_1)(y) \wedge$
$y(i_1) = u_1 \wedge AS\text{--}1(u_2, y)]$

**Figure 7.35: QE-III Translation of "When did who manage whom?"**

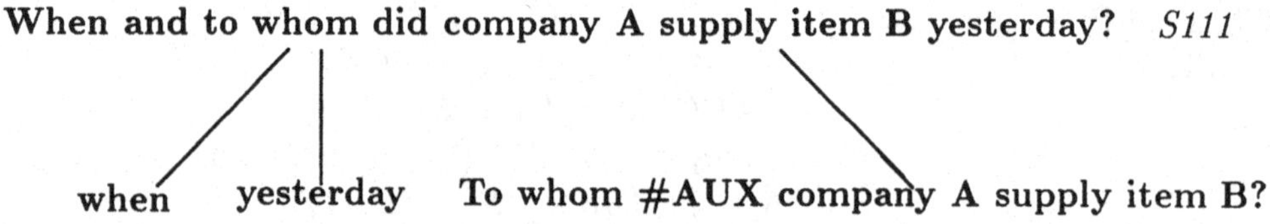

**When and to whom did company A supply item B yesterday?**   *S111*

when   yesterday   To whom #AUX company A supply item B?

**Figure 7.36: QE-III Derivation of "When and to whom did company A supply item B yesterday?"**

time phrases:

**Example 7.14** *When and to whom did company A supply item B yesterday?*

Corresponding to its derivation in Figure 7.36 is the translation of Figure 7.37.

This example uses rule S111:

**S111. [Tensed WHENQ Formation with Specified Time]**
$< F_{111a}, < Tm - Int, Tm, PS >, WHENQ >$
$< F_{111b}, < Tm - Int, Tm, PS >, WHENQ >$
$< F_{111c}, < Tm - Int, Tm, PS >, WHENQ >$

| To whom #AUX company A supply item B? | $\longrightarrow$ | *(as above)* $\exists x[DEPT'_*(i)(u_1) \wedge$ $x(i) = u_1 \wedge COMP'_*(i)(A) \wedge$ $ITEM'_*(i)(B) \wedge REC_3(A(i), B(i), u_1)]$ |
| When and to whom did company A supply item B yesterday? | $\Longrightarrow$ | $\lambda p \lambda i_1[[i_1 < i] \wedge yesterday'(i_1) \wedge p(i_1)]$ $(\lambda i \exists x[DEPT'_*(i)(u_1) \wedge x(i) = u_1 \wedge COMP'_*(i)(A)$ $\wedge ITEM'_*(i)(B) \wedge REC_3(A(i), B(i), u_1)])$ |
| | $\longrightarrow$ | $\lambda i_1 \exists x[[i_1 < i] \wedge yesterday'(i_1) \wedge$ $DEPT'_*(i_1)(u_1) \wedge x(i_1) = u_1 \wedge COMP'_*(i_1)(A) \wedge$ $ITEM'_*(i_1)(B) \wedge REC_3(A(i), B(i), u_1)]$ |

**Figure 7.37: QE-III Translation of "When and to whom did company A supply item B yesterday?"**

$$F_{111a}(\alpha, \beta, \phi) = \alpha\beta \text{ "does" } \phi^*$$

if $\phi$ does not begin with "To," and

$\alpha\beta$ "and" $\phi$ otherwise,

where $\phi^*$ is $\phi$ with the *first verbs* unmarked.

$$F_{111b}(\alpha, \beta, \phi) = \alpha\beta \text{ "did" } \phi^*$$

if $\phi$ does not begin with "To," and

$\alpha\beta$ "and" $\phi$ otherwise,

where $\phi^*$ is $\phi$ with the *first verbs* unmarked.

$$F_{111c}(\alpha, \beta, \phi) = \alpha\beta \text{ "will" } \phi^*$$

if $\phi$ does not begin with "to," and

$\alpha\beta$ "and" $\phi$ otherwise,

where $\phi^*$ is $\phi$ with the *first verbs* unmarked.

**T111.** 
$$F_{111a}(\alpha, \beta, \phi) \implies \lambda p \lambda i_1[\beta'(i_1) \wedge p(i_1)](\lambda i \phi')$$
$$F_{111b}(\alpha, \beta, \phi) \implies \lambda p \lambda i_1[[i_1 < i] \wedge \beta'(i_1) \wedge p(i_1)](\lambda i \phi')$$
$$F_{111c}(\alpha, \beta, \phi) \implies \lambda p \lambda i_1[[i < i_1] \wedge \beta'(i_1) \wedge p(i_1)](\lambda i \phi')$$

This concludes the examples of the kinds of queries expressible in the language QE-III, and the semantics and pragmatics that the fragment provides for them. We now present some of the other additions we have made to the PTQ fragment in order to express certain other common query constructions.

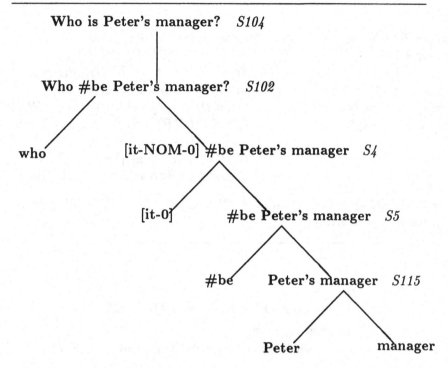

**Figure 7.38: QE-III Derivation of "Who is Peter's manager?"**

## 7.5   Miscellaneous Features of QE-III

The use of possessives is very common in database queries, and is easily incorporated into the fragment as the following rules and examples indicate:

**Example 7.15** *Who is Peter's manager?*

derived as in Figure 7.38.

The phrase "Peter's manager" is formed by the following rule:

**S115. [Possessive Formation]**
$< F_{115}, < T >, DET >$
$F_{115}(\alpha) = \alpha\text{"'s"}$
**T115.** $F_{115}(\alpha) \implies \lambda W \lambda P \lambda Q \exists x[P(i)(x) \wedge Q(i)(x) \wedge$
$\qquad\qquad\qquad W(i)[\lambda i \lambda y AS{-}1(y(i), x)]](\lambda i \alpha')$

The resulting sentence is translated as in Figure 7.39.

An alternative way of phrasing the above question uses "of" instead of the possessive marker:

**Example 7.16** *Who is a manager of Peter?*

| | | |
|---|---|---|
| Peter's | $\implies$ | $\lambda W \lambda P \lambda Q \exists x [P(i)(x) \wedge Q(i)(x) \wedge W(i)$ $[\lambda i \lambda y AS{-}1(y(i), x)]](\lambda i \lambda P \exists y [P(i)(y) \wedge$ $y(i) = Peter])$ |
| | $\longrightarrow$ | $\lambda P \lambda Q \exists x [P(i)(x) \wedge Q(i)(x) \wedge$ $\exists y [AS{-}1(y(i), x) \wedge y(i) = Peter]]$ |
| Peter's manager | $\implies$ | $\lambda P \lambda Q \exists x [P(i)(x) \wedge Q(i)(x) \wedge$ $\exists y [AS{-}1(y(i), x) \wedge y(i) = Peter]]$ $(\lambda i MGR'(i))$ |
| | $\longrightarrow$ | $\lambda Q \exists x [MGR'(i)(x) \wedge Q(i)(x) \wedge$ $\exists y [AS{-}1(y(i), x) \wedge y(i) = Peter]]$ |
| #be | $\implies$ | $\lambda W \lambda z_1 W(i)(\lambda i \lambda z_2 [z_1(i) = z_2(i)])$ |
| #be Peter's manager | $\implies$ | $\lambda W \lambda z_1 W(i)(\lambda i \lambda z_2 [z_1(i) = z_2(i)])$ $(\lambda i \lambda Q \exists x [MGR'(i)(x) \wedge Q(i)(x) \wedge$ $\exists y [AS{-}1(y(i), x) \wedge y(i) = Peter]])$ |
| | $\longrightarrow$ | $\lambda z_1 \exists x [MGR'(i)(x) \wedge [z_1(i) = x(i)]] \wedge$ $\exists y [AS{-}1(y(i), x) \wedge y(i) = Peter]])$ |
| [it-NOM-0] #be Peter's manager | $\longrightarrow$ | $(as\,above)\ \exists x [MGR'(i)(x) \wedge [x_0(i) = x(i)]]$ $\wedge \exists y [AS{-}1(y(i), x) \wedge y(i) = Peter]])$ |
| | $\longrightarrow$ | $\exists x [MGR'(i)(x) \wedge [x_0(i) = x(i)] \wedge$ $AS{-}1(Peter, x)]$ |
| who | $\implies$ | $\lambda P \exists y [y(i) = u \wedge P(i)(y)]$ |
| Who is Peter's manager | $\implies$ | $\lambda P \exists y [y(i) = u \wedge P(i)(y)]$ $(\lambda i \lambda x_0 \exists x [MGR'(i)(x) \wedge [x_0(i) = x(i)] \wedge$ $AS{-}1(Peter, x)])$ |
| | $\longrightarrow$ | $\exists x [MGR'(i)(x) \wedge x(i) = u \wedge AS{-}1(Peter, x)]$ |

**Figure 7.39: QE-III Translation of "Who is Peter's manager?"**

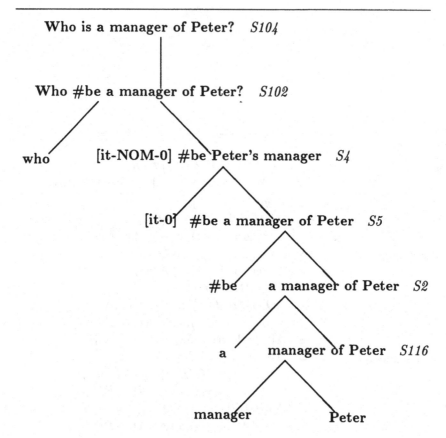

**Figure 7.40: QE-III Derivation of "Who is a manager of Peter?"**

This sentence makes use of Rule S116:

**S116. [Attributive Phrase Formation]**
$< F_{116}, < CN, T >, CN >$
$F_{116}(\alpha, \beta) = \alpha$ "of" $\beta$
**T116.** $F_{116}(\alpha\beta) \implies \lambda x \beta'(\lambda i \lambda y[\alpha'(x) \wedge AS{-}1(y(i), x)])$

Its derivation in QE-III is shown in Figure 7.40, and it ultimately receives the same translation, Figure 7.41.

Note that what might be considered an *equivalent* query in English,

**Example 7.17** *Who manages Peter?*

would be translated as:

$$\exists z[EMP'_*(i)(Peter) \wedge MGR'(i)(z) \wedge z(i) = u \wedge AS{-}1(Peter, z)]$$

| | | |
|---|---|---|
| manager of Peter | $\implies$ | $\lambda x \lambda P \exists y[P(i)(y) \wedge y(i) = Peter]$ |
| | | $(\lambda i \lambda z MGR'(i)(x) \wedge AS\text{--}1(z(i), x))$ |
| | $\longrightarrow$ | $\lambda x \exists y[MGR'(i)(x) \wedge AS\text{--}1(y(i), x) \wedge y(i) = Peter]$ |
| a manager of Peter | $\longrightarrow$ | $\lambda Q \exists z[Q(i)(z) \wedge \exists y[MGR'(i)(z) \wedge$ |
| | | $AS\text{--}1(y(i), z) \wedge y(i) = Peter]]$ |
| #be a manager of | $\longrightarrow$ | $\lambda z_1 \lambda Q \exists z[Q(i)(z) \wedge \exists y[MGR'(i)(z) \wedge$ |
| Peter | | $AS\text{--}1(y(i), z) \wedge y(i) = Peter]])(\lambda i \lambda z_2[z_1(i) = z_2(i)])$ |
| | $\longrightarrow$ | $\lambda z_1 \exists z[[z_1(i) = z(i)] \wedge \exists y[MGR'(i)(z) \wedge AS\text{--}1(y(i), z)$ |
| | | $\wedge y(i) = Peter]]$ |
| [it-NOM-0] #be a | $\longrightarrow$ | $\exists z[[x_0(i) = z(i)] \wedge \exists y[MGR'(i)(z) \wedge AS\text{--}1(y(i), z) \wedge$ |
| manager of Peter | | $y(i) = Peter]]$ |
| Who is a manager | $\longrightarrow$ | $\exists x[x(i) = u \wedge \exists z[[x(i) = z(i)] \wedge \exists y[MGR'(i)(z) \wedge$ |
| of Peter | | $AS\text{--}1(y(i), z) \wedge y(i) = Peter]])$ |
| | $\longrightarrow$ | $\exists z[z(i) = u \wedge MGR'(i)(z) \wedge AS\text{--}1(Peter, z)]$ |

**Figure 7.41: QE-III Translation of "Who is a manager of Peter?"**

The difference between the translations of 7.15 and 7.16, on the one hand, and of 7.17, on the other, is that in these two examples no role (attribute) is specified for Peter. This is because the *neutral* verb "#be" is unable to specify the roles of its subject and object as the verb "#manage" can. This sort of situation could be rectified by means of a meaning postulate that, in this case, would specify the possible roles for an entity that *had* (was associated with) an IC that was a MGR (in this case only an EMPloyee can have a MGR.)

Roles can also be specified by means of the word "as":

**Example 7.18** *Who has Peter as manager?*

derived as in Figure 7.42.

The rule for this kind of construction is the following:

**S117. [Role Specification for Term (I)]**
$< F_{117}, < T, CN >, T >$
$F_{117}(\alpha, \beta) = \alpha$ "as" $\beta$
**T117.** $F_{117}(\alpha, \beta) \implies \lambda P \alpha'[\lambda i \lambda y[P(i)(y) \wedge \beta'(y)]]$

This example, whose translation is shown in Figure 7.43, also illustrates the general translation for the verb "#have."

A final form of role-specification in database queries takes the form of simple concatenation of the role and a Term, as illustrated in this example:

**Example 7.19** *Who sells item 37?*

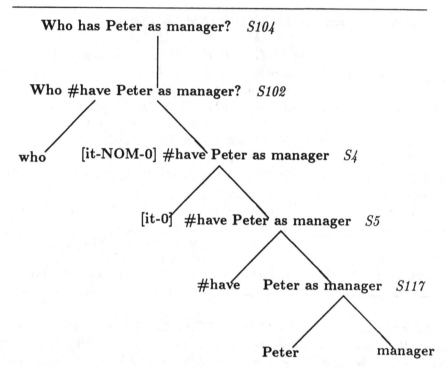

**Who has Peter as manager?**   *S104*

**Who #have Peter as manager?**   *S102*

who        [it-NOM-0] #have Peter as manager   *S4*

[it-0]   #have Peter as manager   *S5*

#have     Peter as manager   *S117*

Peter                 manager

**Figure 7.42: QE-III Derivation of "Who has Peter as manager?"**

| Peter as manager | $\Longrightarrow$ | $\lambda Q(\lambda P \exists x[P(i)(x) \wedge x(i) = Peter](\lambda i \lambda y Q(i)(y) \wedge MGR'(i)(y)))$ |
|---|---|---|
| | $\longrightarrow$ | $\lambda Q \exists x[Q(i)(x) \wedge MGR'(i)(x) \wedge x(i) = Peter]$ |
| #have | $\Longrightarrow$ | $\lambda W \lambda x[W(i)(\lambda i \lambda y[AS\text{--}1(x(i), y)]]$ |
| #have Peter as manager | $\longrightarrow$ | $\lambda x \lambda Q \exists z[Q(i)(z) \wedge MGR'(i)(z) \wedge z(i) = Peter]$ $(\lambda i \lambda y[AS\text{--}1(x(i), y)]) \lambda x \exists z$ $[AS\text{--}1(x(i), z) \wedge MGR'(i)(z) \wedge z(i) = Peter]$ |
| [it-NOM-0] #have Peter as manager | $\longrightarrow$ | $\exists z[AS\text{--}1(x_0(i), z) \wedge MGR'(i)(z) \wedge z(i) = Peter]$ |
| Who has Peter as manager | $\longrightarrow$ | $\exists z[MGR'(i)(z) \wedge z(i) = Peter \wedge AS\text{--}1(u, z)]$ |

**Figure 7.43: QE-III Translation of "Who has Peter as manager?"**

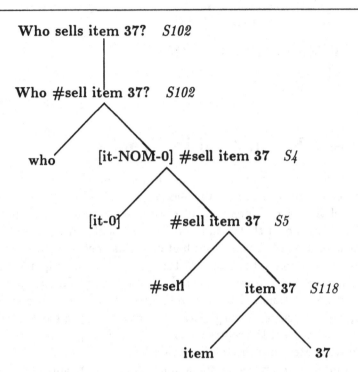

**Figure 7.44: QE-III Derivation of "Who sells item 37?"**

| item | $\Longrightarrow$ | $\lambda W \lambda Q W(i)[\lambda i \lambda y[Q(i)(y) \wedge ITEM'_*(i)(y(i))]]$ |
|---|---|---|
| 37 | $\Longrightarrow$ | $\lambda P \exists x[P(i)(x) \wedge x(i) = 37]$ |
| item 37 | $\Longrightarrow$ | $\lambda W \lambda Q W(i)[\lambda i \lambda y[Q(i)(y) \wedge ITEM'_*(i)(y(i))]]$ |
| | | $(\lambda i \lambda P \exists x[P(i)(x) \wedge x(i) = 37])$ |
| | $\longrightarrow$ | $\lambda Q \exists x[Q(i)(x) \wedge ITEM'_*(i)(x(i)) \wedge x(i) = 37]$ |
| #sell | $\Longrightarrow$ | $\lambda W \lambda x[W(i)(\lambda i \lambda y[REC_2(x(i), y(i)) \wedge$ |
| | | $DEPT'_*(i)(x(i)) \wedge ITEM'_*(i)(y(i))])]$ |
| #sell item 37 | $\longrightarrow$ | $\lambda x[REC_2(x(i), 37) \wedge DEPT'_*(i)(x(i)) \wedge$ |
| | | $ITEM'_*(i)(37)]$ |
| [it-NOM-0] #sell item 37 | $\longrightarrow$ | $REC_2(x_0(i), 37) \wedge DEPT'_*(i)(x_0(i)) \wedge$ |
| | | $ITEM'_*(i)(37)$ |
| Who sells item 37? | $\longrightarrow$ | $(asabove)\ DEPT'_*(i)(u) \wedge ITEM'_*(i)(37)$ |
| | | $\wedge REC_2(u, 37)$ |

**Figure 7.45: QE-III translation of "Who sells item 37?"**

Its derivation tree is in Figure 7.44, and its corresponding translation in Figure 7.45. Rule S118 provides for this construction:

**S118. [Role Specification for Term (II)]**
$< F_{118}^{RC}, < T/T, T >, T >$
**T118.** function application

## 7.6   Query Evaluation in Practice

The evaluation of the translations of English queries into $IL_s$ is given formally by the definition of the pragmatics for the sentences of QE-III and by the definition of the semantics of the logic. Moreover, since we have provided in Chapter 4 a formal definition of the $IL_s$ model that is induced by a given HRDB, this constitutes a full and complete definition of the query evaluation. This does not, however, address the problem of how to *compute* the result of the query. It is anticipated that a QE-III fragment might serve as the front end to an implementation of a relational HRDB that is equipped with a relational algebra or relational calculus interpreter for querying. This section, then, discusses through examples how the pragmatic interpretation of QE-III queries, in terms of the representation of that interpretation as expressions of $IL_s$, could be translated into the relational algebra.

In these examples we are using the symbol "$\Longrightarrow$" to mean, not that the query translates to the indicated logical expression, but rather that the logical expression represents the pragmatic interpretation of the query in question. The logical expression is the result of the translation, plus logical simplifications, plus the pragmatic effect of binding the free time variable $i$ to the constant **now**, and $\lambda$-abstracting over any free individual variables (introduced by WH-Terms.) Evaluating the indicated logical expression in the model induced by the database instance would result in the answer to the query.

We illustrate the process of translating pragmatic interpretations into the relational algebra by means of examples chosen from those used in the earlier sections of this chapter to illustrate the syntax and semantics of QE-III. Each example is numbered as before, and is followed by both its pragmatic interpretation and its translation into the relational algebra. After a few such examples, a sketch of an algorithm that could effect this translation is offered.

**Example 7.1**
**Pragmatic Interpretation:**

John manages Mary $\quad\Longrightarrow\quad \exists y[EMP_*'(now)(Mary) \wedge MGR'(now)(y)$
$\wedge y(now) = John \wedge AS{-}1(Mary, y)]$

**Algebraic Translation:**

$$(\sigma{-}IF_{(EMP\,=\,Mary, MGR\,=\,John), \exists, T}(T_{@now}(emprel))) \neq \emptyset$$

### Example 7.2
**Pragmatic Interpretation:**

Peter earned 25K $\implies$ $\exists i_1 \exists y [1978'(i_1) \wedge [i_1 < i] \wedge EMP_*'(i_1)(Peter) \wedge$
in 1978 $SAL'(i_1)(y) \wedge y(i_1) = 25K \wedge AS\text{-}1(Peter, y)]$

**Algebraic Translation:**

$$(\sigma\text{-}IF_{(EMP\ =\ Peter, SAL\ =\ 25K), \exists, T}\ (\mathcal{T}_{@T\cap 1978}(emprel))) \neq \emptyset$$

### Example 7.3
**Pragmatic Interpretation:**

Peter manages an $\implies$ $\exists w \exists x \exists y \exists i_1 [EMP'(now)(x(now)) \wedge MGR'(now)(w) \wedge$
employee such $w(now) = Peter \wedge AS\text{-}1(x(now), w) \wedge$
that he $EMP_*'(i_1)(x(now)) \wedge SAL'(i_1)(y) \wedge y(i_1) = 30K \wedge$
earned 30K $1978'(i_1) \wedge [i_1 < i] \wedge AS\text{-}1(x(now), w)]$

**Algebraic Translation:**

$(\sigma\text{-}IF_{(EMP\text{-}1\ =\ EMP\text{-}2, MGR\text{-}1\ =\ Peter, SAL\text{-}2\ =\ 30K), \exists, T}$
$(\mathcal{T}_{@now}(emprel) \times \mathcal{T}_{@before\text{-}now}(emprel))) \neq \emptyset$

where *before $-$ now* was defined as the set of all times prior to the present. Note also the (standard) renaming of attributes that is required if a cross-product of a relation with itself is indicated.

### Example 7.4
**Pragmatic Interpretation:**

John worked before $\implies$ $\exists i_1 [[i_1 << (\lambda i_2 EMP_*'(i_2)(Mary))] \wedge$
Mary worked $[i_2 < i] \wedge [i_1 < i] \wedge EMP_*'(i_1)(John)]$

**Algebraic Translation:**

$t_J = \omega(\sigma\text{-}WHEN_{EMP\ =\ John}(emprel)) \wedge$
$t_M = \omega(\sigma\text{-}WHEN_{EMP\ =\ Mary}\ (\mathcal{T}_{@before\text{-}now}(emprel))) \wedge$
$\exists t \in t_J [t < t_M]$

This is one of many ways to express this query algebraically. Note the nesting of the *when* subquery as a parameter to the time-slice of the emp relation, and the necessity for a compound algebraic expression, occasioned by the nested subclause in the English query.

### Example 7.5
**Pragmatic Interpretation:**

Rachel worked before yesterday $\implies$ $\exists i_1 [[i_1 << yesterday'(now)] \wedge [i_1 < i] \wedge$
$EMP_*'(i_1)(Rachel)]$

**Algebraic Translation:**

$$(\sigma\text{--}IF_{(EMP \,=\, Rachel),\exists,T}(\mathcal{T}_{T\cap yesterday}(emprel))) \neq \emptyset$$

**Example 7.6**
**Pragmatic Interpretation:**

Who managed Rachel? $\implies$ $\lambda u\,\exists i_1 \exists y[[i_1 < i] \wedge EMP'_*(i_1)(Rachel)\wedge$
$MGR'(i_1)(y) \wedge y(i_1) = u\wedge$
$AS\text{--}1(Rachel, y)]$

**Algebraic Translation:**

$$\pi_{MGR}(\sigma\text{--}IF_{(EMP \,=\, Rachel),\exists,T}\,(\mathcal{T}_{@before-now}(emprel)))$$

**Example 7.6**
**Pragmatic Interpretation:**

Who manages which $\implies$ $\lambda u_2 \lambda u_1 \exists y[EMP'_*(now)(u_2) \wedge MGR'(now)(y)\wedge$
employees?               $y(now) = u_1 \wedge AS\text{--}1(u_2, y)]$

**Algebraic Translation:**

$$\pi_{MGR,EMP}(\mathcal{T}_{@now}(emprel))$$

**Example 7.8**
**Pragmatic Interpretation:**

What does who supply $\implies$ $\lambda u_3 \lambda u_2 \lambda u_1 COMP'_*(now)(u_3) \wedge DEPT'_*(now)(u_2)\wedge$
to whom              $ITEM'_*(now)(u_1) \wedge REC_3(u_3, u_2, u_1)$

**Algebraic Translation:**

$$\pi_{COMP,DEPT,ITEM}(\mathcal{T}_{@now}\,(supplyrel))$$

**Example 7.9**
**Pragmatic Interpretation:**

who works-for a department $\implies$ $\lambda u\exists x[EMP'_*(now)(u) \wedge DEPT'_*(now)(x(now))\wedge$
such that it sells shoes       $AS\text{--}1(u, x) \wedge ITEM'_*(now)(Shoes)\wedge$
                        $REC_2(x(now), Shoes)]$

**Algebraic Translation:**

$$\pi_{EMP}(\sigma\text{--}IF_{(DEPT-1 \,=\, DEPT-2,ITEM \,=\, Shoes),\exists,T}$$
$$(\mathcal{T}_{@now}(emprel) \,\times\, \mathcal{T}_{@now}(salesrel)))$$

**Example 7.11**
**Pragmatic Interpretation:**

Does Peter earn 30K? $\implies$ $\exists x[EMP'_*(now)(Peter) \wedge SAL'(now)(x) \wedge$
$$x(now) = 30K \wedge AS{-}1(Peter, x)]$$

**Algebraic Translation:**

$$(\sigma{-}IF_{(EMP = Peter, SAL = 30K), \exists, T}(\mathcal{T}_{@now}(emprel))) \neq \emptyset$$

## Example 7.12
**Pragmatic Interpretation:**

When did Peter earn $\implies$ $\lambda i_1 \exists y[[i_1 < i] \wedge EMP'_*(i_1)(Peter) \wedge SAL'(i_1)(y)$
25K? $\wedge y(i_1) = 25K \wedge AS{-}1(Peter, y)]$

**Algebraic Translation:**

$$\omega(\sigma{-}WHEN_{EMP = Peter, SAL = 25K}(emprel))$$

Note that simple when-questions do not actually return a database *relation* but rather a lifespan.

## Example 7.13
**Pragmatic Interpretation:**

When did who manage $\implies$ $\lambda i_1 \lambda u_2 \lambda u_1 \exists y[[i_1 < i] \wedge EMP'(i_1)(u_2) \wedge$
whom $MGR'(i_1)(y) \wedge y(i_1) = u_1 \wedge AS{-}1(u_2, y)]$

**Algebraic Translation:**

$$\pi_{EMP, MGR}(\mathcal{T}_{@before-now}(emprel))$$

## Example 7.15
**Pragmatic Interpretation:**

Who is Peter's manager $\implies$ $\lambda u \exists x[MGR'(now)(x) \wedge x(now) = u \wedge$
$AS{-}1(Peter, x)]$

**Algebraic Translation:**

$$\pi_{MGR}(\sigma{-}IF_{(EMP = Peter), \exists, T}(\mathcal{T}_{@now}(emprel)))$$

Note that the attribute EMP has to be determined from certain information; this would be done by means of an application-specific Meaning Postulate that would specify what sort of individual could be associated ($AS{-}1$) with manager-IC.

## Example 7.18
**Pragmatic Interpretation:**

Who has Peter $\implies$ $\lambda u \exists z[MGR'(now)(z) \wedge z(now) = Peter \wedge AS{-}1(u, z)]$
as manager

**Algebraic Translation:**

$$\pi_{EMP}(\sigma{-}IF_{(MGR = Peter), \exists, T}(\mathcal{T}_{@now}(emprel)))$$

**Example 7.19**
**Pragmatic Interpretation:**

Who sells item 37?   $\implies$   $\lambda u DEPT'_*(now)(u) \wedge ITEM'_*(now)(37)$
$\qquad\qquad\qquad\qquad\qquad \wedge REC_2(u, 37)$

**Algebraic Translation:**

$$\pi_{DEPT}(\sigma{-}IF_{(ITEM\ =\ 37),\exists,T}(\mathcal{T}_{@now}\ (salesrel)))$$

Omitting some details (particularly those for handling nested clauses), the basic procedure for effecting this translation is outlined in the following four steps. Because of the way in which we have encoded the database into the logical model, we are assuming a unique connection between (or among) attributes related in a relationship or association. Without this assumption the logical formulas would essentially consist of a series of disjuncts of the possible interpretations, and this translation procedure would have to be revised accordingly. More work needs to be done on defining formally the precise class of expressions in $IL_s$ into which QE-III expressions translate before implementing an algorithm for this translation into the relational algebra.

1. For each term involving an $AC_n$, or an $REC_n$, find the attributes of the $n$ individuals in the association. Replace the associating term with the relation name that associates these attributes.

2. Form the expression for the cross-product of all of these relations, time-sliced at the *appropriate* times (i.e., the times mentioned in the query).

3. For each individual constant $c$ appearing in these terms, Select-IF the indicated attribute and value from the relation cross-product.

4. Finally, depending upon the syntactic category (in QE-III) of the query, perform one of the following:

   (a) for WH questions, take the projection of the resulting expression onto all $\lambda$-bound variables.

   (b) for when questions, take the "when" ($\omega$) of the resulting expression.

   (c) for yes-no questions, set the resulting expression equal to $\emptyset$.

## 7.7   Conclusion

The problem of modelling the semantics of time is one which is beginning to be explored by researchers in a number of different areas of Computer Science ([Sno86] summarizes much of the recent work in the area). We believe that formal logic can make an important contribution to our understanding and specification of the properties of time that we with to incorporate into our models and systems. Using the logic IL, and the framework of MS, we have presented in this work the essential components of the HRDM model, which is a formalization of the concept of a historical database. HRDM provides for the storage of historical information, the specification of constraints on the way that information can change over time, and a query language for accessing that information with specific reference to its temporal dimension.

To augment the relational query language of HRDM, we have also described a formal English database query language, QE-III, which is defined in a MS framework. QE-III incorporates an account of question semantics that accords with the semantics of HRDM, an account of the semantics of multiple-WH questions, an account of the semantics of time, and a grammar that is conducive to a computer implementation. In addition to its formal syntax and parallel semantics, QE-III is provided with a formal pragmatic component which provides a representation for the answer(s) to a question as a function of its syntax and semantics. We believe that this approach, and the whole area of *formal* pragmatics as a component of language theory, is a fertile area for further research.

# CHAPTER EIGHT

# SUMMARY AND CONCLUSIONS

## 8.1  Summary

### 8.1.1  The Historical Relational Database Model

Under the general assumption that in any scientific enterprise the development of a formal logical theory is a fruitful endeavor, we have attempted in this work to develop such formal theories for the incorporation of a temporal component into a database model, and for the specification of an English query language facility for such a database. Because of the power of the logical formalism of IL developed by Richard Montague [Mon74] we have been able to express both of these theories in terms of the same logical apparatus. Thus two areas which may have seemed only marginally related at the outset were seen to have a closer connection.

Beginning first with formalizing a historical database model, we presented the model HRDM. This model turned out to be a simple extension to an entity-relationship semantics imposed upon the relational database model. The temporal component was included in a very simple but fundamental way as a basic component of the model, and its significance from both the informal, intuitive view of three-dimensional relations extending in both directions of time, and from the formal, model-theoretic view, were discussed. In order to present as general a model of time as possible, we put only the barest of constraints upon the temporal dimension – linear order and density.

The HRDM model was seen as providing a number of insights into the nature of a database and how it functions as a model of the real world. Chief among these were the identification of the database concept of a *key* with the logical idea of an *individual concept* with constant denotation, and of *non-keys* with unconstrained *individual concepts*. The notion of temporal dependencies was explored as an analog to the more familiar functional dependencies of database theory. Certain classes of assumptions were identified that had to be made in order to relate the finite database

173

representation of *facts in time* with the underlying model of time as infinite and dense. Finally various capabilities afforded by the inclusion of a temporal component directly in the database model were discussed and illustrated.

## 8.1.2   The Language QE-III

In the second half of the book we turned our attention to the problem of a formal definition of an English database query language. Again the basis for the theory that we developed was the work of Richard Montague and others working within the framework of the field that has come to be known as Montague Grammar. The contributions of our investigations into this problem are several. In the first place they represent the first attempt to adapt the theory of Montague Grammar to a practical problem. Our results in this respect are modest; a grammar for the language we defined has been implemented [Has82], but the coverage of that language needs significant extension before it could serve as a working query system. Nevertheless we are still convinced that formally specified languages within this kind of logical framework should be the goal of a computer-science approach to this problem.

Our formulation of the query fragment QE-III incorporates three major extensions to the syntactic and semantic components of the PTQ fragment. The first of these is the concept of verb analysis, involving a decomposition of the semantics of verbs into smaller primitive functions defined by the database scheme. This approach, common in Artificial Intelligence approaches to natural language processing, is new to the field of Montague Grammar (but see [Dow79] for related work on *lexical rules* for word analysis) and represents an interesting point of common meeting ground for two fields which have not, in general, looked with favor upon one another. An extension of the treatment of tense and time-denoting expressions is also included in the QE-III. In order to accommodate the treatment that we propose, which allows for direct reference in English to time, we defined the logic IL$_s$, a simple extension to Montague's IL based upon Gallin's Ty$_2$ [Gal75]. The use of this logic also was shown to eliminate some of the confusion in the treatment of indexical expressions in the PTQ fragment's use of IL. Finally the major extension involved the addition of a theory of direct questions in the context of a question-answering system.

We believe that the theory of question interpretation presented in this book is one of its most important contributions. The formal definition of QE-III is presented as a complete semiotic theory, encompassing a syntax, semantics, and pragmatics. Small as the pragmatic component is, we feel that its inclusion raises important questions for the field of natural language analysis. We hope that it will encourage new discussion as to the role of pragmatics in a formal language theory. The pragmatic theory of questions that we offer is quite simple, but it relieves the semantics of a terrific burden. Several examples of this burden were presented in our discussion of this issue, and the simplicity of the pragmatics we present was offered as its major virtue. Under this theory questions denote propositions just as declarative sentences do. The semantic theory is allowed to remain that, namely a theory of reference or denotation. The pragmatic component, using both the syntactic and the semantic analyses, assigns its interpretation of the question based upon its (pragmatic) understanding of *the purpose of the utterance.* Clearly within the context of a database query system the questioner wants the answer; under our theory it is the pragmatics which provides it. Thus the derivation tree (syntax), the denotation (semantics), and the answer (pragmatics) all contribute to the formal analysis of the utterance, in quest of further capturing its elusive *meaning.*

## 8.2 Future Work

### 8.2.1 Time and Databases

The historical database model (HRDM) that we have presented suggests a number of interesting areas for further research. Chief among these is the issue of implementation; database theories are almost inevitably, and quite properly, judged by their practicality. Obviously the picture of each historical relation as a fully specified cube is an idealization. Even if all of the information in the cube were known, a direct implementation would be highly redundant. Furthermore, there may be situations in which the complete history of some attributes may be unknown or uninteresting to the enterprise. Questions of how to implement these relations efficiently, both for storage and retrieval, and of how to handle a mixture of static and historical relations within a single database are among the many interesting implementation questions that remain to be studied.

Since this work was first reported ([CW83]) several additional proposals for extending the relational data model to incorporate the temporal dimension of data have appeared in the literature. These proposals have differed considerably in the way that the temporal dimension has been incorporated both into the structure of the extended relations that are defined as part of these extended model, and into the operations of the extended relational algebra or calculus component of the models. Because of these differences it has been difficult to compare the proposed models and to make judgements as to which of them is *better* or indeed, the *best.* In [CC88b] we propose a notion of historical relational completeness, analogous to Codd's notion of relational completeness, and examine several historical relational proposals in light of this standard.

Although we have incorporated our historical model in terms of the relational model of data with an entity-relationship semantics, the question of how to embed a historical component formally into other models is another area for study. The hierarchical [IMS], network [Gro71] and functional [Shi81] models have all received attention in the database literature and within the database community, and techniques for incorporating a semantics of time within them should be explored. Even within the relational model, the question of other semantic restrictions on the kinds of relations that make sense, within the context of a formalized temporal semantics, is still wide open for future study.

The idea of using a database to model such hypothetical situations as potential futures from a given present situation, and thus provide the ability to answer questions about the implications of such *possible worlds*, is another expansion of the HRDM model that appears to offer promising applications. The query suggested early in our informal discussion of the model, "Will the average salary in the linen department surpass 30K within the next 5 years?" is the sort of question that we envisage could be handled by such an extension. Salary raises built into union contracts, automatic cost-of-living increases, projections of expenditures based upon the expected rate of inflation, etc., are the sorts of applications that a historical database ought to be able to model. (Recent work in [TK89] explored techniques for using both a historical database and *rules* describing the behavior of the enterprise to predict future behavior; earlier work in [SK80] provides an examination of some of these possibilities from a somewhat different perspective.)

In the simple model that we have proposed, existence is synonymous with belonging to an entity set, and we have not allowed an entity to be of more than one sort. An extension to this model would allow entities to fill different (even multiple) roles at various times, as long as they still existed as entities in some *base* or *defining* relation. For example, a particular application, perhaps an expert system, might want to model people with a relation on scheme

PERSON(**NAME** GENDER ... )

and then have relations on schemes like
BORROWER(**NAME** ACCT-NUM ... ) and
DEPOSITOR(**NAME** ACCT-NUM ... ).

People could fill the roles of depositor and borrower in any state at will, provided that state was in their lifespan in the PERSON relation. Meaning Postulates could assert the IS-A hierarchy in the usual manner (BORROWER IS-A PERSON, etc.) and with what appear to be only minor changes in our scheme for encoding a historical database into a logical model the present HRDM approach seems to work and to offer interesting insights into the semantics of this sort of database model.

Another important area that needs more analysis is the nature of the time coordinate in the HRDM model. Such issues as the kinds of constraints that particular applications may wish to make upon the very general treatment that we have defined, strategies for encoding time values and translating from names of times provided by casual users into their (nearest) equivalents in the database representation scheme need to be considered. Allowing more sophisticated Continuity Assumptions, different assumptions for different attributes, modifications to the Comprehension Principle, conceiving of time not as moments but as partitioned into intervals, etc. are also among the many issues relating to temporal semantics in databases that have only begun to be explored.

In this work we have explored how the logical notion of *intension* – in particular Montague's formalization of this concept – can be incorporated into an extended *relational* data model to provide both a coherent and complete view of the temporal semantics of data, as well as a formally-based approach to natural language database querying. In a recent paper [CC88a] we have begun to explore how this same approach can be incorporated into the emerging object-oriented model of database management.

Finally with respect to the database issues, we note the growing interest in expanding the modelling capabilities of existing data models. These efforts, which include the so-called *semantic data models* (e.g. [SS76], [HM78], and [BN78]), proposals for *Knowledge-Based Management Systems* (e.g. [BM86] and [Fro86]), and more recently *Object-Oriented Database Systems* ([Loc85] [CC88a] and [Ozs88]) discuss the need for more powerful database models or languages in order to specify a database semantics that more closely models the complex objects and relationships of the real world. We agree wholeheartedly with this goal, but view with some apprehension the proliferation of so-called Semantic Data Definition Languages (SDDLs) that are nor provided with a formal semantics. While we would not claim that IL$_s$ is the only solution for presenting a clear database semantics, we do believe strongly that an intensional logic like IL$_s$ can serve as a much-needed *lingua franca* in which to compare these higher-level semantic models and languages, and even to provide a basis for constructing proofs that demonstrate their equivalence or differences.

An analogous situation is occurring in the field of Artificial Intelligence, which is witnessing the same proliferation of Knowledge Representation Languages (KRLs): frames [Min75], KRL [BW77], Prolog [Kow79], RLL [GL80], to name only a few. Considerable discussion and often heated arguments have ensued over which language is better. Hayes' *In Defence of Logic* expresses much the same sentiment that we have presented here [Hay77], arguing that logic can serve as a universal tool for clarity and comparison.

Naturally, until the semantics and pragmatics of natural languages are more completely understood, artificial languages such as these SDDLs, clearly more user-oriented than the equally artificial language IL$_s$, are the appropriate kind of vehicle for users to express their database semantics. But we believe that unless these languages are provided with a formal model-theoretic semantics (and possibly pragmatics), there will be no basis for making informed judgements about the expressive power of the languages as a whole, or about the accuracy (or even the precise meaning) of particular statements in these languages.

## 8.2.2 Formalized Natural Query Languages

We believe that our work in providing a formal definition for the semiotics of the query language QE-III demonstrates that Montague's theory of natural languages can be applied to the practical problem of database querying. Naturally we recognize that much more work needs to be done in order to extend the coverage of this language to a point where it could be useable in a real system. For example, a significantly more sophisticated syntactic treatment of questions in English than the one we have provided here would be needed. And many extensions, such as the addition of *list questions* ("Tell me the name, salary, and age of every ..."), aggregate functions ("What is the average salary of ..."), and the simple ability to ignore *noise words* ("please," "could you...") would require considerable expansion of both the syntactic and the semantic components of the theory.

Two other areas of future study that this work suggests are those of portability and evaluation, briefly touched upon in two appendices. Our concern with existing natural language *database front-ends* is, as we have said, that they are not formal theories. This concern is not simply a fascination with formalisms per se, but rather stems from a twofold belief that, on the one hand, informal *theories* are not science, and on the other, that programs not based upon a theory are in the long run unreliable. If we are to propose, then, that a formalism like Montague Grammar is appropriate in the area of natural language querying, we must not only demonstrate that it is appropriate formally, but also that *programs* based upon that formalism are practical. We are currently in the beginning stages of implementing an algorithm for translating the pragmatic interpretations of QE-III queries into the relational algebra. This of course is only one aspect of the problem. It remains to be seen whether a useable interface can be developed to enable database administrators to define *applied* instances of languages expressed in a formalism like QE-III for their particular databases. However, we point out that this problem is not unique to the Montague Grammar framework we have adopted; it is a problem facing every proposed framework for natural language querying systems (see, e.g., [GL81].)

Two final areas of research that appear promising involve the exploration of how many other aspects of the *meaning* of an utterance can be assigned to a pragmatic component in the way that we have construed that term. For example, the pragmatics of a declarative sentence – "John manages Mary." – in a model in which that sentence was False with respect to the current index, might be defined to *update* the model to make it true at the *next* index. Obviously there are considerable difficulties in achieving such a goal formally. (The simplest kind of example that illustrates one kind of difficulty would be the Falsity of "John manages Mary or Peter sells shoes." Would the pragmatics make one or both of the disjuncts True?) Nevertheless there would be considerable advantages to a formal specification of the interpretation of such commands. ([SM82] discusses this approach to database updates.)

A related area suggested by our pragmatic component is the exploration of the similarity between the treatment of question words and unbound pronouns which we have already mentioned. We envision a situation in which we define a formal notion of a dialogue, in which the pragmatic component manipulates a model as the dialogue progresses. Faced with an utterance like "He walks," the semantic component gives its denotation as the set of variable assignments that make it true. If a formal pragmatic component could be defined so as to produce the response "who walks?", it could, upon receiving an answer, say, "Peter," interpret the answer pragmatically as a command to bind the pronoun "he" to the model's representation of Peter. We believe that this view of formal pragmatics, as a way of *responding* to language use, is not only in keeping with the standard conception on the term, but is also an interesting approach to formalizing the notion of the *processing* of language which has been the concern of Artificial Intelligence.

# Bibliography

[ABM84]     G. Ariav, A. Beller, and H. L. Morgan. *A Temporal Model.* Technical Report DS-WP 82-12-05, Department of Decision Sciences, The Wharton School, University of Pennsylvania, December 1984.

[Ajd35]     K. Ajdukiewicz. Die Syntakische Konnexität. *Studia Philosophica*, 1:1–27, 1935. (Translated as "Syntactic Connexion," *Polish Logic*, pp. 207-231, ed. S. McCall, Oxford, Clarendon Press, 1967.).

[AM82]      G. Ariav and H. L. Morgan. *MDM: Embedding the Time Dimension in Information Systems.* Technical Report TR #82-03-01, Department of Decision Sciences, The Wharton School, University of Pennsylvania, 1982.

[And81]     T. L. Anderson. *The Database Semantics of Time.* PhD thesis, University of Washington, 1981. (Unpublished).

[BADW82]    A. Bolour, T. L. Anderson, L. J. Deketser, and H. K. T Wong. The Role of Time in Information Processing: A Survey. *ACM SIGMOD Record*, 12(3):28–48, April 1982.

[Bar54]     Y. Bar-Hillel. Indexical Expressions. *Mind*, 63:359–379, 1954.

[Bel82]     N. D. Jr. Belnap. Questions and Answers in Montague Grammar. In S. Peters and E. Saarinen, editors, *Processes, Beliefs, and Questions*, D. Reidel Publishing Co., Dordrecht, 1982.

[Ben74]     M. R. Bennett. *Some Extensions of a Montague Fragment of English.* PhD thesis, UCLA Ph.D. dissertation; distributed by Indiana University Linguistics Club, Bloomington, 1974.

[Ben77]     M. R. Bennett. A Response to Karttunen on Questions. *Linguistics and Philosophy*, 1:279–300, 1977.

[Ben79]     M. R. Bennett. *Questions in Montague Grammar.* Technical Report, Indiana University Linguistics Club, Bloomington, 1979.

[Ben82]   J. Ben-Zvi. *The Time Relational Model.* PhD thesis, Department of Computer Science, University of California, Los Angeles, 1982. (Unpublished).

[BM86]    M. L. Brodie and J. Mylopoulos. *On Knowledge Base Management Systems.* Springer-Verlag, New York, 1986.

[BN78]    H. Biller and E. J. Neuhold. Semantics of Data Bases: The Semantics of Data Models. *Information Systems*, 3(1):11–36, 1978.

[BP72]    M. R. Bennett and B. H. Partee. *Toward the Logic of Tense and Aspect in English.* Technical Report, Indiana University Linguistics Club, Bloomington, 1972.

[Bub77]   J. A. Bubenko. The Temporal Dimension in Information Modelling. In G. M. Nijssen, editor, *Architecture and Models in Data Base Management Systems*, pages 93–118, North Holland, Amsterdam, 1977.

[BW77]    D. G. Bobrow and T. Winograd. An Overview of KRL - A Knowledge Representation Language. *Cognitive Science*, 1(1):3–46, 1977.

[Car42]   R. Carnap. *Introduction to Semantics.* Harvard University Press, Cambridge, 1942.

[Car47]   R. Carnap. *Meaning and Necessity.* University of Chicago Press, Chicago, 1947.

[CB79]    M. A. Casanova and P. A. Bernstein. The Logic of a Relational Data Manipulation Language. In *Proceedings 6th ACM Symp. on Prog. Lang.*, 1979.

[CC87]    J. Clifford and A. Croker. The Historical Relational Data Model (HRDM) and Algebra Based on Lifespans,. In *Proceedings Third International Conference on Data Engineering*, IEEE, Los Angeles, February 1987.

[CC88a]   J. Clifford and A. Croker. Objects in Time. *IEEE Database Engineering Bulletin*, December 1988.

[CC88b]   A. Croker and J. Clifford. *On Completeness of Historical Relational Data Models.* Technical Report, Department of Information Systems, Stern School of Business, New York University, December 1988. (Unpublished).

[Cha78]   C. L. Chang. DEDUCE 2: Further Investigations of Deduction in Relational Data Bases. In *Logic and Data Bases*, Plenum Press, 1978.

[Che76]   P. P. Chen. The Entity-Relationship Model – Toward a Unified View of Data. *ACM Transactions on Database Systems*, 1(1):9–36, 1976.

[Chu41]     A. Church. *The Calculi of Lambda-Conversion.* Princeton University Press, Princeton, 1941.

[Cli82a]    J. Clifford. *A Logical Framework for the Temporal Semantics and Natural-Language Querying of Historical Databases.* PhD thesis, Department of Computer Science, SUNY at Stony Brook, December 1982. (Unpublished).

[Cli82b]    J. Clifford. A Model for Historical Databases. In *Proceedings of Logical Bases for Data Bases*, ONERA-CERT, Toulouse, France, December 1982.

[Cli85]     J. Clifford. Towards an Algebra of Historical Relational Databases. In *ACM-SIGMOD International Conference on Management of Data*, ACM, Austin, May 1985.

[Cod70]     E. F. Codd. A Relational Model of Data for Large Shared Data Banks. *Communications of the ACM*, 13(6):377–387, 1970.

[Coo79]     R. Cooper. Variable Binding and Relative Clauses. In F. Guenthner and S. J. Schmidt, editors, *Formal Semantics and Pragmatics for Natural Languages*, pages 131–160, D. Reidel Publishing Co., Dordrecht, 1979.

[CR87]      J. Clifford and A. Rao. A Simple, General Structure for Temporal Domains. In *Proceedings Temporal Aspects in Information Systems*, AFCET, Sophia-Antipolis, France, May 1987.

[CW83]      J. Clifford and D. S. Warren. Formal Semantics for Time in Databases. *ACM Transactions on Database Systems*, 6(2):214–254, June 1983.

[Dow78]     D. R. Dowty. *A Guide to Montague's PTQ.* Technical Report, Indiana University Linguistics Club, Bloomington., 1978.

[Dow79]     D. R. Dowty. *Word Meaning and Montague Grammar.* D. Reidel Publishing Co., Dordrecht, 1979.

[DWP81]     D. R. Dowty, R.E. Wall, and S. Peters. *Introduction to Montague Semantics.* D. Reidel Publishing Co., Dordrecht, 1981.

[Fil68]     C. J. Fillmore. The Case for Case. In E. Bach and R. Harris, editors, *Universals in Linguistic Theory*, Rinehart & Winston, New York, 1968.

[Fre92]     G. Frege. Über Sinn und Bedeutung. *Zeitschrift für Philosophie und philosophische Kritik*, 100:25–50, 1892. (Translated as "On Sense and Reference," *Translations from the Writings of Gottlob Frege*, ed. Geach and Black, Oxford, 1952.).

[Fri79]     J. Friedman. An Unlabeled Bracketing Solution to the Problem of Conjoined Phrases in Montague's PTQ. *Journal of Philosophical Logic*, 8:151–169, 1979.

[Fri81]     J. Friedman. Expressing Logical Formulas in Natural Language. In *Formal Methods in the Study of Language*, pages 113–130, Mathematical Center, Amsterdam, 1981.

[Fro86]     R. Frost. *Introduction to Knowledge Base Systems*. MacMillan, New York, 1986.

[FW78]      J. Friedman and D. S. Warren. A Parsing Method for Montague Grammars. *Linguistics and Philosophy*, 347–372, 1978.

[Gal75]     D. Gallin. *Intensional and Higher-Order Modal Logic*. North Holland, Amsterdam, 1975.

[GL80]      R. Greiner and D. B. Lenat. A Representation Language Language. In *Proceedings 1st Annual Natl. Conference on AI, Stanford*, 1980.

[GL81]      Hendrix G. G. and W. Lewis. Transportable Natural-language Interfaces to Databases. In *Proceedings 19th ACL*, pages 159–165, Menlo Park, 1981.

[GM78]      H. Gallaire and J. Minker. *Logic and Data Bases*. Plenum Press, New York, 1978.

[Gol81]     B. S. Goldstein. *Constraints on Null Values in Relational Databases*. Technical Report TR #80/015, Department of Computer Science, SUNY at Stony Brook., 1981.

[Gro71]     CODASYL Data Base Task Group. *CODASYL Data Base Task Group Report*. Technical Report, ACM, New York, 1971.

[Gun81]     T. Gunji. *Toward a Computational Theory of Pragmatics – Discourse, Presupposition, and Implicature*. PhD thesis, The Ohio State University, 1981.

[GV85]      S. K. Gadia and J. Vaishnav. A Query Language for a Homogeneous Temporal Database. In *Proceedings of ACM SIGACT-SIGMOD Symposium on Principles of Database Systems*, pages 51–56, 1985.

[GWCL63]    B. F. Jr. Green, A. K. Wolf, C. Chomsky, and K. Laughery. BASEBALL: An Automatic Question Answerer. In E. A. Feigenbaum and J. Feldman, editors, *Computers and Thought*, pages 207–216, McGraw-Hill, New York, 1963.

[GY88]      S. K. Gaida and C. S. Yeung. A Generalized Model for a Relational Tem-
            poral Database. In *ACM-SIGMOD International Conference on Man-
            agement of Data*, pages 251–259, June 1988.

[Ham73]     C. L. Hamblin. Questions in Montague English. *Foundations of Lan-
            guage*, 10:41–53, 1973.

[Har78]     L. R. Harris. *The ROBOT System: Natural Language Processing Applied
            to Data Base Query*. Technical Report TR78-1, Department of Mathe-
            matics, Dartmouth College, 1978.

[Has82]     B. L. Hasbrouck. *Methods of Parsing English with Context-Free Gram-
            mar*. Master's thesis, Department of Computer Science, SUNY at Stony
            Brook, December 1982.

[Hay77]     P. J. Hayes. In Defence of Logic. In *Proceedings 5th Int. Joint Conference
            on Artificial Intelligence*, Cambridge, 1977.

[Hin74]     J. Hintikka. Questions About Questions. In M. K. Munitz and P. K.
            Unger, editors, *Semantics and Philosophy*, pages 103–158, New York Uni-
            versity Press, New York, 1974.

[Hin88]     E. W. Hinrichs. Tense, Quantifiers, and Contexts. *Computational Lin-
            guistics*, 14(2):3–14, 1988.

[Hir83]     G. Hirst. A Foundation for Semantic Interpretation. In *Proceedings of
            the Association for Computational Linguistics*, pages 64–73, 1983.

[HM78]      M. Hammer and D. McLeod. The Semantic Data Model: A Modelling
            Mechanism for Data Base Applications. In *ACM-SIGMOD International
            Conference on Management of Data*, Austin, 1978.

[HSSS78]    G. G. Hendrix, E. D. Sacerdoti, D. Sagalowicz, and J. Slocum. Develop-
            ing a Natural Language Interface to Complex Data. *ACM Transactions
            on Database Systems*, 133(2), 1978.

[HZ78]      R. Hausser and D. Zaefferer. Questions and Answers in a Context-
            dependent Montague Grammar. In F. Guenthner and S. J. Schmidt,
            editors, *Formal Semantics and Pragmatics for Natural Languages*, D.
            Reidel Publishing Co., Dordrecht, 1978.

[IMS]       IMS/360. *IMS/360 - Application Description Manual*. Technical Re-
            port GH-20-0765, IBM, White Plains, New York.

[Jan86]     T. M. V. Janssen. *Foundations and Applications of Montague Grammar*.
            Centrum foor Wiskunde en Informatica, Amsterdam, 1986. (CWI Tract
            19).

[Kal72]    D. Kalish. Semantics. In Paul Edwards, editor, *The Encyclopedia of Philosophy*, MacMillan, New York, 1972.

[Kar77]    L. Karttunen. Syntax and Semantics of Questions. *Linguistics and Philosophy*, 1:3–44, 1977.

[Kas77]    A. Kasher. What Is a Theory of Use? *Journal of Pragmatics*, 1:105–120, 1977.

[KL83]     M. R. Klopprogge and P. C. Lockemann. Modelling Information Preserving Databases: Consequences of the Concept of Time. In *Proceedings of The Ninth International Conference on Very Large Data Bases*, pages 399–416, 1983.

[Klo81]    M. R. Klopprogge. TERM: An Approach to Include the Time Dimension in the Entity-Relationship Model. In P. P. S. Chen, editor, *Entity-Relationship Approach to Information Modeling and Analysis*, pages 477–512, ER Institute, 1981.

[Kow79]    R. Kowalski. *Logic for Problem Solving*. Elsevier North Holland, New York, 1979.

[KR72]     S. Kuno and J. Robinson. Multiple WH-Questions. *Linguistic Inquiry*, 3(2):463–487, 1972.

[Lan81]    S. P. J. Landsbergen. Adaptation of Montague Grammar to the Requirements of Parsing. In *Proceedings 3rd Amsterdam Colloq. Formal Methods in the Study of Language*, Amsterdam, 1981.

[Lew76]    D. Lewis. General Semantics. In B. H. Partee, editor, *Montague Grammar*, pages 1–50, Academic Press, Inc., New York, 1976.

[LMP79]    H. Laine, O. Maanavilja, and E. Peltola. Grammatical Data Base Model. *Information Systems*, 4(4), 1979.

[Loc85]    F. Lochovsky, editor. *IEEE Data Engineering: Special Issue on Object-Oriented Systems*, December 1985.

[Lum84]    et al. Lum, V. Designing DBMS Support for the Temporal Dimension. In *ACM-SIGMOD International Conference on Management of Data*, pages 115–126, Boston, June 1984.

[Mai83]    D. Maier. *The Theory of Relational Databases*. Computer Science Press, Rockville, MD, 1983.

[Mar59]    R. M. Martin. *Toward a Systematic Pragmatics*. North Holland, Amsterdam, 1959.

[Mar71]    W. Marciszewski. Introduction to Appendix. In J. Pelc, editor, *Functional Logical Semiotics of Natural Language*, Mouton, The Hague, 1971.

[Min75]    M. Minsky. A Framework for Representing Knowledge. In P.H. Winston, editor, *The Psychology of Computer Vision*, McGraw Hill, New York, 1975.

[Min78]    J. Minker. An Experimental Relational Data Base System Based on Logic. In *Logic and Data Bases*, Plenum Press, 1978.

[Mon68]    R. Montague. Pragmatics. In R. Klibansky, editor, *Contemporary Philosophy: A Survey*, pages 102–122, La Nuova Italia Editrice, Florence, 1968. Reprinted in [Mon74].

[Mon70a]   R. Montague. English as a Formal Language. In B. Visentini et al., editor, *Linguaggi nella Societa e nella Tecnica*, pages 189–224, Edizioni di Comunita, Milan, 1970. Reprinted in [Mon74].

[Mon70b]   R. Montague. Pragmatics and Intensional Logic. *Synthese*, 22:68–94, 1970. Reprinted in [Mon74].

[Mon70c]   R. Montague. Universal Grammar. *Theoria*, 36:373–398, 1970. Reprinted in [Mon74].

[Mon73]    R. Montague. The Proper Treatment of Quantification in English. In K. J. J. Hintikka, editor, *Approaches to Natural Language*, pages 221–242, D. Reidel Publishing Co., Dordrecht, 1973. Reprinted in [Mon74].

[Mon74]    R. Montague. *Formal Philosophy: Selected Papers of Richard Montague.* Yale University Press, New Haven, 1974.

[Mor38]    C. Morris. Foundations of the Theory of Signs. In *International Encyclopedia of Unified Science*, University of Chicago Press, Chicago, 1938.

[Mor46]    C. Morris. *Signs, Language, and Behavior.* Prentice-Hall, New York, 1946.

[MW80]     D. Maier and D. S. Warren. *A Theory of Computed Relations.* Technical Report 80/012, Department of Computer Science, SUNY at Stony Brook, 1980.

[MW82]     D. Maier and D. S. Warren. Specifying Connections for a Universal Relation Scheme Database. In *ACM-SIGMOD International Conference on Management of Data*, pages 1–7, Orlando, 1982.

[Nav80]    S. B. Navathe. Schema Analysis for Database Restructuring. *ACM Transactions on Database Systems*, 5(2):157–184, June 1980.

[NG79]    J. M. Nicolas and H. Gallaire. Data Base: Theory vs. Interpretation. In *Logic and Data Bases*, Plenum Press, Chicago, 1979.

[Nic78]   J. M. Nicolas. First Order Logic Formalization for Functional, Multivalued, and Mutual Dependencies. In *ACM-SIGMOD International Conference on Management of Data*, pages 40–46, Austin, 1978.

[NY78]    J. M. Nicolas and K. Yazdanian. Integrity Checking in Deductive Data Bases. In *Logic and Data Bases*, Plenum Press, 1978.

[Ozs88]   Z. M. Ozsoyoglu, editor. *IEEE Data Engineering: Special Issue on Nested Relations*, September 1988.

[Par75]   B. Partee. Montague Grammar and Transformational Grammar. *Linguistic Inquiry*, 6(2):203–300, 1975.

[PBW81]   B. Partee, E. Bach, and B. White. On Friedman et al's Montague Grammar Programs. In *56th LSA Meeting, ACL Session*, New York, 1981.

[Pop76]   E. N. Pope. *Questions and Answers in English*. Janua Linguarum Series Practica 226, Mouton, The Hague, 1976.

[Pri67]   A. N. Prior. *Past, Present, and Future*. Oxford University Press, Oxford, 1967.

[QG74]    R. Quirk and S. Greenbaum. *A University Grammar of English*. Longman, London, 1974.

[Qui53]   W. V. O. Quine. *From a Logical Point of View*. Harper and Row, New York, 1953.

[Qui60]   W. V. O. Quine. *Word and Object*. MIT Press, Cambridge, 1960.

[Rei78a]  R. Reiter. Deductive Question-Answering on Relational Data Bases. In *Logic and Data Bases*, Plenum Press, 1978.

[Rei78b]  R. Reiter. On Closed World Data Bases. In *Logic and Data Bases*, Plenum Press, 1978.

[Rob54]   P. Roberts. *Understanding Grammar*. Harper & Row, New York, 1954.

[RU71]    N. Rescher and A. Urquhart. *Temporal Logic*. Springer Verlag, New York, 1971.

[SA85]    R. Snodgrass and I. Ahn. A Taxonomy of Time in Databases. In *ACM-SIGMOD International Conference on Management of Data*, pages 236–246, Austin, TX, May 1985.

[Sch83]   R. J. H. Scha. *Logical Foundations for Question Answering.* PhD thesis, University of Groningen, 1983.

[Ser80]   A. Sernadas. Temporal Aspects of Logical Procedure Definition. *Information Systems*, 5:167–187, 1980.

[Sha72]   R. C. Shank. Conceptual Dependency: A Theory of Natural Language Understanding. *Cognitive Psychology*, 3(4):552–631, 1972.

[Shi81]   D. W. Shipman. The Functional Data Model and the Data Language DAPLEX. *ACM Transactions on Database Systems*, 6(1):140–173, 1981.

[Shi86]   J. Shiftan. *Assessing The Temporal Differentiation of Attributes as an Implementation Strategy for a Temporally Oriented Relational DBMS.* PhD thesis, Department of Information Systems, Stern School of Business, New York University, December 1986.

[SK80]    M. Stonebraker and K. Keller. Embedding Expert Knowledge and Hypothetical Data Bases into a Data Base System. In *ACM-SIGMOD International Conference on Management of Data*, Santa Monica, 1980.

[SM82]    S. C. Salveter and D. Maier. Natural Language Database Updates. In *Proceedings 20th ACL*, Toronto, 1982.

[Sno84]   R. Snodgrass. The Temporal Query Language TQUEL. In *Proceedings of ACM SIGACT-SIGMOD Symposium on Principles of Database Systems*, pages 204–212, Waterloo, Ontario, Canada, April 1984.

[Sno86]   R. Snodgrass. Research Concerning Time in Databases: Project Summaries. *ACM SIGMod Record*, 15(4):19–39, December 1986.

[SS76]    H. A. Schmid and J. R. Swenson. On the Semantics of the Relational Data Model. In *ACM-SIGMOD International Conference on Management of Data*, pages 9–36, 1976.

[SS77]    J. M. Smith and D. C. P. Smith. Database Abstractions: Aggregation and Generalization. *ACM Transactions on Database Systems*, 2(2):105–133, 1977.

[Sta72]   R. C. Stalnaker. Pragmatics. In *Semantics of Natural Languages*, D. Reidel Publishing Co., Dordrecht, 1972.

[Sto86]   M. Stonebraker, editor. *The INGRES Papers.* Addison Wesley, Reading, MA, 1986.

[TAI87]   AFCET. *Temporal Aspects in Information Systems*, May 1987.

[Tho72]    R. Thomason. *On the Semantic Interpretation of the Thomason 1972 Fragment.* Technical Report, Indiana University Linguistics Club, Bloomington, 1972.

[Tho76]    R. Thomason. Some Extensions of Montague Grammar. In B. Partee, editor, *Montague Grammar*, Academic Press, New York, 1976.

[Tic78]    P. Tichy. Questions, Answers, and Logic. *American Philosophical Quarterly*, 15(4):275–284, October 1978.

[TK89]     A.S. Tuzhilin and Z.M. Kedem. Querying and Controlling the Future Behavior of Complex Objects. In *Proceedings Fifth International Conference on Data Engineering*, IEEE, February 1989.

[Ull80]    J. D. Ullman. *Principles of Database Systems.* Computer Science Press, Potomac, MD, 1980.

[Ull82]    J. D. Ullman. The U.R. Strikes Back. In *Proceedings ACM Principles of Database Systems*, pages 10–23, Los Angeles, 1982.

[vB88]     J. van Benthem. *A Manual of Intensional Logic.* Center for the Study of Language and Information, Stanford, 1988.

[Ven67]    Z. Vendler. *Linguistics in Philosophy.* Cornell University Press, Ithaca, 1967.

[Wal78]    D.L. Waltz. An English Language Question Answering System for a Large Relational Database. *Communications of the ACM*, 21(7):526–539, 1978.

[War79]    D. S. Warren. *Syntax and Semantics in Parsing: An Application to Montague Grammar.* PhD thesis, University of Michigan, Ann Arbor, 1979.

[WKN81]    W. A. Woods, R. M. Kaplan, and B. Nash-Webber. *The LUNAR Sciences Natural Language Information System: Final Report.* Technical Report BBN Report 2378, Bolt, Beranek and Newman, Inc., Cambridge MA., 1981.

# INDEX

Printed in the United States
By Bookmasters